Old Napa Valley
The History
to 1900

by
Lin Weber

Wine Ventures Publishing
St. Helena, CA 94574

Library of Congress Catalog Card
Number 98-96606

ISBN 0-9667014-0-2

Foreword

Lin Weber has written a most original and informative story about Napa County, from the native Americans (our *guapo* Wappos) to the end of the 19th Century. The town of Napa was "Napa City" then and was settled at the time of the Gold Rush. What is now our Napa Valley was more like the old Wild West. So much we've forgotten or never knew! Lin researched every detail, from the cinnabar, gold and silver mining here, to the Napa Valley Railroad and the Chinese population.

We travel with Charlie Hopper, Joe Chiles and other pioneers on the wagon trail, relive the famous Bear Flag revolt and the rescue of the Donner Party. The report on the Napa Valley wine industry of the last century is a discovery and a treasure.

Lin is not only totally knowledgeable about our region, but entertaining, too, and you can't wait to turn the pages. The bibliography is extensive, but *Old Napa Valley* reads more like an adventure than a history text.

Thank you, Lin, for this wonderful book. It's a must for reference and for fun.

--Margrit Biever Mondavi

Acknowledgements

Writing this book has been a joy. It's been a bit of an obsession, too, but mainly it's been a joy. The inspiration for it came to me about 7 years ago when I happened to take a drive down to the very end of Spring Street in St. Helena. The Spanish moss hung from the oak trees like tattered shrouds, giving the place a haunted feeling, as if someone from another era might emerge from the shadows at any moment. Surely, I thought, ghosts must be here.

This sense of an ancient past led me to the St. Helena Library, where (with the help of Julie Fraser) I discovered unpublished manuscripts and microfilm of Napa Valley newspapers dating back to the 1850's. There I found the answers to all sorts of questions I've always had concerning the communities where I've lived and worked my entire adult life. Over the next several years, whenever I had the chance, I'd scurry over to the Library to read about how the landscape was formed, how come there's a Seventh Day Adventist enclave here, how the wine industry came to be, why "Silverado" is an important word here and scores of other why's and how comes that piqued my curiosity.

Just as I was pondering the Napa Valley's ancient past, Virginia Snowden suggested I actually write a history of the area. She is the Godmother of *Old Napa Valley*. Without her permission-giving encouragement I doubt I would ever have written it.

Bob Lamborn has also played a key role in its development. He introduced *Old Napa Valley* and me to the staff at the *St. Helena Star*, and was instrumental in its being serialized there before it came out (or was even finished) as a book. I also offer my special thanks to Lucy Shaw and Christie Tadiello for positively hounding me to publish my work. Lucy even found a publishing mentor for me, James K. Stevenson, whose assistance I have deeply appreciated.

I'm thankful, too, for the assistance I received from the staff at the Napa City and County Library, especially in using their microfilm collection. Their California history section is wonderfully well stocked, and it, too, has one-of-a-kind, unpublished materials.

I am indebted to Robin Lail, John Livingston and John York, who read early drafts of the book and offered me excellent advice on its development. I am grateful, too, to Earl Couey and the late Yolande Beard, who reviewed my material on the indigenous peoples of the Napa Valley and corrected me when I strayed from fact. Gerry Shelley, member of the Board of Los Californianos, did the same for me with the Spanish/Mexican period and sent me copies of rare material I never would have guessed existed. Nancy Sange Haynes helped me by proofreading the book. Geri Raymond's assistance was also invaluable.

Dick and Carol Cavagnaro were kind enough to give me very useful information regarding the histories of their families, which I was able to incorporate into the text. So did John York, Julie Coffield Farley and Sarah Boggs.

I was lucky enough to have the talented graphic artist Matthew Shelley help me with the photos and prepare cover design. I truly appreciate the time and effort he put into the project. Also helpful were Brouck Haynes, Peter Fenczik, Loren Sorensen, Ken Stanton, Dave Toboni and Kelly Christensen who provided technical support; and Darryl Sattui, Reginald Oliver, Clyde Low, Kathy Merritt, Bob and Peg Beardsley, Julie Prince, the Napa County Historical Society (especially the late Jess Doud), the Sonoma County Historical Society and the staff at the Vasquez House.

Finally, I would like to extend my sincere thanks to Margrit Biever Mondavi, for the kind words she has written in the foreword. A generous contributor to the arts, she is truly one of New Napa Valley's most important assets.

Most of all, though, I thank my husband, Chris, who brought me to this beautiful part of the world in 1971 and has shared it with me so lovingly ever since--LW

Old Napa Valley

The History to 1900

To Chris, with love

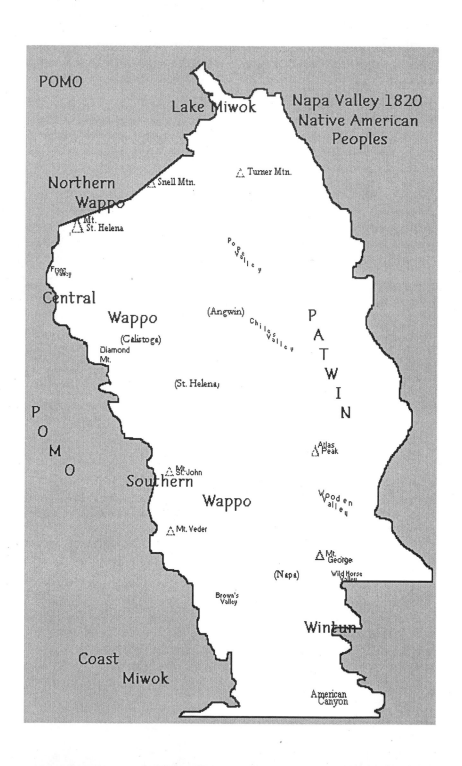

POMO

Lake Miwok

Napa Valley 1820
Native American
Peoples

△ Turner Mtn.

Northern
Wappo

△ Snell Mtn.

△ Mt.
St. Helena

Pope
Valley

Central

Wappo

(Angwin)

Chiles
Valley

P
A
T
W
I
N

(Calistoga)

Diamond
Mt.

P
O
M
O

(St. Helena)

△ Atlas
Peak

△ Mt. John

Southern

Wappo

Wooden
Valley

△ Mt. Veder

△ Mt.
George

(Napa)

Wild Horse
Valley

Brown's
Valley

Wintun

Coast
Miwok

American
Canyon

Chapter One

The First People

Several years ago, archaeologists exploring a dry, dusty dig at Borax Lake in Lake County, California, found traces of ancient hunters who may have made their home there as much as 12,000 years ago.[1] They left bits of hard evidence about their lives everywhere, including on the fertile alluvial plain that would one day be called the Napa Valley. These proficient warriors buried their dead face down, wore ornaments made of shell and tipped their weapons with heavy points. They had use of a technological marvel that made them masters wherever they chose to live: They had the *atlatl*, a spear-thrower that helped them fell the largest animals.

There was plenty of big game to fell. Giant lions, sloths, mammoths, cave bears and dire wolves prowled the forests and lush meadows, and the hunters speared them, perhaps hastening their extinction. Lesser game was also plenty, and big fish splashed in the year-round river that ran down the A-shaped valley to the south.

Some archaeologists believe that these first people and their big weapons moved on. Where did they go? The most recent discoveries suggest they may have migrated as far away as South America.[2]

Another group of prehistoric people appears to have taken their place. If so, it may have been a geological phenomenon that provided

---

[1]Yolande Beard, *The Wappo--A Report*, self-published, St. Helena, CA, 1977, p. 1.

[2]Rick Gore, "The Most Ancient Americans," *National Geographic*, Vol. 192, No. 4, October, 1997, pp 93-99. Radiocarbon dating reveals that ancient peoples with technology similar to the Borax Lake dwellers may have traveled as far south as Chile.

the impetus for the new group's arrival.[3] The Sierra mountain range was growing taller and was snatching the rain clouds that formerly irrigated the Great Basin area. This created a "rain shadow" where little rain fell. The land became too arid to support an ecology friendly to humans, so the inhabitants left for greener pastures. Thickly verdant with grasses and redwood, oak and madrone, California of 4500 BC was certainly that.

The people themselves had a much different explanation for how they came to inhabit their homeland. Their tradition had no legend of migration. According to their myth, Taikomol, the Creator, laid sticks on the floor of a house that Coyote built. To make men he used large sticks, and to make women he used smaller ones. He produced children by scattering little sticks around the larger sticks. He and Coyote taught the people the rituals they would need to know and showed them how to hunt and gather. Then he brought them to life as *Ukomno'm*, "in the valley."[4]

However it was that these people turned up in Northern California, they thrived. They populated a broad area bounded in the south by the Russian River and by what is now Eureka in the north. In this stronghold they developed their language, a tongue like no other in North America, and one that some linguists say is the oldest Native American language in California.[5] This unique speech pattern is tonal, like Chinese, where the pitch in which a word is spoken is a meaningful part of the word.[6] Today we call their language

---

[3]See Philip Kopper, *The Smithsonian Book of North American Indians: Before the Coming of the Europeans*, Washington, DC, Smithsonian Institution, 1986, pp. 187-199.

[4]Virginia P. Miller, *Ukomno'm: The Yuki Indians of Northern California*, Ballena Press, Socorro, NM, 1979, p. 11. The valley peoples' neighbors called them the "Yuki."

[5]Earl Couey, Consultant/Historian to the Mishewal-Wappo, correspondence to the *St. Helena Star*, 9-10-97. Couey cites studies done by Kroeber (1925), Whistler (1977, 1980) and Elmendorf (1980).

[6]Robert Heizer, ed. "The Archaeology of the Napa Region," *Anthropological Records*, Vol. 12, No. 6, University of California Press,

"Yukian."

The basics of the Yukian culture grew out of the long stay in their ancestral homeland. They usually cremated their dead and practiced the Kuksu religion, a totemistic belief system common among central and northern California natives. In time they spread south into what are now Napa, Lake and Mendocino Counties.[7]

Their occupation of this large domain was uninterrupted for thousands of years until the Pomo, Miwok and Wintun--each speaking their own languages--pressed in on the borders of the Yuki language group. The intruding newcomers finally cut off the southern branch from their cousins in the north, which had consequences for the subsequent development of their language. They came to refer to themselves as *Onastis*, the "outspoken people" who spoke "our" language and fished the river of *Talahalusi*, "beautiful valley."[8] Everybody else was a "them"-- outsiders. Some of the outsiders, however, had names for these people. The Pomo called them the "Ashochimi," and official Spanish records from the 1830's refer to them as the "Satoyomi." To the Spanish soldiers, though, they were *guapo*, "courageous,"[9] an attribute they demonstrated in their refusal to be dominated. *Guapo* soon became "Wappo," and the name stuck.

The pioneer George Yount described them as averaging about 5'4" tall. They were beardless and had straight black hair. The men wore clothing only in the winter, for warmth, and the women covered

---

Berkeley, 1933.

[7]Peter M. Knudtson, *The Wintun Indians of California and Their Neighbors,* Naturegraph Publishers, Inc., Happy Camp, CA, 1977. Knudtson refers to the period from 4000 to 2000 BC as the "Early Horizon Culture." Indigenous people of the "Middle Horizon Period"-- 2000 BC to 300 AD--sometimes buried their dead in a flexed position, with the knees drawn up to the chin.

[8]Charlie Toledo et al, "Native Americans" in *The Valley of Legends,* Napa, 1997.

[9]*Guapo* also means "handsome."

themselves front and back with a kind of double apron made of fur, buckskin or woven grasses.[10]

We know a lot about the Wappo now. The main body of the group lived in northern Sonoma and southern Lake counties, but there were many Wappo in the Napa Valley. All told there were probably about 1,650 in the Valley itself when the missionaries came in the 1830's and 4,600 in the general area, including both sides of Mount St. Helena.[11]

Within the larger Wappo clan there were three main subgroups: the *Mishewal* (Northern Wappo), *Mutistul* (Central Wappo) and *Meyahk'mah* (Southern Wappo). The late Yolande Beard, who studied the Napa Valley's earliest people, said there were several permanent settlements south of Mount St. Helena. These small villages had names, and individuals would refer to them as their communities of origin. For example, in the Napa Valley there were the *Mallocamas* in the Calistoga and Mount St. Helena area, the *Callajomanos* around St. Helena, the *Kaimus* in Yountville and perhaps the *Napatos* in Napa between Napa Creek and the Napa River.[12] Like modern-day campers, they always set up their dwellings near water.

Other groups of Native Americans penetrated the area shortly before the Spanish came.[13] The Wintun (or Wintu) people spread south from their stronghold in Shasta and set up an encampment near what is now Vallejo. From there a splinter group migrated up into the Napa Valley, making at least two permanent living sites near the future Napa City. One site, to the east of the present city, was called

---

[10]Harold E. Driver, "Wappo Ethnography," *University of California Publications in American Archaeology and Ethnology*, Vol. 35, No. 3, Berkeley, 1936.

[11]Beard, p. 43.

[12]Ibid, p. 45.

[13]A. L. Kroeber, *Handbook of the Indians of California*, California Book Company, Berkeley, 1953. Kroeber offers a detailed description of all the identifiable indigenous peoples in California.

Ulucay. The other , south of the city, was *Suscol*.[14]

A branch of the Wintu, the Patwin, settled in Berryessa Valley. They established a community called *Topay*. A small stem of that group made a settlement in Pope Valley. They referred to themselves as the "Re-ho" people, [15] and the Berryessa Patwin called the Re-ho the "Tu-lo-kai-di-sel". The anthropologist A. L. Kroeber says that Lake Miwok also peopled Berryessa Valley.[16]

The Wintu/Patwin newcomers exchanged certain aspects of their culture with the Wappo. The Wintun took on some of the Wappo's beliefs and tribal customs, while the locals came to resemble the newcomers physically as they intermarried. Linguistically, the Wintu and Patwin could understand each other, but both had difficulty following the language of the Wappo.

The Wintu/Patwin people had round faces and were often rather obese as children. They were short in stature and had straight, bristly hair. In general their heads were smaller than the Wappo's. Many had widow's peaks descending their low foreheads and very prominent noses that appeared to be triangular: small at the base but very wide at the nostrils. The Wappo were generally lighter skinned and often had more prominent chins.[17]

To the west of the Wappo lived the Pomo people. They also impacted upon the local Napa Valley group. The Pomo spoke "Hokan," a language different from either the Wintun, Patwin or Wappo. They wove fine baskets. In time the Wappo learned to produce baskets in the manner of the Pomo, and their styles and patterns, if not their speech, became almost indistinguishable from

---

[14]Beard, p. 45.

[15]Stephen Powers, *The Tribes of California,* University of California Press, Berkeley, 1976, p. 228. Powers was an ethnologist who lived among the Wappo briefly in the 1870's. He wrote that the Pope Valley Re-ho were Miwoks and not Wintu/Patwin.

[16]See A.L. Kroeber, *The Patwin and Their Neighbors,* University of California Press, Berkeley, 1932, appended map.

[17]Idem.

each other.

Still another large group of people lived to the northwest and southeast of the Valley. These were the Miwok, an artistically endowed group who carved soapstone and traded shells and raw iron. The Coast Miwok to the southeast were the natives who greeted Sir Francis Drake when he made an emergency landing in June of 1579 in what is now called Drake's Bay.

Some writers have said that the indigenous peoples of America did not have a concept of owning the land. While this may have been true for native groups elsewhere, the Wappo and those around them were definitely territorial, at least about some things. They zealously guarded their fishing holes, for example, and regarded them as family treasures. They would fight to protect them.[18]

Inter-tribal warfare was not the rule among native Californians in this area, but the Wappo eventually grew very irritated with the encroachment of others onto their territory. Some native groups became fearful of treading into their hunting grounds, lest the Wappo retaliate. A Wappo going to battle would dress for the occasion by painting his chest and wearing head feathers of bird wings. The attacks usually came at night. There is some disagreement among historians as to what the Wappo did with their vanquished. They did not take scalps.[19]

Despite their xenophobia, the Wappo could not hold back the tide of newcomers descending on their Valley. Contact with outsiders became common. A major reason for this was the obsidian deposit

---

[18]Powers wrote of an instance where a native from a neighboring tribe was hunting with a white man. The white man shot a deer just beyond the boundary that marked Wappo territory. Even though the native was hungry, he refused to take the deer from Wappo land for fear of retaliation. (Powers, p. 196)

[19]One of George Yount's chroniclers, Charles Camp, reported that after a Wappo party raided Yount's cattle on Christmas, 1837, Yount sent "scouts" to Pope Valley to find them. According to Camp, the scouts--perhaps white men--brought back four scalps (see p. 27).

at Glass Mountain,[20] which drew natives from all parts of the region. The obsidian was used to make spearheads, arrow points, knives, scrapers and other cutting tools. The natives mined it by using sticks to pry the glassy rock loose from its bed of soft, white pumice.[21] Obsidian that had been exposed to the sun was considered spoiled.[22] Other tribes traded with the Wappo for the privilege of extracting the obsidian. It is still possible to mine the obsidian nodules used by the Wappo in the Bournemouth/Swanston Road area of St. Helena. The Napa Valley is littered with obsidian arrowheads.

The Wappo themselves ventured onto their neighbors' lands regularly. Twice a year, for example, they crossed Pomo and Miwok country to make a two-day trip to Bodega Bay, where they gathered shells to use as money and decoration. Like modern tourists at the Coast, they feasted on saltwater specialties like crab and abalone while they were there. Seaweed was also on the menu. Members of all the Wappo communities traveled annually to the primary settlement in Mendocino County, northwest of Napa, for convocations---huge meetings of all the Wappo.

The native people of the Napa Valley walked wherever they went, and many of the roads in the Napa Valley follow old native footpaths, according to Beard.[23] The Silverado Trail and Spring Mountain Road, for example, are ancient Wappo routes, she says, as is Langtry Road on Spring Mountain in St. Helena. Butts Canyon Road north of Pope Valley, Hardin Road in the Chiles Valley area and Monticello Road in Napa all follow or parallel roads walked by the indigenous peoples of Napa County.

---

[20] off the Silverado Trail in present-day St. Helena. There is a more famous Glass Mountain north of Bishop, CA, which equaled or exceeded the Napa Valley one as a neolithic tourist draw.

[21] Robert F. Heizer and Adam E. Treganza, "Mines and Quarries of the Indians of California," in *California Division of Mines Report*, v. 40, No. 3, Ballena Press, Ramona, CA, 1944.

[22] Beard, p. 56.

[23] Beard, pp. 59-60.

A typical Wappo settlement featured three types of structures. The first was the primary dwelling place, an oval house about 30' long with multiple doors and a smoke hole for the fire of each sub-family that dwelled within. These apartment-like living quarters were built from a framework of bent saplings and included a main living area with a menstrual room that was separated from the rest of the house by a woven screen. Individuals slept in hollows dug near the walls, on pillows of grass or fern. Several of these homes were clustered together to make a small permanent village.[24]

The second type of structure in the Wappo encampment was a dance house--a roofless, circular enclosure. It was bad luck not to have one. Learning how to dance well was a priority among many native peoples, and a good dancer enjoyed prestige in the community.

Each village also had a sweat lodge (called a *hotsa*),[25] which was a rounded structure with a pit for heated rocks in the center and a domed, mud-covered roof. It was often built next to a cold stream. The sweat lodge served social, spiritual and medicinal purposes for men. (Children and women contented themselves with bathing in the cold water.) As often as twice a day, tribal males could gather there around lava rocks that had been superheated in huge bonfires until they glowed from within. Lodge leaders enhanced the experience by sprinkling offerings of tobacco and sweet-smelling herbs on the fiery rocks. Participants filled the hot, pungent air with chanting and song, purifying themselves, they believed, both within and without, by sweating in this ceremonial sauna.

The Wappo had a marriage ceremony of sorts.[26] The prospective groom entered the dwelling of his would-be bride and laid a dowry of shell beads or some other valuable item at the feet of her father. Suitor and parent sat in silence. The father appeared nonchalant about the amount tendered. After what may have seemed like a very long time, the father either accepted the offering (and the young man)

---

[24]Ibid, p. 45.

[25]The Wintun word for sweat lodge was *temescal.*

[26]Powers, pp. 198-199.

or rejected him and his gift. A spurned suitor could try sweetening the pot by adding more shells. If the father consented to the match he broke the silence by calling for the daughter to join them. The young lovers would sit at her father's knees. The father joined their hands together, spoke a few words of advice, and a new Wappo couple was created. Divorce was possible with mutual consent, and single-parent children lived with their mother. Surviving accounts of Wappo customs indicate that Wappo men may have taken several wives.

The Wappo were patriarchal. Grooms, for example, could speak and dine with their new in-laws, but brides could never eat with theirs and could only speak with them when necessary. Some ethnologists say that the Wappo considered it bad luck for a woman to be present in certain key places, like fishing sites,[27] but women did have some power, because the Wappo were matrilineal, with the inherited position of chief passing through the female side.[28]

A distinguishing characteristic of the people was their experience of *couvade*, a psychosomatic condition where the father of a newborn child feels labor pains. After the delivery, Wappo fathers took to their bed for four days, during which time they fasted from meat, fat and fish and refrained from smoking their pipes.[29]

Steelhead salmon were prolific in Valley streams back in Wappo times. They called the salmon *melka wa*.[30] They caught them by hand or harpoon, free-swimming or in weirs of baskets constructed for the purpose. For extra luck, a fisherman might fasten a few clamshell beads to the weirs before they submerged them. Another trick for catching luck (a necessity for fishermen of all ages) was to throw four handfuls of beads into the stream. Tradition had it that Coyote taught the people to chum the waters this way back at the beginning

---

[27]Driver, Loc. Cit.

[28]R. F. Heizer and M.A. Whipple, *The California Indians--A Source Book*, University of California Press, Berkeley, 1971, p. 31.

[29]Beard, p. 48.

[30]Driver, Loc. Cit.

of time.

They caught freshwater eel (*cot*) by hand as the fish lay curled up in the stream. Driver claims that the Wappo could snag a trout (*mets'ekititi*) by tying a grasshopper to a hair and extending it from a short stick.[31] The fish's teeth supposedly caught on the hair. Wappo fishing appears to have required great concentration.

Wappo cuisine featured fish prepared in several ways. Fishermen ate them raw on the spot, dried them in the sun or gutted and smoked them by draping them over lines hung above the family fire. Dried fish could be pounded up, bones and all, and eaten straight as a snack food or drunk in a mixture of water and pounded acorn flour. Sometimes they stored prepared fish by stringing them through poles or twine and hanging them up among the rafters, where they probably attracted other *a la carte* items, like rodents, which they also ate.

There seems to have been a friendly division in the Wappo clans between men who fished and men who hunted. Driver says that for luck, hunters could eat no fish before hunting, and fishers could eat no meat before fishing.[32]

The Wappo hunted deer, antelope, elk and a host of small mammals. Before a hunt they invoked friendly spirits and rubbed themselves with strong-smelling plants, like fennel or yarrow, to camouflage their scent and perhaps to fend off bad luck. Hunts began at dawn. Like most native American people, they utilized all parts of the killed animal, including hoofs (for shamans' rattles) and brains (for curing deerhide). They may have made pets of bear cubs and fawns. Bear had divinity status among the Wappo, as did Coyote and Lizard.

Unlike their ancient predecessors, the Wappo did not use spear-throwers, perhaps because the game they encountered was smaller than the animals of the Late Ice Age, and this technology would not have been useful. Deer were among the largest targets. To kill one, a

---

[31]Idem.

[32]Idem.

hunter would don a deer head disguise (an *onan*) and paw the ground to make deer sounds until one approached. Other hunters then drove the animal along a blind made of brush (an *owiluk*) and clubbed or shot it with arrows. The hunter with the highest status got to divide the carcass, unless a newlywed happened to be in the hunting party, in which case, Driver says, the new groom would carry the deer home and share it with his mother-in-law.[33]

Wappo men used bows that were about 3' to 4.5' long and wound around with deer tendons to provide elasticity.[34] They tipped the arrow shafts with obsidian points, made fast with more deer tendon. The arrowheads of the Wappo were significantly smaller and more elaborately crafted than those of the earliest Valley dwellers, miniaturization being the result of improvements in the arrowhead industry, where smaller was better.

Birds were another favorite food item. The Wappo caught woodpeckers by placing a basket over the tree hole in which they nested. They drove quail into nets and trapped ducks in snares made of bulrushes. They also ate insects, particularly grasshoppers, which they drove from the grass by setting small fires and plucking them up as they tried to escape the flames.

While the Wappo men were hunting, the women gathered. Their major staple was neither corn nor wheat, for they were not agricultural, but acorns, which they boiled, leached to remove the bitter tannin, ground into a meal and stored in large woven containers which resembled beehives. So important were acorns to their diet that Wappo shamans offered regular prayers for the oak tree's safe passage through each season of the year. A bad year for oak trees meant a bad year for Wappo. According to Driver, several of the moons, or months, in the year were named for the phases of the

---

[33]Idem.

[34]See Alexander Forbes, *A History of Upper and Lower California*, San Francisco, John Henry Nash, 1937. Forbes was an early pioneer who settled in the Central Valley well before the Gold Rush. He wrote his history in 1835.

oak tree's cycle. January was *pi-po-tso-hin*, the "white oak earth" moon. February was *kotico-pele-hin*, "black oak leaves" moon. March was *pi-po-pele-hin*, the moon of white oak leaves. They named May after the flour made when they pounded the acorns: *wa 'ate-hin*.

The word for summer (*hell-u-wen*) meant "fire season," and accordingly, June was "burn-the-valley" moon, *t'olacuk-hin*. This might have referred to the temperature, but it also could have pointed to the Wappo's practice of regularly clearing the fields by burning them. This caused a stampede of potential menu items and encouraged growth of the foliage favored by deer and elk. The Wappo burned down their sweat lodges and homes every couple of years, as a means of sanitizing their living environment.[35]

Another gathered item in the Wappo household was the root of "amole," or soap plant. When pounded, the large, soft bulb yielded a soapy lather the Wappo used for cleaning. Beard writes that the bulb was also effective as a poison for catching quantities of fish. The lather apparently stunned fish in shallow waters and allowed them to be gathered by hand. Because these and other roots were gathered by California native groups like the Wappo, the American pioneers referred to this group in general as "Diggers," a derogatory term.

When a person became sick, his or her family employed a "dreaming doctor" to extract the offending poison from the person's body, which he did after lacerating the sufferer with a sharp flint stone.[36] If the patient didn't heal, (or even if he did) the doctor determined who the "poisoner" was, and appropriate retribution was made. The "poisoner" was usually considered to be a person or persons from another nearby tribe, the poison having been transmitted by evil thoughts. Retaliation for such ensorcellment could require a battle, which the accused could prevent by making peace offerings: a kind of civil litigation. Heizer said that if the cure succeeded, the patient's family paid the doctor in magnesite beads or

---

[35]Driver, Loc. Cit.

[36]Heizer, Loc. Cit. These practices were common among totemistic peoples.

clamshells, and the doctor rested in isolation for four days. If the cure failed, the doctor went without pay, and the deceased was washed, adorned with flowers and feathers, wrapped in a blanket and burned on a pyre with all his belongings while his relatives wailed in unison and cut their hair and, often, their bodies. Afterwards they either smeared the ashes on their faces or buried them in a hole under the pyre. The ghost of the deceased was said to hang around for a good while afterward.

The Wappo also employed "singing doctors," but their remedies were considered temporary. They dressed themselves in elaborate costumes of feathers and furs and tried to dance and chant the pathology away.

Powerful as it may have been in the minds of the Wappo, the doctors' expertise was no match for the smallpox virus. Two epidemics of it struck, interspersed with an outbreak of cholera.

The first big smallpox epidemic hit in the winter of 1828-29. Smallpox virus spreads via the tiny droplets that are expelled in a cough or sneeze, and its incubation period is 10-12 days, so a person might be infected with the virus without showing symptoms immediately. Muscular ache and a high fever develop, and then in another two days or so a rash appears on the face and spreads to the rest of the body. As in chicken pox, the rash elevates and scabs, and when the scabs are disturbed, scars form. Blindness is a common side effect, but among the native Californian people, death was the usual result. The population of indigenous people in Northern California was decimated by the Europeans' diseases.

The worst smallpox epidemic struck in 1837. The carrier was Ignacio Miramontes, an employee of General M.G. Vallejo's who had gone to Fort Ross with a shipment of hides and other trade items. He returned with word that smallpox had struck the Russian outpost, not knowing that he was carrying it now too.[37] The resulting outbreak among the Wappo was so severe that in many cases no one was left to bury them.

---

[37]Heizer, Loc. Cit.

Chapter Two

The Napa Valley Is "Discovered"

The Napa Valley was once part of a huge, wild region called "Alta California," the final claim of the Spanish Empire. Spain's realm still spanned much of the globe in the early 19th century, and at first she had only two real competitors for this remote land--the substantial native population and the Russians, who had established a farming community in Fort Ross in 1812.[1]

In 1817 the Spanish started a mission in San Rafael. It gained them access to a new pool of natives from which to find converts to the Catholic Church, one of the major motivations for Spain's era of exploration. It also afforded them a northern perch from which they could spy on the Russians while trading with them for much-needed supplies.[2] Spain lost Alta California in 1821, when Mexico broke away from its mother country. The non-native population swore allegiance[3] to the Empire of Mexico and called themselves "Californios."

The new Mexican government reevaluated things right away. One of the first problems they considered was the state of affairs at Mission Dolores in Yerba Buena (later known as "San Francisco"), where the natives, used to warm, dry weather, were suffering badly.

---

[1] For an in-depth and detailed history of the Spanish occupation of California, see Hubert Howe Bancroft's massive collection, *The History of California,* originally published in 1886. See also Fr. Zephyrin Engelhardt's four-volume work, *The Missions and Missionaries of California,* James H. Barry Company, SF, 1912.

[2] Bancroft, Vol. XX, p. 115.

[3] often begrudgingly.

The padre in charge was the enthusiastic and aggressive Jose Altimira of Barcelona. Still loyal to Spain, he secretly refused to sign the oath of allegiance.

Altimira knew that his natives needed to relocate to a sunnier climate. His politically ambitious plan was to leapfrog the mission in San Rafael and establish a mission and military presence somewhere to the north, with himself in charge. He would populate it with natives from both Mission Dolores and San Rafael as well as with *neophytes*, "beginners" to Christianity recruited from the native population.

Secretly encouraged by the Governor, Luis Arguello, Altimira seized an opportunity to outfit an expedition that would survey the unexplored territory to the northwest of the San Pablo Bay. It was during this exploration that the first non-natives officially set foot on Napa County soil.[4]

Altimira and 20 soldiers entered the Napa Valley from the southwest on June 28, 1823, the fourth day of the trip. In his diary, he recorded that after leaving their launch in an estuary of Sonoma Creek they headed northeast and crossed a range of hills that the Indians were getting ready to burn. The soil, he remarked, was good for pasture, and there were no thick woods into which livestock might stray.

They crossed a small canyon with a warm spring. Altimira attributed the elevated temperature to the heat of the day and the lack of shade. The ground there, he noted, was white and sticky, similar to a region near Barcelona: good, perhaps, "for cleansing purposes."[5] They mounted the hill on the other side and saw a more extensive canyon with 200-300 head of elk. He also commented on the presence of deer, antelope and bear.

Altimira wrote that the Napa Valley was so-named because of the

---

[4]For a complete reading of Altimira's diary, see Robert Smilie, *The Sonoma Mission*, Valley Publishers, Fresno, 1979.

[5]Bancroft, Vol. XIX, pp 497-498. The white substance might have been pumice, a product of vulcanism.

Indians who lived there. He may have been referring to *Napato* (or *Napajo*), a permanent native community somewhere between Napa Creek and the Napa River. He seems to have come upon the creek first, which he said had little current, but he did see several small ponds which would be good watering holes for cattle. Then he and his men came to a large waterway, clearly the Napa River, which they christened the "San Pedro" in honor of the Feast of St. Peter (June 30). They spent the night there.

The next morning they said Mass and continued northeast. Altimira said that the natives were burning more fields and assumed it to be a warning that he was coming, although field-burning was a normal native activity for the month of June ("burn-the-valley-moon"). He wrote of large, dry stretches which he said might be suitable for vineyards, and of numerous groves of tall oak trees. He also mentioned the plentiful supply of rocks all about on the mountains they then ascended to the east: enough to "build a new Rome," he said. From there he and his men continued another 15 miles into the Suisun Valley by way of Suisun Creek. Altimira noticed, as many others have since, that it's warmer in Suisun than in Napa or Sonoma.

After a friendly meeting with the natives near Cordelia, Altimira and company returned home. They killed three bears between Cordelia and the Napa Valley. This time they went farther north before crossing into Sonoma and found an outcropping of limestone as well as more potential vineyard land.

In summing up the adventure, Altimira decided that the Sonoma Valley, having more timber and more water than he observed in Napa, would be the best place for the new mission, while Napa would be very suitable for cattle tending. From this new location, he felt, the Californios would be able to convert the natives and subdue any who resisted their soldiers.

He started building. By the end of 1824 his new mission, "San Francisco de Solano," housed 693 neophytes, most of them natives transferred from Mission Dolores, San Rafael and San Jose. The rest were the result of "recruitment." An inventory of the surrounding ranchos tallied 1,100 cattle, 4,000 sheep, 430 horses and a few mules.

Staple crops of wheat, corn and beans had been planted.[6]

Not all the indigenous people, however, were interested in being recruited, much less subdued. In the fall of 1827 a native force attacked and burned the mission. Altimira transferred elsewhere, and when his many Californio enemies discovered that he had not signed the oath of allegiance back in '21, they forced him to leave the New World altogether.[7]

It was obvious to the Mexican government that some of the natives, particularly the Wappo, posed more of a problem than they had anticipated. Ensign Cayetano Juarez received orders to proceed to Sonoma to "keep the Indians there and in the Napa Valley in subjection."[8] Each morning and every night he and his contingent of soldiers patrolled the area around Sonoma, monitoring the natives' activity.[9]

In 1829 Juarez got news that 2,000 natives[10] were attacking the mission in San Jose. The leader of the raid was a native, Estanislauso, whose name is remembered in Stanislaus County. Juarez was among the contingent of soldiers that Vallejo dispatched to the site. Juarez *et al* found the mission devastated and the priest in charge cowering in the tule marsh. He rounded up as many of the mission's natives as he could find and pursued the offenders. He was wounded when an arrow pierced the seven layers of his rawhide armor and penetrated about 3/4 of an inch into his chest.[11]

While the Californios grossly inflated their estimate of how many Indians attacked them, the magnitude of their public relations problem with the natives was truly enormous. It further exasperated

---

[6]Bancroft, Vol. XIX, p. 506.

[7]Beard, p. 21.

[8]Idem.

[9] Lyman Palmer, *The History of Napa and Lake Counties*, Slocum & Bowen, NP, 1881 pp. 494-499.

[10]Nellie Van de Grift Sanchez, *Spanish Arcadia*, Powell Publishing Company, San Francisco, 1929, p. 111.

[11]Palmer, Loc. Cit.

them that the Russians enjoyed prosperity without hindrance from the natives. The new Governor, Figueroa, sent his top military man, Mariano Guadalupe Vallejo, age 29, to Fort Ross to learn the secret of the Russians' success and to determine whether they posed a threat to Mexican interests.

Vallejo saw that the Russians did not attempt to convert the natives. Some of them had taken native wives, and mission Indians who had managed to elude their Spanish "recruiters" found a welcome there. Vallejo wrote a strongly worded letter to Figueroa. Forcibly baptizing the Indians and turning them into unpaid laborers, he said, was the main source of their hostility. Armed soldiers sometimes dragged young native men from their camps. The soldiers themselves came from the worst elements of society. California was anything but a desired military assignment; indeed, as the most remote outpost in the Empire it had been a kind of Botany Bay for Spaniards.

Vallejo built a large adobe in Sonoma and settled in, while his soldiers continued to "recruit" the surrounding natives to work in the mission. One who was "recruited" to Mission Dolores as a boy and later transferred to Sonoma was a 6'7" Suisun. Baptized "Francisco Solano Suisun," the powerful, giant of a man became an alcalde and later a labor boss. Vallejo made "Chief Solano" (aka "Prince" Solano) a Captain in the Mexican Army. His commanding presence was a visual affidavit to his peers that Vallejo and the Californios meant business.[12]

As Commander of the Presidio in Sonoma, Vallejo tried other means of settling the surrounding countryside. He imported a shipload of potential colonists from Mexico and helped them start a community in the present Mark West Springs area. (Mark West was an early land owner there.) But the would-be pueblo failed, because the people feared the natives and doubted that Vallejo's military could really protect them.

---

[12]Clyde Low, personal conversation with the author. See Low's informative article, "Chief Solano, the Legend Examined," *Solano Historian,* May, 1986, pp. 1 and ff.

By 1830, 650 natives had been baptized at Sonoma, most of them from Napa and Sonoma Valleys. The total number of natives was listed as 760. In addition, 370 had been buried. Bancroft lists the names of the native communities with people at the mission, which reads much like a death toll of the native American culture in the Bay Area:

> *Aloquiomi, Atenomac, Canoma, Carquin, Canijomano, Caymus, Chemuco, Chichoyomi, Chocuyem, Huiloc, Huymen, Lacatiut, Loaquiomi, Linayto, Locnoma, Mayacma, Muticolmo, Malaca, Napato, Oleomi, Putto, Polnomanoc, Paque, Petaluma, Suisun, Satayomi, Soneto, Toleni, Tlayacma, Tamal, Topanto, Ululato, Utinomanoc, Zaclom*[13].

Forbidden from their custom of burning down their dwellings in order to sanitize them, the natives soon became dirty and louse-ridden. Paralytic depression was also a persistent problem. The afflicted native would become lethargic and refuse to eat or move around much.

Day in the neophytes' lives began just before dawn, when they left their dwellings outside the mission wall to attend Mass.[14] Breakfast of cereal made from corn or grain was served from large iron kettles. As soon as breakfast was over, work began. Women labored within the mission walls, weaving blankets and coarse clothing. Men did heavier work in the fields or around the mission. Many natives from both genders prepared hides and tallow, the only real exports from the entire Alta California region. They had Sundays and holidays off.[15]

They ate dinner (more grain from the kettles, sometimes with meat or other seasonal vegetables added) at noon, then relaxed for a two-hour siesta. Work began again for the afternoon, and the

---

[13]Bancroft, Vol. XIX, p. 506.

[14] Fr. Zephyrin Engelhardt, *The Missions and Missionaries of California*, II, James H. Barry Co., SF, 1912, pp. 253-254.

[15]Irving Berdine Richman, *California Under Spain and Mexico, 1535 - 1857*, Cooper Square Publishers, Inc., NY, 1965, pp. 335-336.

workday ended at around 5:00, when the neophytes returned to church and then had supper, which was more or less a soupy, watered-down repeat of breakfast and dinner. With no dried fish, no acorns, no grasshoppers and no venison, the bill of fare at the missions may have been as unpalatable to the natives as native food would have been to the missionaries.

Neophytes were collected from all the tribes in the general area, and new converts were shipped from nearby missions. Some Napa Valley natives were transported to more distant locations. Beard writes, for example, that 200 Wappo from the *Kaimus* village in Yountville were taken to the mission in San Jose. Natives whose tribes had been at odds with each other now had to work side by side.

Relatives of neophytes set up camp near the missions where their loved ones resided in a kind of loose captivity, so a steady supply of free labor was virtually guaranteed. Prostitution, which was unknown among the family-oriented Wappo, became common, as did the presence of syphilis, which the natives contracted from the soldiers.

To protect native girls from the unwanted affection of love-starved men, unwed women were housed separately and supervised by an older matron. Suitors could court their maidens through the bars in the windows. If the courtship was successful, the young woman told her father, and if he approved, a wedding was arranged. The new couple then took up residence in a house built among the other native homes outside the mission.

The King of Spain had instructed the missionaries to start schools for the neophytes in 1793, but few of the natives had seemed interested in learning to read or write.[16] By the time Altimira had established San Francisco de Solano, the imperative to impart literacy had been all but abandoned. It should be noted that the Californios themselves did not place high value on literacy; Vallejo was one of the very few lettered men in the region.

The natives received no recompense for their work, and,

---

[16]Engelhardt, pp. 472-475.

depending on the philosophy of the priest in charge, punishments could be severe. A malfeasant could find himself locked in the *calabozo*, and if he tried to escape he could be hunted down, flogged and put in leg irons as an example to the others. They were never referred to as slaves, but there was no graduation from neophyte status, and the children of neophytes were also called neophytes.

Not all the natives were recruited to the missions by force. Many came voluntarily. What would have induced the Wintu, Miwok and their neighbors to leave their freedom for life in the missions? The primary attraction may have been food. The Californios' voraciously grazing livestock elbowed out the elk, antelope and other large wildlife, driving away the natives' customary food supply. The Californios slaughtered wild animals for tallow and hides. A Frenchman visiting the mission in 1827 described riders on horseback lassoing scores of deer and cutting their leg tendons to prevent them from fleeing. The fat was then removed from their bodies, while the flesh and skin remained for consumption by bears. [17]

The Wappo and their neighbors were punished for burning the fields, because it destroyed the grass that the cattle needed for grazing. Field burning, however, was an important element in the maintenance of their ecology.

A drought added to their misery. No rain at all fell for the 24 months between 1828 and 1830, diminishing the acorn crop and interrupting the cycle of grass regeneration, which affected the domestic livestock as well as the native animals.[18] Fishing, always a family affair among the Wappo, could not make up for the increasing scarcity of game. Quite naturally, the hungry Wappo tried substituting beef and horseflesh for deer meat. This brought recriminations from the soldiers, who were especially upset over the loss of their horses.

Awe of the Spanish and their cultural attainments may also have drawn some to the missions. The soldiers' God must have seemed

---

[17]The French explorer was named Leperouse. From Forbes, p. 2.
[18]Bancroft, XIX, p. 115.

very powerful to the natives, and worshiping him might have seemed pragmatically expedient. True spiritual conversion is also probable, despite the militarism surrounding it.

Scarcity of food, severe penalties for rustling and the shanghaiing of neophytes resulted in hostility among the tribes, especially the Wappo, who attacked other natives who collaborated with the missionaries. The native population had to choose between hunger and loyalty to the old ways, or food and submission to the new.

Old rivalries among the tribes were rekindled in the final days of Wappo society. The war that came to be known as the "First Satoyomi Campaign" had its roots in the natives' dilemma of supporting the old ways or joining forces with the new.

The war had a prosaic enough beginning.[19] A Pomo stole a mule from Vallejo, probably to eat. A Wappo tribelet sheltered the thief. Vallejo sent an interpreter (perhaps another Wappo) to get the mule and the thief, but the Wappo tied up the interpreter and laid him where the soldiers would find him. Angered by this message of non-compliance, Vallejo deployed a contingent of soldiers, who were ambushed in a ravine by Wappo wielding flint-tipped spears. The Wappo were led by a chief named Succara. Six soldiers were killed and 32 wounded. The Wappo also captured and hung 30 Pomo who had allied with Vallejo. (This was a very non-Wappo behavior, and was probably inspired by what they saw the Californios do.) The Wappo warriors fled north to present-day Mendocino County, leaving behind about 300 of their own men, women and children, who were taken prisoner by the Californios.

Mariano Vallejo's brother Salvador pursued the warriors and soon came upon a Pomo friendly to the mission who had been strapped all over with fine thongs and left in a cave. The Wappo and the soldiers finally clashed in a place called Valle de Tuche, where about 200 of the natives were slain, dying mostly of saber- and lance-wounds,

---

[19]Anecdotes of Californio/Wappo clashes are from Robert Heizer, "The Archaeology of the Napa Region," *Anthropological Records,* Vol. 12, No. 6, 1953.

Cayetano Juarez

*Mariano Vallejo, above, was
the military commander of
Mexico's Northern Frontier,
administrator of mission San
Francisco de Solano and
grantee of several* concedos,
including Rancho Nacional
Suscol *in what would become
Napa County. His brother,
Salvador, right, was a
military officer and grantee of*
Rancho Napa.

implying that the fighting was done close up. There were no Californio casualties.

Chief Succara was now far from his home and was carrying his own supplies, so he dared not launch another attack. Mariano Vallejo sent to the governor for reinforcements. Four hundred troops marched into the Wappo camp behind the leadership of Salvador Vallejo. Succara surrendered and handed over 20 of his warriors as hostages, along with a promise to return all the uneaten horses.

Another battle between the Wappo and Vallejo occurred in 1836, this also over the theft of livestock. A Pomo friendly to Vallejo stole back from the Wappo four horses that the Wappo had stolen from Vallejo. A large party of Wappo, led by a chief named Coton, attacked the Pomo group, killing 20 and wounding 50 more. Salvador Vallejo gathered 50 soldiers and about 100 friendly Indians and chased the Wappo to the Geysers area. Vallejo won. A treaty was signed, gifts were exchanged, and the Wappo and Pomo agreed to respect each others' territory. The Wappo agreed to return fleeing neophytes to Vallejo.

More skirmishes occurred despite the truce. Salvador Vallejo and the Wappo entered into a second treaty in 1837. Among its 11 articles was an agreement that Wappo warriors would not come to Sonoma Valley in numbers greater than 30 at one time, while the Californios would seek permission of the Wappo before entering into their territory.

The treaty was solemnly sworn to in a special ceremony, but it is unlikely that either side honored it. Indeed, the condition was on its way to deteriorating. Cayetano Juarez told his biographer that 24 natives whom Vallejo was training to be soldiers escaped with their guns. All but one got away.[20]

Charles Camp, a biographer of the pioneer George Yount,

---

[20]Palmer, p. 497. The one who didn't was apprehended at the Napa River near Carneros Creek.

described warfare between the natives and the white pioneers.[21] On Christmas Day, 1837, he said, Yount awoke to find half of his cattle missing. The culprit, Yount believed, was La Jota, a high-ranking neophyte from the Pope Valley area who had apparently escaped from the mission. Fearing the Wappo were getting ready to attack him, Yount appealed to Vallejo for help. Vallejo sent Chief Solano and 25 young native men to apprehend La Jota and his followers "dead or alive." Meanwhile, Yount himself and some cohorts went to Pope Valley, and his scouts took four scalps. That night Solano, Yount and their followers attacked La Jota and burned the natives' settlement.

On paper, the plan for all the missions in Alta California had been to stay for 10 years, then turn the land over to the Christianized natives and colonists wishing to start ranchos. In practice it did not turn out this way. The missions remained intact for scores of years. In 1830 Governor Encheandia issued a law enforcing the 10 year rule.

When his successor, Governor Figueroa, toured the missions he found that on the whole the natives were in no condition to self-govern, even if they had wanted to. From today's perspective it is easy to see why. The Californios naively expected a single generation to pass from a hunter/gatherer ethos to that of a modern European society. In actuality disease, the collapse of the native's world and the incompatibility of their culture with their conquerors' had reduced them to a state of dependency as well as a depressive lassitude.

Figueroa recommended that the northern frontier be secured for Mexico by the immigration of Mexican colonists, with natives receiving land grants whenever possible. Only one Wappo is known to have received land from Vallejo, a *Kaimus* villager from what is now Yountville. His name was Camillo Ynita. Ynita became chief of a settlement called Olompali in Marin. He was unable to trade the wheat he grew, however, and Vallejo had to act as his middleman. Ynita figured in the Bear Flag rebellion and is said to have been killed by his own people in 1856.

---

[21] Charles Camp, *George C. Yount and His Chronicles of the West*, Old West Publishing Company, Denver, 1966, p. 13.

Favored Mexican citizens were to be granted ranchos: large tracts of land on which they could run and breed cattle, horses and sheep, and live if they dared. The Californios considered the Napa Valley, situated in the heart of Wappo country, too dangerous for non-native occupation. Vallejo ran cattle there and employed native labor to husband the livestock. The workers were paid in food. By the end of the 1830's 25 families had settled on the "northern frontier," almost all of them gathered around the little garrison in Sonoma.

Not that Sonoma was all that peaceful. In the winter of 1837 a band of about 50 Californio soldiers threatened to mutiny and kill the Vallejos. Mariano Vallejo called upon his old stalwart, Cayetano Juarez, to resolve the difficulty. Juarez learned that the soldiers' complaint was that they had not been provided with warm clothing for the chilly December weather. The matter was resolved.[22]

The first American pioneer with courage to pitch his tent permanently in Napa County was George Yount, a North Carolina man who had emigrated to Missouri. Yount had lost most of his money to a scoundrel friend and skipped town, leaving behind his impoverished wife, son and two daughters. He trapped beaver in the Southwest with grizzled mountain men like Ewing Young, James Ohio Pattie, William Wolfskill and Antoine Robidoux. With the price of beaver declining and the natives growing more hostile, Yount went to Northern California to pursue the sleek, 5'-long otter that dined on abalone in the coastal surf.[23] Guy Fling, a mountain man who eventually settled in Napa, claimed to have guided Yount through the Napa Valley as early as 1831.[24]

Along the way in his adventurous life, he had learned to make wooden shingles for siding in houses. This skill brought him to the attention of Mariano Vallejo, who employed him and a fellow

---

[22]Palmer, p. 497.

[23] Walton Bean, *California: An Interpretive History*, McGraw Hill, NY, 1973, p. 74.

[24] Clarence Smith and Wallace Elliott, *Illustrations of Napa County, California, with Historical Sketch*, Oakland, 1878, p. 2.

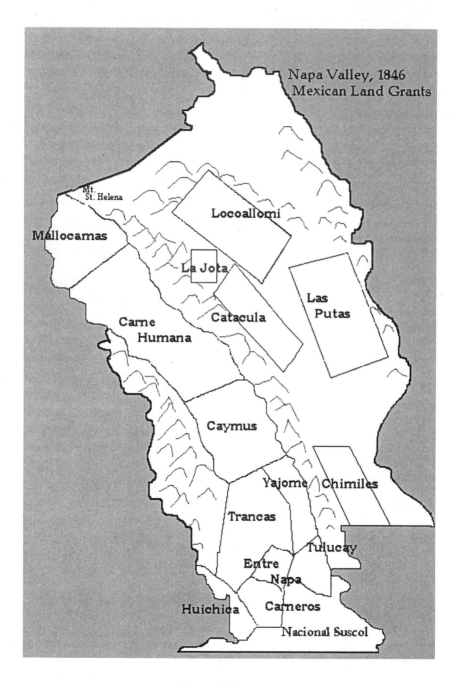

Napa Valley, 1846
Mexican Land Grants

Mt.
St. Helena

Locoallomi

Mallocamas

La Jota

Carne
Humana

Catacula

Las
Putas

Caymus

Yajome Chimiles

Trancas

Tulucay

Entre
Napa

Huichica Carneros

Nacional Suscol

pioneer, George Brown, as carpenters. In payment, Vallejo offered Yount a large grant of land in the heart of Wappo country, on the condition that he become a Mexican citizen and a Catholic. Ready to retire from the rigors of matching mountains, Yount agreed to both and in 1836 received about 12,000 acres in central Napa Valley, a huge parcel that encompassed what is now Yountville, Oakville and Rutherford. He called it *Rancho Caymus*, after the natives who had first occupied the land. A few years later he applied for and received a grant on Howell Mountain, which he called *Rancho La Jota* for the Wappo leader whose village he had helped destroy.

"Captain Buckskin," as the Californios sometimes called him because of his unusual homemade garb,[25] was the quintessential mountain man: brave, illiterate, ugly, industrious and thoroughly knowledgeable about the outdoors. A master craftsman as well, he was up to the task of securing the land given him. He constructed a small log cabin (the first wooden house in California) in a style called the "Kentucky Blockhouse." The bottom story of the house was about 18 feet square, and the second floor overhung the first by five feet all around. He slept on the upper level, peering out narrow windows to keep watch on the native Wappo, who set up camp just north of him. He kept his muzzle-loader rifle at the ready, with bullets he molded himself.[26]

The natives were definitely hungry, probably quite curious about the white man and possibly hostile. Any plans they may have harbored to mount an attack on him were thwarted the next year, however, for in 1837 a massive smallpox outbreak hit. Smallpox vaccine was available, and Mariano Vallejo was able to vaccinate his soldiers. He attempted to defeat the disease among the natives by sending a boat to Santa Cruz for lime, with which the Indians were instructed to whitewash their houses. Most of it was used to disinfect

---

[25] Rev. Orange Clark, "Chronicles of George C. Yount," *California Historical Quarterly*, II, 1923-24, p 10.

[26] Capt. William Kerr, ed., *History and Bibliography of the Mexican Ranchos of Napa*, San Diego, Nd. Pages unnumbered.

the dead.

After the epidemic Yount dismantled the blockhouse and built a long, narrow, fort-like home with a red tile roof and portholes in its thick adobe walls.[27] Natives who had survived the smallpox plague continued to camp nearby.

Other mountain men on their journeys through the West often stayed at Captain Buckskin's place, swapping tall tales in the true oral tradition. A man described as "an old Frenchman" (probably a French Canadian trapper) appears to have lived with him for several years.[28] In the next decade, many American pioneer families sought out George Yount for his hospitality, while others exploited his generosity by squatting on his land.

Shortly after Yount built his Kentucky Blockhouse, a former alcalde (judge) of Sonoma, Nicolas Higuera, received for his services two large grants of land bordered by the Napa River and Carneros Creek, which he called *Entre Napa* and *Rincon de Carneros*, respectively. Higuera ran 2,000 head of cattle and 3,000 horses at *Entre Napa* and on the 2,557.68 acres of his *Carneros* rancho to the south and west.[29]

Entre Napa lay on real estate now occupied by the southern portion of Napa City. Higuera erected some corrals and built a primitive house of mud and wicker there, although he also maintained a residence in Sonoma.[30] By an interesting quirk of fate, the property upon which his little hut was built later fell into the hands of an Englishman named John Patchett. Patchett employed a young German, Charles Krug, to make wine for him to sell. Thus the first wine ever produced commercially in the Napa Valley was made on land that once belonged to Napa City's first identifiable

---

[27]In 1873 a Yountville farmer named John Finnell erected a mansion on the foundation of Yount's adobe (*Napa Reporter*, 4-12-1873).

[28]Ralph Kingsbury, *The Napa Valley to 1850*, LA, unpublished Master's Thesis, USC, 1939, p 44.

[29]Davis, p. 32.

[30]Idem.

homeowner.

Tidy as this coincidence may seem, however, it is unlikely that Higuera's was the only domestic cell in the proto-Napa City area in the late 1830's. There are vague references in historical documents to the "Pueblo de Salvador"--a small Mexican town--somewhere between the ancient path up the valley and the tidewater of the Napa River (at First Street).[31]

In 1838, Salvador Vallejo became the county's third landholder, taking a large tract between Higuera's and Yount's parcels. If Don Salvador owned the land today he would count the western and northern parts of downtown Napa, all of North Napa and Browns Valley as parts of his realm.

Don Salvador's place went by two names--*Rancho Napa* and *Trancas y Jalapa*. The boundary between Salvador's rancho and Higuera's *Entre Napa* was Napa Creek. The name "Napa" derives from the *Napato* village that Altimira said was once there, artifacts from which may have been those excavated earlier in the 20th century at the corner of Franklin and Laurel Streets, a residential area just south of the business district. A *trancas* in Vallejo's time was a metal or wooden bar erected to keep cattle from natural river crossings. Such a barrier is said to have existed at the tidewaters' head, and was a well-known landmark.[32] *Jalapa* may have referred to the *Yulupa* native settlement located somewhere within the nearby area. The rancho's name may also have been a clever pun. *Trancas* can mean, simply, "sticks," and *jalapa* can mean "morning glory," a common weed. The moniker "Sticks and Weeds" would have seemed aptly descriptive of the rancho, in the middle of what was then nowhere.

William Heath Davis, a pioneer who was Vallejo's contemporary, wrote in his memoirs that 5,000 to 6,000 head of cattle and 2,000

---

[31]Hoover, pp. 290-291.

[32]Gudde, p. 367.

horses ran in S. Vallejo's Napa Valley kingdom.[33] Salvador also managed a soap factory on his premises.[34]

In 1841 Mariano Vallejo's stalwart ensign, Cayetano Juarez, was rewarded for his courage and counsel with a substantial land grant: 8,865.58 acres, bounded on the west by the Napa River, and on the east by the ridges and mountains the explorer Altimira thought could rebuild Rome. Juarez called his rancho *Tulucay* after an old Wintun settlement. He boasted of having more than 1,000 natives living on his property, onto which he, too, eventually moved.

Juarez married a Higuera, Maria de Jesus, and his family hosted fiestas typical of the Mexican Pastoral period. After his annual rodeo he held a "Bull Bake" to feed his guests, where he roasted entire steers.[35] Less than 50 years later, Juarez's land would become the heart of East Napa, the Valley's "Little Italy." Another rancho, *Llajome*, or *Yajome*, lay mostly on the eastern side of the Napa River, from (roughly) the present-day Yountville Cross Road to Hagen Road in Napa. The Mexican government gave this slightly elevated shelf of land to a soldier, Damaso Antonio Rodriguez, who never lived there.[36] Salvador Vallejo annexed the property in 1852 when Rodriguez died.

The City of Napa is thus an amalgam, a nexus where the estates of several Californios converged. Higuera's *Entre Napa* formed the bulk of the present downtown area west of the Napa River, extending as far south as Highway 121 and as far west as Old Sonoma Road. Its northern boundary was First Street. Everything north of First Street (Napa Creek) belonged to Salvador Vallejo, and across the river to the east, the land belonged to Juarez and Rodriguez.

---

[33] William Heath Davis, *Seventy-Five Years in California*, J. Howell, SF, 1929, p. 32.

[34] H.H. Bancroft, *California Pastorale*, p. 444.

[35] Sarah Scott, "Los Californios," in *Late Harvest: Napa Valley Pioneers*, California Indigenous Arts Organization, 1984.

[36] Hoover, p. 283.

While his wealthy Californio neighbors managed their estates from Sonoma, the contented George Yount planted pear trees, roses and strawberries and let large herds of cattle roam in the wild oats and other grasses that grew almost as tall as he was.[37] He employed natives and *vaqueros* (cowboys) to tend his livestock. He put in a small vineyard of mission grapes and made wine from them for his own enjoyment and that of his frequent guests, using the Spanish method of storing the fruit in hides and allowing the juice to ooze out, drop by fermented drop.[38]

On December 27, 1840, a runner came to his adobe with a plea from Mariano Vallejo for Captain Buckskin to bring whomever he could and meet him at a *trancas* by the Napa River for a military activity that was about to take place. The trancas he had in mind was not at his brother Salvador's place, but a river crossing called "Suscol" south of Higuera's land grant. Natives--primarily Wappo--were massing there for a battle, and Vallejo believed that the target of their aggression would be the garrison in Sonoma.

Vallejo deployed men to the north and south of the Wappo war camp and hid them. Then he and a half-dozen of his soldiers took a very visible position on a knoll and commanded the natives to disperse. As Vallejo had anticipated, they approached instead in a large arc formation, dressed for war. Vallejo gave the order for his flanks to attack, and when the "Battle of Suscol" was over, 34 natives had been killed and the rest scattered or taken prisoner. A few years later, General Mariano Vallejo himself owned the battleground. He accepted a large grant of land, *Rancho Nacional Suscol*, in the American Canyon/Vallejo area.

A particularly chilling postscript to the Battle of Suscol followed in 1841. Salvador Vallejo and a gang of American hunters murdered more than a dozen Wappo men as the natives emerged, one by one,

---

[37] Ibid, p. 281. Hoover says Yount may have had a gristmill on his property as early as 1843. He rebuilt it in 1854 with lumber hauled down from Howell Mountain.

[38] *Napa County Reporter (NCR)* 1-3-1879.

from their sweat house.[39] The incident occurred in what is now Lake County, where another grisly episode would take place 10 years later.

Joining the mountain man, the judge, the bully and the soldier in 1841 was a hotheaded man with a mysterious past: Edward Turner Bale, whose reconstructed Bale Mill functions today. Bale was born in England (London? Manchester? historians disagree) around 1810 and arrived in Monterey sometime in the 1830's, perhaps by shipwreck.[40] He claimed to be a doctor and evidently possessed skill of some kind, because Mariano Vallejo appointed him surgeon-in-chief of the Army in 1840. Like many other frontier MD's, he may have received his training on the job by assisting the ship's doctor on his voyage west.

Bale made his way to Yerba Buena, which in the 1830's wasn't much more than a pile of dunes and sandy hills with a few freshwater creeks running through them. He became friends with Nathan Spear, an entrepreneur who co-owned a store in Monterey. Spear also operated Yerba Buena's first grist, or flour, mill.[41] It was an association that benefitted Bale and the Napa Valley in general, as will be discussed later.

Much of the social life in Yerba Buena occurred aboard ship on the larger vessels that came there to port. A visiting English nobleman, Sir James Douglas, noted in his diary that a doctor named Bale came aboard with the customs officers, had tea with them, and was still hanging around at 6 o'clock. Bale told Sir James that everybody who was Anybody would be in the ship's ballroom that night, and that he himself would be the "master of ceremonies" and could invite whomever he chose. Unconvinced, the nobleman and his party

---

[39] Davis, p. 236.

[40] Jennie and Denzil Verardo, "Dr. Edward Turner Bale and His Grist Mill," *Gleanings,* Napa Valley Historical Society, Vol. 2, No. 3, June, 1979.

[41] which came to Yerba Buena in 1839, prefab. It was made in Boston, came around the Horn, and was put together as a two-story wooden building on the north side of Clay Street, between Kearny and Montgomery. Davis, p. 133.

demurred. They learned later that Bale himself hadn't even been invited.[42]

Along with his social aspirations, the "free and easy doctor," as Douglas described him, had a problem with substance abuse. He was jailed eight days for selling alcohol from his medical offices and was sharply criticized for dispensing medicine at doses dangerously higher than usually prescribed. Moreover, in what proved to be a foreshadowing of future troubles with the judicial system, he was sued for breach of contract when "a Frenchman" paid him for mules which Bale never delivered. (The "Frenchman" might have been the same one who lived with Yount.)

Despite these mottles on his reputation, Bale married the Vallejo brothers' very attractive niece, Maria Guadalupe Soberanes. He received a 17,000-acre land grant covering the length of the Napa Valley from the northern border of Yount's rancho to Tubbs Lane in present-day Calistoga. The city of Saint Helena would be in the center of it.

Bale named his rancho *Carne Humana,* which means "human flesh." He was making a pun out of *Canijomano,* the Spanish name for a nearby Wappo community, as well as a macabre reference about what he feared might be his own fate. (The Wappo did not practice cannibalism, however.) He built a small rectangular adobe on what is now Whitehall Lane, south of present-day St. Helena. His dwelling was deep in the heart of Wappo country.

Not long after their marriage, a scandal occurred in the household of Edward and Maria Bale which would have set Napa Valley tongues wagging, had there been tongues to wag. There are two versions of the story. In the first version, Bale returned to *Carne Humana* unexpectedly and found Salvador Vallejo and Maria (Edward's wife, Salvador's niece) embracing. Socially sensitive gentleman that he was, Bale challenged Salvador to a duel with swords, as was de rigueur for the era. He was soundly defeated, and Salvador had him publicly whipped for the insult. In the second version, (perhaps the one for

---

[42]Verardo, p. 8.

public consumption) Bale accused Salvador of lying, and Salvador had him whipped for this.[43]

In July of 1844 Edward Bale, seething, rode into Sonoma with 14 Americans. He fired two shots at Salvador from behind, as the latter was walking down the street with Cayetano Juarez. Bullets grazed Salvador's neck and hit Juarez on the left jawbone. Bale then ran to the home of Jacob Leese, perhaps hoping to pay Leese to hide him. But Bale was apprehended by a group of Wintu. The natives were preparing to lynch him (a custom which was not de rigueur for them) when Salvador interceded and turned him over to the custody of Sgt. Jose de los Santos Berryessa. Berryessa put Bale in leg irons. He awaited trial in the *calabozo*, after unsuccessfully attempting to bribe the guard to release him.

Bale was found guilty. When the case was sent to Governor Manuel Micheltorena for sentencing, however, Micheltorena ordered it dropped. Bale was English by birth, and Micheltorena may have feared angering the English, because their Hudson's Bay Company was a major purchaser of hides and tallow from Northern California, and trade in hides was the heart of the economy. Bale was released.

Hudson's Bay Company, like the Rocky Mountain Fur Company and John Jacob Astor's Astoria Fur Company employed trappers. Hudson's Bay made a fortune for its owners by bartering expensive animal pelts for cheap household items. Their ships were floating general stores whose arrival was eagerly anticipated by the Californios.[44] Its Napa Valley connection was forwarded by another land grant recipient, an American trapper-cum-entrepreneur, Jacob Primer Leese, Yerba Buena's first real socialite.

When Jacob Primer Leese married Rosalia Vallejo, the sister of Mariano and Salvador, he became, like Edward Bale, part of The Family. Unlike the pseudo-doctor, however, the Ohio-born adventurer Leese had real talents and actual ability.

---

[43] George Lyman, MD, "The Scalpel Under Three Flags," in *California Historical Quarterly*, IV, No. 2, June, 1925, p. 153.

[44] Bil Gilbert, *The Trailblazers*, Time-Life Books, NY, 1973, p. 61 ff.

Leese emigrated from Ohio to hunt for beaver as a very young man (about 21), and arrived in the mountains of New Mexico around the same time Yount left that area. Indeed, his career in the West trails Yount's by about three years. While Yount remained on the supply side as a hunter, however, Leese got involved with the business part of the profession. He made his way to Monterey in 1836, where he attracted two other businessmen, William Hinckley (who owned ships) and Nathan Spear (who owned stores).[45] Conveniently, Spear's nephew, William Heath Davis, clerked at the store and piloted Hinckley's schooner.[46]

Inspired, encouraged and bankrolled by these older men, Leese set up shop in the next good port up the coast, Yerba Buena. He became the second settler there, the first being an old sea captain, William Richardson, for whom Richardson Bay and Bridge are named.[47]

With Hinckley and Spear as silent partners,[48] Leese and Salvador Vallejo ran little vessels along the inland coast, collecting hides and other products of the cattle industry, and offering much-needed goods to the settlers there in return. His dealings always turned a handsome- -indeed, usurious and monopolistic--profit. Because others were at his unyielding fiscal mercy, he was not loved.

He built a large home with attached general store for his wife and himself on what is now the southwest corner of Grant Avenue and Clay Street. He and Rosalia hosted many parties for the captains, supercargoes and other visiting dignitaries who dropped anchor in "Yerba Buena Cove" (San Francisco Bay). Not long after they built their home, they threw the first big party ever in Yerba Buena--a Fourth of July party to celebrate American Independence Day.[49] The

---

[45]Kerr, p. 72.

[46]W. H. Davis' autobiographical *Seventy-five Years in California* is an eye-witness account of life before the American conquest of California.

[47]Hoover, p. 293.

[48]Idem.

[49]Adrian Michaelis, "Jacob Primer Leese--Founding father of Yerba Buena."

next year they hosted a "September 16" bash to celebrate Mexico's independence from Spain The Leeses were also responsible for another first: their daughter, named Rosalia for her mother, was the first non-native child born in Yerba Buena.[50]

In 1841, Leese sold his house and store to the Hudson's Bay Company, the huge British-owned organization with global trading connections. His decision to sell might have had something to do with the fact that his relationship with Nathan Spear had turned sour, a situation some historians have blamed on Leese's temper. He also incurred the displeasure of Mariano Vallejo. Nevertheless the Mexican government granted Leese five leagues of choice grassland bounded by Carneros Creek on the east, extending into what is now Sonoma County. He and Rosalia called their spread *Huichica*, for a native community that had been there. The Leeses bred horses and cattle at *Huichica*, but lived in Sonoma and Yerba Buena. Untiringly creative in his quest for profit, Leese sailed to China for goods to trade, masterminded a lucrative drive of horses to Oregon for Hudson's Bay, and when the rush for gold seized the spirit of men from around the world, pocketed hefty sums for selling cattle at the digs for very high prices.[51] For a while, Leese's life seemed charmed with good fortune.

William Pope, aka Julian Pope, received a Napa Valley grant about the same time as Bale and Leese. Like them, Pope hunted for fur, trapping with James Pattie and Kit Carson. James Pattie has gone down in history as being at least as savage as the "savages" he encountered and engaged in several bloody battles with the natives of the southwest. His predations on the Apache and Comanche helped whip those peoples into an anti-Caucasian frenzy that, among other things, disrupted trade to Northern California for a time. Kit Carson figures more directly in the history of the Napa Valley. For example, during the Bear Flag Revolt, Carson murdered three members of the family who owned the grant adjacent to Pope's.

---

[50]Ibid, p. 293.

[51]Hoover, p. 293.

After a brief stay with George Yount, Pope came to Napa permanently in 1842 with his wife, eight members of his family and a company of 12 men,[52] including William Gordon, who also eventually owned land in the Napa Valley. Pope was given title to *Locoallomi* rancho, now called Pope Valley. Pope was better suited to trapping, however, than to ranching. The year after acquiring his land grant he severed an artery while using his axe, and died.[53]

Jose Jesus Berryessa, his brother Sisto, their nephew Jose de los Santos Berryessa and another relative, Ignacio Berryessa, all came from a large, well-respected Mexican family who had already received grants in other parts of Alta California. They all received land in the Napa Valley in 1843. (One of the Joses had stolen a horse in Monterey in 1835,[54] but that was all behind him.) Jose Jesus and Sisto married two daughters of *Entre Napa's* Nicholas Higuera, Maria Anastacia and Maria Nicolasa. [55] Their *Las Putas* grant in what became known as Berryessa Valley was a pun. Putah Creek (so-named by the natives who had lived there) irrigated their 8 square leagues of land, and *las putas* is the Spanish word for "whores," a good-natured joke, perhaps, directed toward their wives. (Californio humor tended to be a bit vulgar: viz. "*carne humana*".)

Jose de los Santos Berryesssa was grantee of the *Mallocamas* grant north and northwest of present-day Calistoga. His 17,742.72 acres were also known as *Muristul y Plan de Agua Caliente*. For many years the entire area north of Yount's domain was known as "Hot Springs," *Agua Caliente*. Jose de los Santos was the man who apprehended Bale and sent him to the *calabozo* in 1844.

A plot almost identical in size to Jose de los Santos' holding fell to Ignacio Berryessa on the exact opposite side of Napa County. *Rancho*

---

[52]Bancroft, XXI, p. 782.

[53]See John T. Beales, *The Saga of Locoallomi*, Piedmont, CA, unpublished, 1978.

[54]Bancroft, XXI, p. 718. See also Irene Soberanes, "The Berryessa or Berreyesa Family History, 1776-1957."

[55]Hoover, p. 284.

Chimiles, bounded by today's Moskowite Corners, Circle Oaks, Wooden Valley Road and Suisun Creek, was snatched from Ignacio very soon after the treaty of Guadalupe Hidalgo ended the war with Mexico in 1848. The Berryessas, having experienced death and robbery at the hands of Americans, were long reputed to be hostile toward the newcomers who started filling the valley.

Historians call the years during which Mexico City governed Alta California the "Mexican Pastoral Period." The Pastoral Period was late in arriving in Napa, and because Mexican Pastorale ended abruptly with the American takeover in 1846, it was very short north of San Francisco. Cayetano Juarez was the Californio in the Napa Valley best remembered for enjoying many of the aspects of the period.

During the years before the Mexican-American War, nearly every able civilian male Californio was a *vaquero,* a cowboy.[56] Vaqueros spent most of their waking hours with cattle, which roamed wild and often unbranded throughout the large ranchos. They herded, bred and slaughtered them and converted their skin and fat into hides and tallow, often using natives for the more laborious aspects, like scraping and stretching the skins.[57] Cowhides were the usual currency of exchange. They also wore them. Leather vests and leggings protected the vaqueros from the chaparral and grasses, and they rode on leather saddles with leather shields *(tapaderos)* over their stirrups.

They ate a diet whose main feature was beef. At noon the men gathered on the open patio at the land owner's adobe for the main meal of the day. The women stacked piles of fresh tortillas and helpings of beef and beans on long tables, and all hands would chow down. After lunch the men rolled cigarettes, took a siesta or strummed their guitars for a while and then returned to work until nightfall.

---

[56]De Nevi, *Sketches of Early California,* Chronicle Books, San Francisco, 1971, p. 11.

[57] See Richard Henry Dana, *Two Years Before the Mast,* P.F. Collier & Sons, New York, 1909, pp. 156-7 for a complete how-to on curing hides the old-fashioned way.

The vaqueros spent most of their days on horseback, and many writers of the time comment that they much preferred riding to walking. The only other way to get around was by *carreta*, cart, the wheels of which were solid O's of oak with a hole in the center that was slightly larger than the wooden axle. The axle was lubricated with a lather of soap, and soap buckets always came along in the carts, which squeaked loudly no matter how many soapsuds were applied.[58]

Horses ran free and seemed to be available and at large, like driverless taxis.[59] The horses were not particularly sturdy, nor were they treated well, and the life expectancy of a range horse was no more than a couple of years. Great care was taken, however, of the vaquero's saddle and bridle, which were often embellished with silver and other elaborate ornamentation. At *fiestas* the vaqueros dressed in their finest and entertained themselves and their audiences of ladies, older men and natives with breathtaking displays of horsemanship.[60] In the Napa Valley it was cows, however, and not horses that were the true focus of their working lives.

Time had a different feel to it than it has today: less urgency and much less complication. Parties, weddings, and rodeos were important: more meaningful, for example, than learning to read and write were for most Californios.[61] The wedding thrown by Don Jose Martinez and Don Ygnacio Peralta for their children was a case in point. The festivities lasted a week. A hundred or more guests came from all around to dance all night every night, with picnics and bullfights offered in the daytime.[62] The dances themselves required considerable athletic ability. One favorite, *la Bamba*, required the participating *senorita* to balance a full glass of water on her head while

---

[58]De Nevi, p. 96.

[59]Ibid, p. 28.

[60] Tom Gregory, *History of Solano and Napa Counties,* Historic Record Company, Los Angeles, 1912, p. 35.

[61]Ibid, p. 31.

[62]Idem.

performing intricate dance steps.[63]

Like all social groups, the Californios observed a caste system. The vaqueros threw *fandangos*, where everyone was invited, but the Vallejos and their upscale peers held formal *bailes*, balls, where the guest list was carefully considered.

Beneath the festivities, however, trouble brewed. It was clear to all that Mexico City would not/could not defend the land from aggression by foreigners. Any government could send a fleet of ships into Yerba Buena Bay and gain a strategic position from which they could claim sovereignty over the land. Alta California had no ships of any kind, military or otherwise, harbored there, and the cannons hadn't worked since the early 1830's. Moreover, having a one-product economy, the grantees worried about the security of their trade agreements. Some, like *Huichica's* Jacob Leese, took considerable profit as middlemen in the industry, angering the ranchers.[64]

The final man given a land grant by Mexico was of a different type from the others. An American like Pope and Yount, he was not a trapper, but an artisan. Joseph Chiles was the Adam of a generation of pioneers who traveled in parties from the Mississippi Valley to try their luck and test their mettle in the Far West. His story and those of other key settlers of the Napa Valley will be told in the next chapter.

---

[63]Bean, p. 71.
[64]Bancroft, XXII, p. 93.

Chapter Three

The Americans Are Coming!

T he High Sierras had stood forever as California's fortress against the eastern part of North America. By 1841, however, American adventurers had begun to penetrate the mountain range. At first it was just a few gangs of greasy mountain men. But then there were other people, many of them ne'er-do-wells chased west by their own shortcomings. Some of the pre-Gold Rush pioneers, however, were practical idealists, willing to overcome great odds to pursue what would be termed their "manifest destiny."

Some of those fortunate enough to be land owners in Mexican Alta California saw the advantage of befriending the Americans as a new source of manpower. A well-placed Californio could claim the whole place for himself if he had a retinue of supporters, because California's capital, Mexico City, was poorly run and in a perpetual state of chaos.

Several men could actually have been King of California. One who wanted to be was a Swiss entrepreneur, John Augustus Sutter. Sutter slipped out of Basel-Land to avoid going to debtor's prison, leaving behind his wife and five children and a bankrupt dry-goods business.[1] He traveled extensively throughout the west and even sailed to Hawaii and Alaska as a seaman before finally arriving in Alta California. Calling himself "Captain Sutter of the Royal Swiss Guard of France," (a delusion if not a lie) he convinced the Mexican governor, Alvarado, to sell him a boat and give him the rights to a huge expanse of land up the Sacramento River. There he built a fort,

---

[1]Bean, p. 83.

established good relations with the natives and accumulated enough credit from his agricultural and milling enterprises to buy the inventory and structures (including cannons) at Fort Ross when the Russians pulled up stakes in 1841.

Sutter was grandiose to the point of mania. He conducted himself like a feudal lord, employing everyone who wanted work, buying everything that was for sale and running up enormous debts. He maintained a militia of natives and paid a German officer to command them.[2] Virtually every American who came to Northern California after 1840 spent some time with Sutter at his fort, which he considered to be the capitol of an agrarian kingdom he intended to call "New Helvetia," New Switzerland. He was not, perhaps, the sanest of men.

Governor Alvarado's motivation for giving this odd Swiss duck a little kingdom in the Sacramento Valley may have been so that Sutter could serve as a check on another, potentially more dangerous man.[3] Mariano Vallejo was administrator of the mission in Sonoma, grantee of spreads in Sonoma and Napa, and military commander of the entire northern frontier. The Vallejos were very well aware of Mexico's inability to govern and protect its holdings. Friendly, intelligent and surprisingly sophisticated, Mariano Vallejo was an aristocrat who would not have seemed out of place in the courts of Europe. He was loyal to his superiors in Mexico City, but as will be seen, his efforts to obey their directives were not necessarily rigorous. His brother Salvador was a well-bred bully with no flair for statesmanship. There is no evidence, however, that either Vallejo aspired to any power beyond that which he already held.

John Marsh would have loved to have been King of California, but Governor would also have done nicely.[4] A Missourian, he headed west after graduating from Harvard with a Bachelor's degree and

---

[2]DeNevi, p. 93.

[3]Bean, p. 83.

[4]For more on this important American pioneer, see George D. Lyman, *John Marsh, Pioneer,* Charles Scribner's Sons, New York, 1930.

idealistic hopes of teaching the natives to read and write. He fell deeply in love with a woman who was half Sioux and half French-Canadian and involved himself in championing the rights of the Sioux. His pro-Sioux fervor prompted him to sell them guns, which was a federal offense. He and his wife fled to California to avoid prosecution, where, tragically, she died. Marsh plunged into a deep depression, from which he never fully recovered.[5]

He managed to pass himself off as a medical doctor to the Californios, who were unable to translate the Latin on his Harvard diploma. In time he actually became an accomplished physician, learning his craft on the job. In return for his services the Californios gave him an enormous piece of land in the San Joaquin Valley and a large number of cattle, oxen and other livestock.

Marsh knew that as a former American he was not fully secure in the existing political situation, but he reasoned that if California became an American province, he could continue in the style to which he was becoming accustomed. He wanted to populate the area with American emigrants who would eventually help the States seize the area, with himself playing a prominent role. He therefore wrote letters to friends back in Missouri, extolling California as an earthly paradise and urging Americans to come settle, the sooner the better. His letters were reprinted in America by the prairie presses. They had a profound impact, not only on their readers in the Mississippi Valley, but on the officials in Mexico City, who jailed Marsh on suspicion of sedition. He talked his way into a quick release and, furious about being jailed, stubbornly redoubled his efforts at letter-writing, posting dispatches with each eastward-bound trading caravan. He also sent a letter to Washington describing the jailing incident.

In the Fall of 1840, while Marsh was writing his letters, a French Canadian trapper/trader named Antoine Robidoux was promoting the Far West to packed audiences in Marsh's home state.[6] Robidoux

---

[5]Bean, p. 82.
[6]Ibid, p. 84.

had trapped with George Yount and William Pope in New Mexico.[7] California was a place, Robidoux said, where there was no sickness, friendly people and wonderful farmland.

John Bidwell, a school teacher, was among his listeners. Bidwell and his friends formed the "Western Emigration Society" and took a pledge to leave together when the snows melted the following spring. Each man who signed the pledge promised to buy a wagon and provisions and meet in Sapling Grove, Missouri, in May. Five hundred men signed the pledge.[8]

Likewise, in Independence, Missouri, a public meeting was held on February 1 to air the idea of a westward settlement expedition, with John Marsh's letters as the rallying point. William Baldridge, a wheelwright, was on Marsh's mailing list, and he showed his letter to his best friend, Colonel Joseph Chiles. Chiles had also heard Robidoux.[9]

Joe Chiles was a tall, lean young man from Kentucky. He had emigrated to Missouri with his wife, Polly Ann. Six years after they were married, she died, leaving him with four children whom he loved but had no idea how to raise. He left them in the care of relatives and became a soldier, fighting the Seminoles in the Florida War. On the way back from Florida he stopped in New Orleans and bought a fiddle, which he learned to play and carried with him.[10] Blessed (or cursed) with a well-developed taste for adventure, Chiles heard in Robidoux's message an opportunity to start over. He planned to find a suitable spot in California for a homesite and guide his children across the plains as soon as they were old enough to travel.

During the winter of 1840-41, however, the people in Missouri heard other voices. A New York lawyer published a newspaper

---

[7]Gilbert, p. 77.

[8]DeNevi, p. 50.

[9] Helen S. Griffen, *Joseph Chiles, Trail-Blazing Pioneer,* John Howell Books, San Francisco, 1969, p. 6.

[10]Ibid, p. 16.

GEORGE C. YOUNT.

article presenting a much more sour picture of California. Many who had signed the Sapling Grove pledge backed out. By May, Bidwell was the only pledge-signer in Platte County who was still willing to go on the adventure. The group from Independence had dwindled severely, too. Chiles' buddy, Billy Baldridge, was among the dropouts, having entered business contracts he was obliged to honor. Joe promised to come back for Billy as soon as he had scouted out a place to settle.

The California-bound party who eventually assembled at Sapling Grove numbered 32 men, one woman and one child. A friend of Chiles', John Bartleson, demanded to be made captain of the entire party. Since Bartleson knew the greatest number of people, and since he had the only instructions on how to get to Marsh's rancho, he was considered too valuable to lose and thus got his way. Bidwell was voted secretary of the party.

The president was a man who called himself "Talbot Green." He was actually a bank clerk named Paul Geddes, on the lam after embezzling significant amounts of cash from his employer.[11] (He will turn up again, briefly, later on.)

The only people allowed to vote on the party's decisions were those considered to have a financial stake in the venture's outcome. Some of the party members--including Chiles--may have brought slaves along with them. These people would not have been mentioned on the company's roster, since they would have been considered unqualified to vote.[12]

The regional presses rolled with news of Bartleson-Bidwell's departure. General Almonde, Mexico's Minister of War, was quickly informed of the event. He sent word to Mariano Vallejo to arrest the party as soon as they showed up if they lacked appropriate passports.

Many of Chiles' compatriots on the Bartleson-Bidwell Party were destined to become his neighbors in the Napa Valley. One of these

---

[11]Bancroft, XX, pp. 765-66.

[12] Kenneth G. Goode, *California's Black Pioneers*, McNally & Loftin, Santa Barbara, 1973, p. 24.

men was Elias Barnett, age 36, who had deserted his wife and five children several years earlier. He carried with him messages to Marsh from some of Marsh's Missouri friends and a letter from a financial concern, Barnett & Hague, also addressed to Marsh. B&H may not have been entirely certain that Barnett would survive the trip. They gave a duplicate to another emigrant, Michael Nye, a friend of Barnett's, to be handed to John Sutter.[13] In the letter, Barnett & Hague reported that many people in Missouri were interested in emigrating to California, but that doubts had arisen "as to the practicability of the routes for wagons and families." Elias Barnett and Michael Nye, it said, had come to explore the territory and return with reports about it. Specifically, the letter requested that mules be sent back to Missouri, "for the animals had been depleted in Missouri by immigrant caravans outfitting for the Oregon and Santa Fe trails." They also wanted Marsh and Sutter to provide a description of the resources in California.

B&H promised to bring out 200 to 400 families within four or five years, regardless of the fact that California was part of a foreign country whose relations with the US were growing increasingly hostile.

Another future Napan in the party was Charles Hopper, a 41 year-old mountain man who knew Yount and eventually settled near him. Hopper Creek and Canyon in Yountville were to become his. Like many of the others, Hopper was married with children.

The Kelsey family--Andy Kelsey, Sam Kelsey and Ben Kelsey and his wife Nancy, age 18, with their 2 year-old daughter--was also to live in the Napa Valley. The Kelseys' second child had died in February, shortly after his birth, and Nancy, still grieving, would be the second white woman to cross the Sierra Nevada into California.[14]

---

[13] " Henry P.Scalf, "Overland California Letter Carried by Prestonburg Man," *Floyd County Times*, Prestonburg, KY, June 28, 1962.

[14] See Philip H. Ault, "Pioneer Nancy Kelsey: Where My Husband Goes, I Go." *The Californians*, Vol. 9, No. 5, March/April, 1992, pp. 32-41.

The Kelseys' friend Bill Fowler joined up, too.[15] Bill was the footloose oldest son of a hard-working family who had emigrated to Illinois from Virginia. The Fowlers and Kelseys knew how to build mills, and Bill's mission was to procure contracts for constructing these community focal points. His parents and brothers would then come west and build as contracted.

Just before pulling out of Sapling Grove, the Bartleson-Bidwell party was joined by a group of nearly the same size which was heading for Oregon.[16] Five women were part of the company--three married, one a widow and one an eligible young single. There were also some Catholic missionaries under the guidance of Father de Smet, and a first-rate mountain man, Tom Fitzpatrick, known by the natives as "Broken Hand." Fitzpatrick was the real leader of the Bartleson-Bidwell party. The group, along with a substantial portion of Napa County's early history, would probably have perished without him.

For organizational purposes, the party divided itself into smaller groups called "messes," each with a leader. Joe Chiles was leader of his mess.[17] The messes ate together and generally watched out for each other. A representative from each mess stood guard at night against natives, who occasionally bothered the livestock.

Most of the wagons in the westward-bound pioneer party were ordinary topless hauling carts. When they sensed trouble, the emigrants bunched their wagons together, sometimes with the tongue of one hitched to the rear of the next, like a train--hence the term "wagon train." At night they formed a square, corralling the draft oxen as well as the horses and mules. No cattle came with the Bartleson-Bidwell party.[18]

The main meal was cooked at midday. Oddly, the travelers feared

---

[15]Fowler Mallett, *Geneological Notes and Anecdotes*, unpublished, Berkeley, 1953, p. 81.

[16]DeNevi, p. 55-56.

[17]Bancroft, XXI, p. 267.

[18]For more on Bidwell and the trip west, see De Nevi and Ault.

making fires at night, lest the smoke and firelight alert the natives, as if the voluminous clouds of dust they raised did not.

Near the Platte River, in what is now Nebraska, one of the party, Dawson, who had been out hunting with his mule, ran back into camp half naked, unarmed and without the mule.[19] Wild-eyed, he exclaimed that he had been surrounded by "thousands" of Indians. With the exception of Fitzpatrick, the entire party panicked and drew the wagons into a square. Soon a group of about 40 Cheyenne pulled up and pitched their tents. Fitzpatrick and one of the hunters approached the natives, and after a short parley it was revealed that Dawson had gotten so upset when he saw the Cheyenne it was necessary for them to take away his gun lest he hurt somebody. He lost his clothes in the process and left the mule behind. The Cheyenne were returning the mule and the gun, which Fitzpatrick accepted. Dawson's clothes were never retrieved.

Farther down the Platte, the plains seemed to transform into a moving black carpet of buffalo. At first the men just shot at the animals for sport and for their tongues and marrow as the Rocky Mountain hunters often did, but after a while they felt wasteful and only killed them when they needed food. Being trampled by the thundering woolly herds became a legitimate fear, and the party started building nighttime fires and shooting guns to scare them away.[20]

A waterspout spun up a little farther along and came within a few hundred yards of the wagon train, preceded by a heavy shower and a storm that left a pelting of hailstones four inches deep.

They crossed the Rockies at a place called the South Pass, in present-day Wyoming. The crossing was not too difficult, since the mountains were somewhat lower there. Shortly after that, Bartleson's mess revealed that they had several cases of whiskey, which they proceeded to sell to a band of white trappers who were in the vicinity. Very soon after leaving the wagon train with their purchase,

---

[19]DeNevi, p. 60.
[20]Ibid, p. 61.

several of the trappers were killed by natives. Bidwell, who later ran for President as a Prohibitionist, blamed their fate on the whiskey.

Some of the original members dropped out along the way and high-tailed it back to Missouri. One man accidentally shot and killed himself while removing his gun from his wagon. A few changed their minds about California and joined with the Oregon faction, including two of Ben Kelsey's brothers, one of whom married the aforementioned eligible single woman. Music for the ceremony was provided by Joe Chiles and his fiddle.[21]

At a place called Soda Springs in present-day Idaho, the party split up as originally planned, with the Oregon-bound group heading for Fort Hall along the Snake River. The Bartleson-Bidwell group headed south to Utah, placing their lives on the lines of Marsh's ambiguous letter. The way to California had never been mapped, and the directions in Marsh's letter were based on hearsay. Marsh himself had come to California via Santa Fe and never crossed the Sierra.

Roughly, the instructions were:

1. Follow the Oregon Trail (Lewis and Clark's route) westward to Ft. Hall.

2. Locate the "Portneuf River," a branch of the Snake. This led southwest, to the desert.

3. Find "Mary's River," a northwest-flowing stream that emptied into "Mary's Lake," which had no outlet. (They were given the gruesome advice that if they went too far south they would perish in the desert, while if they went too far north they would become hopelessly lost in endless canyons.[22])

4. Go southwest through the "Snowy Mountains."

5. Pass through a gap where a river went south. This emptied into the San Joaquin River, which would bring them to a valley of the same name.[23]

It was late August when they started looking for the all-important

---

[21]Griffen, p. 16.

[22]DeNevi, p. 72.

[23]Lyman, p. 29.

"Mary's River." The animals strained to pull the wagons through the sagebrush, and mirages lured the pioneers off their course. The group was forced to abandon the wagons and trudge over the salt and sand on horseback or on foot. Nancy Kelsey, whose moccasins had worn out earlier in the trip, alternately rode horseback and walked, barefoot, carrying her toddler. Joe Chiles spelled her from time to time with the child.[24]

Chiles, Kelsey, Hopper and the rest trudged painfully through the salty wilderness, looking for Mary's Lake. Food gave out, and the pioneers started killing off their horses and oxen to eat. Occasionally jackrabbit, sage hen or coyote found their way onto the meager menu, but the emigrants were finally reduced to foraging for acorns. Bidwell became increasingly irritated with Bartleson, who kept insisting the group had to make better time, not only to preserve the food, but to escape being trapped by snow in the "Snowy Mountains." Bidwell himself got on everyone's nerves by wasting a day hiking for pleasure in the mountains. The group actually pulled off without him at one point.

Aware of their hunger, a band of natives sold them a native delicacy, crunchy honey-flavored balls scraped from the tule rushes that lined the riverbanks. The pioneers were delighted and gobbled them up greedily. The crunch, they soon learned, was provided by the carapaces of hundreds of insects. Upon learning this, the pioneers' appetites for honeyballs waned dramatically.[25]

After almost two weeks of fruitless wandering through the desert southeast of Lake Tahoe, the hungry party finally found a river that flowed south, the Walker. Believing they had found the San Joaquin and that their journey would soon be over, they were chagrined to encounter the solid wall of the Sierra, which indeed were "Snowy Mountains."

When they reached the summit on October 18, 1841, they had good news and bad news. The bad news was that snow had already

---

[24]Griffen, p. 16.
[25]DeNevi, p. 74.

fallen and was deep. The good news was the approach of a single Indian crying "Marsh, Marsh." He guided the starving, bedraggled crew the rest of the way to Marsh's rancho.

If the trip west had been harrowing, their first view of California was truly dismaying. An 18-month drought had killed the wheat crop and parched the fields. This was not the Eden promised in Marsh's letters.

Marsh himself improved their spirits by providing them with a feast and plenty of brandy. Eager for American company, he talked to them long into the night. The sudden introduction of heavy food and alcohol after weeks of acorns and honeyballs caused the travelers to become ill. During the night, however, sick or not, Chiles and his friends killed an additional steer and slaughtered Marsh's best work ox. When Marsh discovered this the next morning, he was outraged.

In order to stay in California, the Americans needed passports. These could be issued in the nearby pueblo of San Jose. Everyone except Bidwell set out for San Jose, but at a river crossing they were stopped by some soldiers. They were arrested and thrown in jail, per the orders of Mexico's Minister of War, General Almonde.

They were brought to Mariano Vallejo, who had heard about their conquest of the Sierra and rode to San Jose to intercept them. Already in possession of Almonde's orders, Vallejo asked them their business. One of the group produced Marsh's letter inviting them to come. Vallejo sent for Marsh and demanded to know what business Marsh had suggesting that American emigrants populate Alta California. Marsh denied any seditious intentions, and, while Vallejo didn't necessarily believe him, he opted to let the emigrants stay, provided Marsh would sign a bond assuring their good behavior. Fearful of being assessed for any trouble these scruffy personages might create, Marsh refused, perhaps thinking of the slaughtered steer and ox.

The group confided that they were prepared to shoot their way out of the jail, where they had now been for four days with the door open. This convinced Marsh to sign the bond. Marsh was apparently unwilling to let this small, desperate party of grizzly hotheads wreck his dream of populating the region with Americans. Perhaps hoping to gain favor with what he thought would be the winning team, Vallejo himself offered to provide security for whatever Marsh wouldn't cover.[26]

In the narrative he provided years later, Hopper said that "the Spaniards" were lacking mechanics and had special needs for a millwright.[27] This prompted some shrewd thinking on Chiles' part. Billy Baldridge, his good friend in Missouri, knew milling. Chiles scheduled a private meeting with Vallejo in Sonoma, where he would make him a pleasing proposal.

With Marsh as the guarantor of the group's good behavior, Vallejo issued passports to everyone but Bidwell, who was still back at Marsh's adobe. Marsh charged $5.00 per document. No one had any money at all. They gave Marsh whatever of any worth they possessed, although Chiles was able to hang onto his fiddle. When Bidwell later went to get his own passport he found that they were free, and that Marsh had fleeced the group of the few paltry objects they had been able to salvage from the trip.[28]

At this point, the pioneers dispersed, but many of them would meet again. Joe Chiles and Charlie Hopper went to Yerba Buena, the future San Francisco, which Hopper described as a "miserable place, nothing but a lot of sand hills."[29] William Richardson, the proprietor of the only tavern in town--which Hopper said was also the only building at all--claimed they were out of food, but he eventually located some beef to broil for them.

From Yerba Buena they took a small boat to the landing in Sonoma, perhaps the same landing Altimira had used long ago. It was stormy, and they sloshed through the rain to make their scheduled appointment with Mariano Vallejo.[30] Chiles proposed to build a

---

[26] Franklin Beard, *Charles Hopper and the Pioneers of the Pacific*, Southern Mines Press, LaGrange, CA, 1981, p.11.

[27] Idem.

[28] De Nevi, p. 86.

[29] F. Beard, p. 12.

[30] Idem.

Joe Chiles built the gristmill above and lived in the adobe, below. Both were among the first of their kind in the area.

W. Baldridge

sawmill for cutting logs into boards for building--something Vallejo knew would considerably hasten the development of the region.

In return, Vallejo would give Chiles a land grant, provided, of course, he convert to Catholicism. This would have been hard for Chiles, who was a Baptist. A Jacksonian through and through, Joe Chiles held fast to the ethnocentrism of his times, and in 1842 Catholicism seemed foreign and strange to many Americans.

George Yount was elated to hear of the arrival of the Americans. Charlie Hopper and Yount were old friends, and Hopper was up-to-date with news of the family Yount had abandoned: his wife had remarried, his son had grown up, and one of his daughters was about to tie the knot with a fellow named Bartlett Vines.

Hopper was feeling his age (41), and Yount suggested he and Chiles go up to *Aguas Calientes*, the hot springs region at the head of the Napa Valley, to partake of the curative waters. This they did. Along the way Hopper shot seven deer and a mountain lion and explored the terrain over the eastern hills. He paid a visit to Nicholas Higuera at his rancho in soon-to-be Napa City.[31]

Refreshed by both the waters and the hunting, Hopper and Chiles headed over to Sutter's fort and immediately left for Missouri via the Santa Fe trail, bearing two mules as a gift from Yount to Yount's new son-in-law, Bartlett Vines. Because of the shortage of mules in Missouri, they would have been the equivalent of a brace of Mercedes, and were intended as a wedding gift. Chiles and Hopper promised to return as soon as possible with Yount's family, Chiles' family, Billy Baldridge and a sawmill.

The Kelseys went straight from Marsh's to the Napa Valley, where they squatted on a plot of land about a mile south from present-day Calistoga. They were the first Caucasians to erect a dwelling in that part of the Valley. Ben and Nancy were cut from very rough cloth. They were a hard-fighting couple who had little respect for authority and no real interest in putting down roots.[32] Kelsey used his

---

[31]F. Beard, Loc. Cit.

[32]See Ault, pp. 32-41.

makeshift Napa Valley dwelling as a headquarters for hunting and established several camps in the general area. Other men of similar swagger set up camps nearby, and largely because of Kelsey the northern part of the Napa Valley began to attract American hunters.

One of the Kelseys' new neighbors was Elias Barnett, who built a rough cabin nearby. He had delivered Barnett & Hague's letter to Marsh and made his way to John Sutter's fort. Sutter put him to work planting seed acquired from the purchase of Ft. Ross. The seed was for wheat and eventually yielded a good crop. When spring came, Barnett decided to explore the general area. He worked briefly at Mark West Springs, helping to build an adobe, and spent some time with George Yount. He gave up whatever plans he may have had for returning to his wife and children in Missouri, and for giving feedback to the financial firm of B&H.

While exploring the general vicinity, Barnett passed through a valley that ran parallel to the Napa, just to the east. There was a house there, occupied by the widow Juliana Pope and her large family. He "squatted" nearby (took up residence without proper authorization), and in 1843 he married her and became the new patriarch of Pope Valley.

John Bidwell was insulted to the core by John Marsh's tight-fistedness. After lingering at Marsh's for a few days he struck out on his own and soon found himself in territory that had been granted to a British expatriate named Livermore. He spent the night at the adobe of Senor Amador, a Californio, and there encountered a young American sailor who had jumped ship from a whaler and was hiding until the vessel left for sea. The man called himself "Harrison Pierce."[33] Bidwell and Pierce walked together to Sutter's fort, and from there Bidwell leaves as a central figure in this story (to go on and become, among other things, the founder of Chico). Harrison Pierce, however, has a greater part to play in terms of the history of the Napa Valley, as shall be seen.

Ben Kelsey was an expert hunter, but in 1843 he took up a second

---

[33]DeNevi, p. 98.

profession, that of professional wrangler. Along with his brothers, he, Nancy, and their small children left the Valley briefly to drive a herd of about 100 head of cattle to Oregon, where there were more settlers and thus a better market. The Kelseys fought natives all along the route: fights which they very likely provoked themselves. In Oregon they acquired a young native boy whom they utilized as a slave.

Meanwhile, a politically ambitious young lawyer named Lansford Hastings was leading a group of Americans south over the Cascades from Oregon to California. His party included 16-17 men and about as many women and children, plus an armed contingent of two dozen. They encountered little trouble until they crossed paths with the Kelseys and their cattle drive, who were coming up the other way.[34] From then on, due in large part to the Kelseys' habit of antagonizing the natives, the Hastings party had to fend off increasingly hostile Indians. Hastings himself was also guilty of fomenting trouble. He fired on a small group of natives, killed their cow and served it to the party. The natives retaliated by wounding one of the emigrants with an arrow to the back. The Hastings party ended up killing as many as 20 natives in all.

Lansford Hastings was a piece of work. After contributing to the deterioration of pioneer/native relations, he returned East to write *The Emigrant's Guide to Oregon and California*, which was worse than useless as a guidebook, but fabulously successful as a publicity gimmick for luring American settlers to Mexican California. It was *The Emigrants' Guide* that persuaded the Donner Party of 1846 to take a deadly detour that led to their starvation in the Sierra.

The Emigrant's Guide reveals the blatantly chauvinistic attitude held by many Americans.[35] Hastings said Americans could and should grab whatever lands they wanted in paradisical California. He characterized the Californios as shiftless semi-barbarians, thus prejudicing the waves of settlers who would read his best seller and

---

[34]Bancroft,XXI, p. 390.

[35] Lansford Hastings, *The Emigrant's Guide to Oregon and California*, De Capo Press, NY, 1969 (reprint of 1845 edition).

come pouring into the territory in the decade to come.

Hastings contemplated the political vulnerability of California and seems to have envisioned himself as future president of a Pacific republic (as opposed to a King of California).[36] His timing--an intuitive faculty prerequisite for any would-be conqueror--was poor, however, and he failed to take a leading role in the exciting events that exploded four years later, although he helped in his own way to bring them about.

One member of the Hastings Party was a young man whose contribution to society was actually destined to be very positive. While Lansford Hastings wove dreams of empire, Nathan Coombs was doing what was necessary to become a true leader of his peers.

Handsome, earnest Nathan Coombs left Massachusetts with his widowed mother and headed with her to the Iowa Territory, where she remarried. When Nathan was 17 he, his mother, and her new husband hitched up with a wagon train led by Lansford Hastings and went to Oregon. Nathan disliked the rainy climate (and perhaps his new step-father), however, and he set off for California with Hastings' 1843 emigration.[37]

Coombs obtained a California passport from Sutter and recovered from his trip by doing manual labor for him. He then went to Bodega Bay to work for an entrepreneur named Stephen Smith, who had imported a steam engine--California's first.[38] Finally he went to the rancho of a recently arrived American, William Gordon in the Cache Creek area of what is now Yolo County, 10 miles east of Woodland.[39] There he became naturalized as a Californian. He married his boss's daughter, Isabel: all this within his first two years in California.

At Cache Creek Nathan had an experience that was to mark him for life, literally. While riding through the brush he was attacked by

---

[36]Bean, p. 87.

[37]Gregory, pp. 882-883.

[38]Bancroft

[39]Hoover, p. 199.

a grizzly bear, which yanked him from his horse and left deep claw marks in his chest and left arm.[40] In 1843, being mauled by a bear in the Napa Valley was a much greater risk than being attacked by a hostile native. The region that would soon be Napa, Lake, Yolo and Glenn Counties was an ideal habitat for grizzlies as well as black bears. Berries, a staple food for bears, grew profusely beside the rivers and creeks, and the tall-growing grasses provided shelter for small animals, which were *a la carte* items for the bears. The bears ate the grass as the salad course. They also liked to eat the fish that abounded in the Napa River.[41]

Even more desirable in terms of bear's markets were the cattle slaughter corrals. Bears came by for free pickings, and young Californio men laid in wait to rope them and, if they could, drag them through the pueblo as proof of *machismo*.[42]

George Yount told of seeing 60 bears in a single day, and one settler in the Calistoga area reported catching a different bear in his traps every night for a solid month. Charlie Hopper claimed to have killed eight grizzlies within a mile of his home in the summer of 1848. It is likely that there were more bears in Napa County after the settlers came than had been previously. They would have been attracted to the farm smells of feed and manure[43] and perhaps to the presence of the pioneers' pigs.

Bear-baiting and bull vs. bear fights were common Californio spectator sports, especially on the festival day of the local mission's Saint.[44] In the latter, a bear was chained to a foreleg of the bull to give

---

[40]Gregory, p. 883.

[41] Dorothy Hinshaw Patent, *The Way of the Grizzly*, Clarion Books, New York, 1987, p. 7.

[42]De Nevi, p. 20.

[43] Andy Russell, *Grizzly Country*, Lyons & Burford, New York, 1967, p. 54.

[44]The feast day at the Sonoma mission, for example, which was named for St. Francis--San Francisco--was October 4.

the bull a fighting chance.[45] The surviving animal won, and so did those who bet accordingly. Sometimes bear abuse was done from horseback, with the vaquero lassoing the bruin, dragging it for a while, and then tieing it to a tree for further torture if it was still alive. Wounded, unhappy and therefore angry bears may have been commonplace.

Not long after his encounter with the grizzly, Nathan Coombs moved to a more civilized zone: Higuera's *Entre Napa.*

About half of the group who came west with the Bartleson-Bidwell party went back to Missouri within weeks of reaching California, some because they hated the place and couldn't wait to leave, and the rest to recruit their friends and family to settle in California forever.[46] Joe Chiles, Charlie Hopper and six others made it back to Missouri via the Santa Fe Trail by September of 1842, escaping a band of angry Apache by the skin of their teeth. (The Apache, not the meekest of people, had been enraged by the behaviors of James Pattie and his mountain men, as described earlier.) On the way, they crossed paths with John C. Fremont, who was leading an expedition to chart the wilderness and provide a reasonably accurate topography of the route west. Fremont may have had other, more sinister motives on his agenda, as well.

Chiles went to the home of Yount's ex-wife, as he had promised, and presented the brace of mules along with Yount's offer that they all join him in Napa. The former Mrs. Yount and her new spouse declined. So did Yount's son Robert, who was still bitter about his father's 15-year disappearance. Perhaps mollified by the mules, the newlyweds Bartlett Vines and Frances Yount agreed to go west, as did Yount's youngest daughter, Elizabeth. (Robert came west too, eventually.)

Chiles and his friend Billy Baldridge were reunited, and Baldridge put together the parts for a sawmill, which he lashed to a wagon.

---

[45]De Nevi, p. 21.

[46]Bancroft, XXI, p. 347.

They prepared for the trip to California.

Bill Fowler, who had met with the Kelseys in Oregon, also returned to Missouri, with word that there was plenty of work for his family. It was the custom those days on the Midwest frontier for travelers to stop at the nearest farmhouse when it got dark, where friendly farmers gave them dinner and lodging. One of Fowler's stops was at the home of the John Trubody family, whom he regaled with tales of the Far West as an agrarian paradise. Because of Fowler, the Trubodys soon built a wagon, sold their home, and bought four yoke of oxen. In a few years, Napa would be their home.

In May of 1843 Chiles left Independence with a group of about 50 men, women and children.[47] On the roster of his wagon train were John Wooden and John Conn, who would settle in and name little Napa County valleys. The Vines and Elizabeth Yount were part of the party. So were future Napans Milton Little, Charles McIntosh and an old Army officer named John Grant. The families loaded their wagons with food, furniture and other possessions they deemed indispensable. Before departing, Chiles also met with his own children, but he decided they were still too young to undergo the grueling passage west. He promised to come back and get them in 1848.

Compared with his first adventure west, Joe Chiles had a relatively easy trip most of the way, but by the time the party reached Fort Hall, Idaho, supplies were running low. To conserve food the group split up, with Chiles and nine or ten horsemen going ahead to Sutter's Fort. They ate what they could kill along the way. Chiles paid the mountain man Joe Walker $300 to guide the remaining families and wagons the rest of the way. The plan worked well for the horsemen but poorly for the wagon train. As the oxen struggled to pull their wagons through the sand, the families had to discard their heavy items piece by piece. Finally Baldridge had to ditch the sawmill itself. It was discovered rusting away on the desert a few years later by puzzled miners.

---

[47]Palmer, pp. 387-88.

Chiles and company found Sutter's fort, rested very briefly, then headed East again to the Sierra to rendezvous with the wagon train. Neither Chiles nor Walker had a map (there were no maps yet), and the two contingents missed each other, the main party crossing the Sierra east of Visalia and dodging death in a major snowstorm. The wagons all broke down. Walker guided the settlers all the way to Monterey before he could find the trail to Sutter's Fort, and Chiles, driven back by snow, returned to Sutter's. There the two factions--immensely relieved--met at last. Chiles, Baldridge, the Vines, Elizabeth Yount, a young woman named Mary Ayers and perhaps Chiles' manservant hopped on a schooner that was bound for the embarcadero in Napa with a shipment of lime for Nicholas Higuera. Then Chiles and Baldridge went to Sonoma. After promising to build a gristmill instead of the sawmill originally agreed upon, they received Vallejo's blessing. Chiles accepted the last Napa Valley land grant, *Rancho Catacula*: an 8,000-acre strip southeast of Pope Valley.

Back in Missouri Bill Fowler hooked up with another wagon train and left for Oregon. He brought his father, William Sr., his brother, Henry, and their good family friend, William Hargrave. Along for the ride too were the Kelsey brothers' sisters. Bill Fowler married Becky Kelsey en route, and when they arrived in Oregon the Kelseys and the Fowlers worked together to build and operate mills. In 1844 the two clans headed down to the Napa Valley together.

As soon as they reached Sutter's fort, Sutter issued them passports. He also performed a marriage ceremony for Becky Kelsey Fowler and another man.[48] The despondent Bill Fowler applied to the American consul in *Alta California*, Thomas Oliver Larkin, for help with his domestic nightmare. On Christmas Eve, 1844, Larkin wrote to the estranged couple, in the first recorded instance of marital counseling in the West:

> You complain that your wife has left you and refuses any longer to live with you, that she has no cause for leaving, that you have ever treated her well, boarded and clothed her in a loving manner, and to the best of your means. In case what you state to be true,

---

[48]Bancroft, XXI, p. 698.

your Wife has no right to leave you...But in case your Wife will not live with you, it remains for you to point out some respectible [sic] house where she shall live. She has no right to go from place to place without your permission...

Well-acquainted with the ways of young adventurers, he added this advice:

Should there once have been cause on your part to make your [Wife] unhappy I would advise you, as you value your peace of mind, your character, and future wealth and well being, to exert yourself in doing all you can to make your Wife's situation with you pleasant and happy.[49]

That same night, Larkin also wrote to Becky:

Your husband say [sic] that if you will return and live with him, he promises you and myself, to do his best to make your situation and life a happy one, and that should you hereafter ever have reason to complain of him, you have his full consent to apply to me for advice and assistance...[50]

The counseling appears to have failed.

Why would sane people leave behind all they had ever known and risk their lives to move to a foreign country they knew only by hearsay? Missourians like the Trubodys, Fowlers and Hargraves were not members of a persecuted religion; the natives they had supplanted were becoming subdued; crops did poorly that year, but there was no enduring famine.

The causes of America's westering trend are complex, and have held the interest of historians ever since. Politically, the acquisition of California--a potential Northern state because slavery was not an institution here--would provide a counterweight to the hoped-for acquisition of Texas, which would be a slave-holding state.

---

[49]George P. Hammond, ed., *The Larkin Papers*, Vol. II, University of California Press, Berkeley and LA, 1952, pp. 334-35.

[50]Ibid, p. 336.

Commercially, having a good port on the west coast of North America would be advantageous for the whaling industry, which in some ways was to the 19th Century what the petroleum industry was to the 20th. Shipping and international commerce in general would also benefit from a West Coast headquarters, since travel to the Orient depended on a dangerous passage 'round the Horn or a treacherous journey through the jungles of Panama.

Politics and commerce are not in themselves enough, however, to motivate everyday people to perform acts of extreme courage, like risking their lives to go to a new land. Spain and Mexico learned that lesson, to the great disappointment of Vallejo, when they tried to lure settlers to the Northern Frontier. What actually caused regular down-home human beings to head West? One of the main motivators was economics.[51] In a nutshell, the situation was this. The Bank of the United States (BUS) had been chartered by Congress in 1816 to issue currency and approve local banks' extensions of loans and credit. Practically everyone hated the BUS, because times were hard, and while the rich got richer, the poor could not get out from under. As the continent gradually opened up for settlement, folks were itching to bust whatever bonds they felt bound them and farm the horizon. For this they needed loans.

President Andrew Jackson stacked Congress with his own supporters, and, being a man of the people, saw to it that the BUS lost its charter. Congress gave local state banks the authority to finance speculation on land and issue money at their own discretion and promised the banks a share in the federal surplus that they anticipated. The people and their bankers rejoiced, and pioneers had financial backing to try their hand at farming the new regions in the Mississippi Valley. Eager to partake of America's prospects for growth, England also poured money into the country.

Enthusiasm for settling the frontier, both on the part the people and their local banks, far outstripped the frontier's readiness to be settled. The "Panic of 1837" ensued practically the minute Jackson

---

[51] Michael Kraus, *The United States to 1865*, University of Michigan Press, Ann Arbor, 1959, p. 358.

left office, leaving an impossible dilemma for his successor, Martin Van Buren. Plows broke, epidemics killed the children, Indians burned down the barns and the houses and stole the cattle, rain didn't come or came at the wrong time in the wrong quantities. Crops failed. The United States imported more than it exported, and there was no federal surplus. Stung by losses on their American investments, banks in England toppled, and soon the local banks, once the good guys, became the villains. Mortgages were called, loans were refused, and settlers all over the newly opened frontier lost their farms.[52]

Left with nothing, many settlers in the Mississippi Valley looked west again for the Land O' Goshen: deliverance from the captivity of economic forces beyond their understanding. Oregon was the original land of promise. Images of its lush pasturage were alluring to Midwestern farmers with their thirsty cattle. England and America owned Oregon jointly. California, on the other hand, was an arid region in a foreign country with whom America had uncomfortable relations, where one needed a passport to move about and had to become a Catholic to own land: a prospect abhorrent to many Americans at the time, because to them being Catholic meant honoring the Pope, a foreigner. Chauvinism--blind, intense, aggressive national allegiance--was pronounced. Most white Americans in the years between Jackson and Lincoln were chauvinistic and ethnocentric as patriots, as members of their own geographical regions and as Christians.[53]

Christianity was an essential element in the character of most people. Americans saw themselves as God-fearing folk with God-given rights, whom God had protected from outsiders with natural divides like oceans.[54] The family Bible was both a treasured heirloom

---

[52]See also Charles and Mary Beard, *The Rise of American Civilization*, Macmillan, New York, 1936.

[53]See Merle Curti, *The Growth of American Thought*, Harper & Row, New York, 1964, esp. pp. 387-413.

[54]Ibid, p. 398.

and a basic textbook. Moreover, missionary zeal was as alive among Americans as it was among the Spanish, although the system through which it was implemented was quite different.

Seeking relief from their difficult, often painfully frustrating lives, some looked to the Bible for secret messages of better times to come, ASAP. A preacher named William Miller and his disciple, Joshua Himes, pored over Revelation and the Book of Daniel and by 1831 had come up with what they considered to be proof that Jesus Christ would return in the fall of 1844. Only a few thousand of the truly pure (144,000, to be exact) would be elected to join Jesus in heaven, while the rest of the corrupt world came to a devastating but richly deserved end. As many as a million people gathered together on rooftops on the appointed night, dressed in the white robes that they felt were suitable for the advent of the Kingdom of Heaven.[55]

One of those who was disappointed when dawn broke the next morning was a young lady named Ellen G. Harmon. She soon married a preacher named James White. Ellen G. White wrote letters of encouragement to the despondent former Millerites. She traveled the country and later the globe, preaching a gospel of spiritual perfectionism through healthier living and personal piety. Considered the primary prophet of Seventh Day Adventism, Ellen G. White would eventually bring her message and many of her followers to the Napa Valley.[56]

The world having failed to end or get much better, either, 1845 would see a veritable explosion of the pioneer population in the Napa Valley. The most notable new arrivals were the York, Hudson and Grigsby families, all of whom were very prominent in the Valley's initial development, and all of whom arrived together in 1845 in what has become known as the Grigsby-Ide party. Their descendents are still numerous in Napa County.

Demographically, the York and Hudson clans were typical for

---

[55]Curti, p. 303.

[56] Warren Jakes and Richard H. Utt, *The Vision Bold*, Review and Herald Publishing Association, Washington, DC, 1977, p. 12.

JOHN YORK.

David Hudson

their times. The Yorks were a large family of English descent who originally came to America in the 17th Century.[57] Many Yorks settled in the southeast, and the branch that blossomed in St. Helena can be traced back to a stem in North Carolina, which at that time was on the edge of civilization. Those Yorks kept moving west, along with the frontier. The John York who traveled with Grigsby-Ide was born in the eastern Tennessee mountains in 1820 and emigrated to the middle part of the state when he was 13. In 1841, John headed west to Dade County, Missouri, and shortly afterward married Lucinda Hudson, sister of his friends and neighbors David and William Hudson, whose parents had owned a farm that was manned by slaves.[58] The Hudsons were Virginians. The Hudsons and the Yorks sold their lands, built wagons and carried on their families' westering tradition. Like the Hargraves and the Fowlers, they were Southerners who admired Andy Jackson, kept moving west, stuck together loyally and intermarried.

The Grigsby-Ide party had minimal trouble with the natives along the way, although at times the natives killed the livestock. One night while on watch John York shot at a rustling Indian, and the experience upset him so much that he threw down his gun and refused to fire on the natives again. York's yellow dog also made the arduous journey, exhausting himself by chasing buffalo.[59] Young Lucinda York's greatest hardship, one not to be minimized, was the birth of twins in the Humboldt Sink area. The one who survived was named David.

One of the most difficult problems the first wagon trains encountered was that of hauling their goods up the sheer, sharp rise of the Sierra. Prior parties were forced to dispose of their animals and possessions and arrived in California with whatever they could carry. When the Grigsby-Ide party reached the Sierra, co-leader William Ide

---

[57] John W York, "Enoch York," unpublished, 1989, p. 1.

[58] Rodney McCormick, "A Short Story History of Grandfather York," unpublished, September, 1938, p. 1.

[59] Ibid, pp. 2-3.

surveyed the way ahead and established a route where trees and boulders could be used as anchors to pulley up first the oxen, one ox at a time, and then the wagons themselves. The men and their animals were sweaty, bloody wrecks attempting this feat, but they survived intact.[60]

As soon as they breached the summit, York, Hudson and the rest got the disconcerting news that they would be arrested by the Californios when they descended the mountains.[61] Some members of the party considered not coming down at all, but they wisely determined that winter might be difficult at such an elevation. Others in the party raced ahead, wanting to be the first to grab whatever lands might be available. While the rest sat about gathering their courage, a huge explosion leveled the wagon belonging to a future Napan, Thomas Knight. Knight had left his worldly wealth in a strong-box that another party member obliterated with gunpowder. It is unclear whether the box was exploded after the thief got the money.

The Hudson and York families found their way to the Napa Valley and prepared crude hunting camps for themselves near where the Kelseys had pitched tent. Farmers rather than mountain men, however, they sought a more enduring domesticity, and soon each family built a cabin. The Yorks' place was in what is now known as Kortum Canyon in Calistoga, and David Hudson settled nearby, where Kortum Canyon Road intersects with Highway 29. The Kelseys' hunting camps were seasonal lean-to's, the Wappo's dwellings were only meant to last a season or two, and the other Americans had settled in the side valleys. Bale's home was farther south, below present-day St. Helena. No Californios had built dwellings in the upper valley.

After squatting on the land for the winter (with Bale's permission),

---

[60]Simeon Ide, *Who Conquered California? The Conquest of California by the Bear Flag Party,* "Rio Grande Press, Inc., Glorieta, NM, 1967, pp. 37-39.

[61]Ibid, p. 40.

the Hudsons and John York went to Sonoma and applied to Mariano Vallejo for passports and work, both of which they received after Yount agreed to sponsor them. York split redwood rails, hauling them down to Higuera's embarcadero at Napa for shipment to Yerba Buena, where they were used for fencing.

North of Rutherford, at the end of what is now Whitehall Lane, a pioneer named Ralph Lee Kilburn had finished building an adobe house for the English "doctor" Edward Bale and his Californio wife, Maria. Ralph Kilburn was a true adventurer. He emigrated to Oregon and didn't like it, but rather than return east or go overland to California, he and a partner built a small ship, the "Oregon." They sailed down the coast with at least one passenger--possibly another old sea dog, Peter Storm. Kilburn tried to buy a compass from the Hudson's Bay Company for the journey, but they refused to sell him one, hoping, perhaps, to discourage him and his mates from such a perilous enterprise.[62] Amazingly, they survived. Kilburn settled in the Napa Valley to raise sheep and cattle and work as a carpenter. In 1845 he married one of the daughters of William Pope, Maria, age 14. By 1844 Kilburn was ready for his second project, a mill for grinding wheat into flour. One of his assistants in this endeavor was another erstwhile sailor, Harrison Pierce, the man who had walked many miles with Bidwell.

The Bales had some long-term house guests, the growing family of a Yankee adventurer-turned-businessman named Nathan Spear. After sailing the seas (and trying unsuccessfully to start a colony in Hawaii[63]) Spear settled down for a while in Monterey and went into business as a trader. For several years his store was virtually the only one in Northern California and therefore not just a place to buy or trade for things, but a meeting place, as well. Spear had joint business ventures with many of the first pioneers, including Jacob Leese, Salvador Vallejo, Thomas Larkin and William Richardson. In 1839

---

[62] John T. Beales, *The Saga of Locoallomi*, unpublished, p. 33.

[63]Edwin Bryant, *What I Saw in California*, Lewis Osborne, Palo Alto, 1967, p. 329.

Spear sent to Callao, Peru, for a gristmill, a two-story wooden structure that he erected on the north side of Clay Street in Yerba Buena, between what are now Kearny and Montgomery Streets. It was powered by mules.

Spear's health was deteriorating, so he sought sunshine at Bale's rancho. While he was there he advised Bale in constructing a gristmill on his property. Like Spear's, the completed structure was to work by mule-power,[64] but Bale was dissatisfied with it and ordered another to be built several miles up valley, where there was a water supply which he felt could more amply power a mill. Gristmills were vital to the development of towns, for it was there that whatever grains had been grown were processed into flour for baking bread. In some ways the local gristmill was analogous to today's grocery store, as it was the place where local people ran into each other and caught up on domestic happenings. Gossip--the other grist of gristmills--has always played a formative, if not formidable, role in the homogenizing of communities.[65] Bale, Yount and Chiles each had a mill, all built around the same time. Bale's big, new up-valley one was the best known and may have been the most used. The mill wheel was 20' high. The water power in the creek behind it was too weak to turn it, so a series of improvements had to be made. Kilburn retired from gristmill building before actually completing the project and started work on a sawmill for Bale instead, at the site of the present-day Charles Krug Winery.

Remote though their rustic encampments might have seemed, the first Valley pioneers did not live in isolation. They were about to become the instigators of an international incident.

---

[64]Davis, p. 133.

[65] Sheila Skjele, *Edward Turner Bale: A Pioneer Miller in the Napa Valley*, p. II-2. Skjele notes that Bale also used Indian laborers.

Chapter Four

1846-47

A condition of tension had existed for years between America and its much weaker neighbor to the south. Multiple administrative upheavals had plagued Mexico ever since it broke away from Spain in 1822. The young nation was not solidifying. To add to its woes, Americans who had emigrated to the Mexican region known as "Texas" defied the Mexican government in 1836 and established an independent, American-leaning Republic.[1]

After Texas fell from Mexico's tree, the world turned its eyes toward the other apple, Alta California. Lacking a large enough population to qualify as a full state in the Mexican republic, the "Territorio de las Californias" created a defense system composed of volunteers.[2] Everyone, including the Californios, knew there was too little manpower to protect Alta California from a real invasion. Moreover, of the 790 *concedos*--land grants--made by 1846, 15% were given to naturalized citizens.[3] The greatest concentration of Anglo grantees was in the Northern Frontier. Californios in Sonoma and Yerba Buena debated the relative merits of falling to Britain, France or America. So ripe for plucking was the region that as early as 1842, all three contenders for the prize had warships cruising the Pacific,

---

[1]Unless otherwise noted, most of the material in this chapter is from Bancroft, XXII, pp. 1-172. There are numerous inconsistencies in the eye-witness reports among the Bear Flaggers as to what happened during the month between June 10 and July 10, 1846.

[2] Rodolfo Larios, *The American Invasion of Mexican Alta California, 1842-1847*, unpublished, 1983, p. 142.

[3]Ibid, p. 142.

ready to pull into Monterey Bay if the moment presented itself.[4] Of the three, many considered the British to be the most serious threat because of their imperialistic activities elsewhere on the globe and because their ships and their 104 guns were the best.[5]

A very telling false start to this effect occurred in October of 1842, when Commodore Thomas Ap Catesby Jones of the United States Navy attacked San Diego harbor, then sailed into Monterey (the capital of Alta California) with his ship flying Mexican colors. After seizing several of the vessels in port, Jones raised the Stars and Stripes and claimed Monterey for the United States.[6] He was reacting to a rumor that war had been declared between the US and Mexico and that a British warship was on the way to lay claim to the countryside. None of these things was true. The embarrassed Jones withdrew the American flag and fired a salute to the Mexican one, and the 24-hour American occupation ended with banquets and dancing hosted by the Californios. Governor Micheltorena fired off a furious but secret letter to Mexico City about the incident.[7]

With many Americans slavering over the prospect of grabbing California, Sonoma's Mariano Vallejo grew frustrated with Mexico's general mismanagement of the province. He retired from command of the Northern Frontier in 1842, pointing out that while the Russians had left the previous year and the natives were dead or subdued, there had been a significant influx of armed Americans in recent months.

To better defend the territory, Governor Manuel Micheltorena beefed up the local forces with an army of conscripts that was little more than a band of marauders. Micheltorena himself was well meaning, but the army was so objectionable to so many that a brief military coup occurred under Jose Castro. Almost everyone joined

---

[4]Bancroft said there were eight French vessels, four English and five American ships cruising the Pacific at the time. (IV, p. 340.)

[5]Idem.

[6]Larios, p. 64.

[7]Bean, p. 91.

in the fray. Elias Barnett, pushing 40, fought with Sutter and Marsh on the side favoring Micheltorena and The Establishment, such as it was. He was surprised to find that the other side was also supported by American adventurers.

Castro and the rebels won. Mexico City recognized Castro as the military leader of Alta California, and then to avoid further trouble they diluted his power by giving control of the civil government to a politician, Pio Pico. Pico moved the capital to the small pueblo of Los Angeles, while Castro remained headquartered in Monterey. The two disliked and mistrusted each other.

In the Fall of 1845 California was in delicate equilibrium, with Pico and Castro snarling at each other from a distance, American politicians poised to claim their manifest destiny from the East, and foreign ships of war prowling the Pacific. One man, one incident could tip the balance.

The man turned out to be John Charles Fremont. Fremont might have had orders to provoke an incident, but the occasion was provided for him by Napa County's first American residents. A native of Savannah, Georgia, and a West Point graduate, Fremont married the daughter of Thomas Hart Benton, a very powerful Senator from Missouri. Benton was convinced that England wanted to snatch California. He strongly urged that the US do so first. (Perhaps he was impressed by the disastrous outcome of the British banks' involvement in the Mississippi Valley.)[8]

Among other things, Fremont was a surveyor. He was commissioned by the United States Army to explore and chart the route west from Independence along the Oregon Trail. He crossed paths with Chiles and Hopper on their return to Missouri. The reports he wrote of his first two expeditions were blockbuster reading for the folks back home, with whom he was rapidly becoming a hero.[9]

This time, Fremont-- "The Pathfinder"-- was to survey the political

---

[8]Bean, p. 96.
[9]Gilbert, p. 166.

terrain of California along with its topography. Fremont and a band of 60 armed "scientists" (including the mountain man Joe Walker and several future Napans) penetrated California via the Sierra in December of 1845, just ahead of severe blizzards and just behind the Grigsby-Ide party. His topographical engineers were crack shots who wore three guns each and had plenty of ammunition.[10] Passing over the South Fork of the American River and noticing nothing unusual,[11] they proceeded to New Helvetia. Sutter issued them passports, and part of the group went south.

General Castro demanded to know what Fremont meant by marching his men through California. Fremont said that they were on a scientific expedition and would stay well out of the way of settled areas. They were only in Monterey to re-outfit their men, he said, and to scout a suitable route to the Pacific. He promised to head for Oregon immediately. When it became clear that Fremont's troops were in fact continuing to move south after Monterey, and that they were not avoiding populated areas, Castro ordered them to leave the country. General Castro recruited as many people as he could to prepare a defense against the intruders--an act the politician Pico misinterpreted as a bid to start an uprising against Pico himself. Perhaps hoping to lure Castro into the hoped-for "incident" that might ignite a war, Fremont and his men played cat-and-mouse with Castro, but the Californios did not pursue. Fremont finally headed to Oregon as he had promised.

On May 8, an agent of US Secretary of State James Buchanan met Fremont in Oregon. This man, Lt. Archibald Gillespie of the US Marines, had a secret packet for Fremont and a message for Thomas Oliver Larkin, who served as the United States consul. The message appointed Larkin as "confidential US agent" (aka spy) and told him to monitor any rival nations' interest in taking over California. In addition, Larkin was to encourage American emigres to align themselves with their country of origin, if this could be done

---

[10]Bean, p. 97.

[11]DeNevi, p. 108.

without aggravating Mexico. If war did break out, Larkin was to take California for America.[12] The ultimate aim, however, was the peaceable annexation of California by the United States. Larkin let his business partner, *Huichica's* Jacob Leese, in on the plan.[13]

Fremont's packet contained copies of the instructions to Larkin as well as a sealed envelope from Senator Benton. (The exact nature of the contents is still unknown. Maybe it was a personal letter from Fremont's wife.)

After talking late into the night, Fremont and Gillespie finally went to sleep. They were awakened when a small contingent of Indians fell upon two of Fremont's men, killing them with axe blows. In retaliation, Fremont's man Kit Carson and several of the topography corpsmen randomly raided native communities. They killed as many natives as they could between Oregon and the camp that they finally established not far from Sutter's. The illiterate Carson dictated anecdotes about these and other exploits,[14] and his thrill-seeking American readers hailed him as a hero.[15]

The first week in May, 1846, when Gillespie was looking for Fremont, the largest wave yet of transcontinental pioneers started its roll westward. An estimated 2,000 people, with 500 teams of oxen and seas of livestock, flowed out of Independence, Missouri. Throngs of well-wishers cheered and sobbed and waved farewell as the covered wagons, festooned with jingoistic signs like "The Whole or None," became bouncing dots on the horizon and were swallowed in their own dust. Many of the travelers turned back, and many headed for Oregon, but a substantial number made California their destination.[16]

---

[12]Bancroft, p. 89.

[13]Bean, p. 95.

[14]Bancroft, XXII, p. 25, footnote.

[15]Gilbert, p. 81.

[16] The historian Bernard Devoto estimated that in 1846 there were as many as 7000 Americans living in Oregon and only about 800 in California.

As before, "place in line" was critically important: the folks in the front of the wave got good water, and their teams got good grass. Perhaps because he was wealthy, Andrew Jackson Grayson was among the first. "Jackson" Grayson was a southern dandy who was also a talented painter, greatly influenced by the works of John James Audubon. His wife, Jane Francis Timmons ("Frank"), would later become a prominent St. Helenan.[17] The Graysons became close friends with another member of their wagon train party, a journalist named Edwin Bryant, whose book about the trip west--*What I Saw in California*--became, like Fremont and Carson's writings, a blockbuster. Grayson volunteered to be captain of his party, but wisely turned over command to a seasoned guide, Col. W.H. Russell.

Another well-heeled gentleman was not so wise. The elderly Jacob Donner was the titular head of about 100 hopeful settlers from Tennessee, Illinois, Ohio, Missouri, the Iowa territory and Europe. The party included several senior citizens and quite a few infants and children. With no mountain man to guide them and lacking a strong leader, the Donner Party was a tragedy waiting to happen. Many of the survivors stayed or settled in the Napa Valley, especially in the upper valley area. Key members of the relief parties that eventually rescued the lucky ones also came from--or to--the Valley.

Several people who would eventually rescue the Donner Party brought up the rear of 1846 emigration. The "Smith Company," captained by the famous mountain man Jedediah Smith, suffered gravely from their poor position. Stampedes by their starving cattle, sickness from polluted water, predations by irritated Indians, even freaks of weather blighted their travels. Families in Smith Company named Tucker, Ritchie, Stark, Owsley, Harlan and Cyrus would survive the ordeal and make names for themselves in the lush, A-shaped California valley that beckoned them.

The best known among his peers in the Emigrant Class of 1846 was a man who eventually made his home in Napa City. Lilburn

---

[17] Lois Chambers Stone, "Biography of Andrew Jackson Grayson," in *Andrew Jackson Grayson, Birds of the Pacific Slope*, SF, Arion Press, 1986, unnumbered ms.

Boggs, father of seven sons and two daughters, had been governor of Missouri. During his political career he had enjoyed much popularity but had alienated not only Missouri's powerful Senator Thomas Hart Benton (Fremont's father-in-law), but the Mormons and their prophet Joseph Smith, as well. With great theatricality Joseph Smith prophesied that Boggs would soon die, and shortly thereafter a Mormon shot Boggs while Boggs relaxed with his family after dinner. He survived the attempt and lived out the rest of his long life with two bullets lodged in his head.

Folks who knew Boggs deemed him "not quite right" after the assassination attempt. The neuropsychiatric consequences of brain trauma such as Boggs received would probably have included, among other things, confusion, fatigue, and loss of higher executive functions such as judgment, as well as social and emotional inappropriateness.[18] Little wonder he left Missouri.

The W.H. Russell party, Boggs party, Donner party, Smith Company and others passed each other several times after leaving Independence, just as cars going long distances on a highway will pass and be passed by fellow travelers. Members of nearby subgroups often became acquainted by face and even by name.

On May 13, 1846, the US declared war on Mexico over incidents occurring in Texas. California was not yet included as part of the war zone. On May 25, word reached Jose Castro that Fremont and his armed men were back in California: on their way, rumors said, to seize Monterey. Castro tried to warn Pico of the dangerous situation that seemed to be developing, but the latter continued to view the former as threatening a military coup. Pico made a show of gathering forces. He arrived with about 80 men in Santa Barbara a month later, but he secretly suspended Castro as military chief and may have been planning to use the army to unseat Castro.

Rumors of war flew wildly throughout the Napa Valley--leaked,

---

[18] Jonathan M. Silver, "Neuropsychiatric Sequelae of Traumatic Brain Injury: Assessment and Management," in *Currents in Affective Illness,* XIV, No. 10, October, 1995, pp. 5-13.

in many cases, by Fremont.[19] The Napa Valley settlers were convinced that it would only be a matter of days before they would be ordered from their camps and cabins and forced to leave the country, to perish in the mountains and desert they had just crossed. Word circulated that Castro had a large army that was preparing to effect this, and that he had ordered local natives to burn the emigrants' crops and houses.

Castro did in fact issue a proclamation declaring that the purchase of land by people who had not become naturalized citizens would be null and void, and that these people would be subject to expulsion from California at the discretion of the government. This was no new ruling, however, just a restatement of the policy that already existed. The truth was that Castro was more worried about Pico than either Fremont or the frightened American pioneers.[20]

Ben Kelsey, William Hargrave, Granville Swift and several others from the Napa Valley rushed to Fremont's camp and urged him to protect the American settlers by striking first. Fremont explained that he could only attack the Californios in self defense.[21]

Fremont's protests notwithstanding, on June 9 about a dozen of his men under the leadership of future Napan Ezekiel Merritt intercepted and stole a drive of more than 200 horses that were en route to Castro's army. The two Californio officers who were in charge of the round-up (Lieutenants Arce and Alviso) were advised by their boasting captors that the next step in the "revolution" would be the capture of Sonoma and New Helvetia.[22] Merritt dispatched the horses to Fremont's camp. Another dozen or so men from Napa and the surrounding valleys joined him, and a grizzly looking band of pioneers headed toward Sonoma. After eating at Billy Gordon's Cache Creek rancho, they crossed Berryessa and Pope Valleys and spent the night at Elias Barnett's house. (Barnett himself wasn't there.

---

[19]Bean, p. 98.

[20]Bancroft, XXII, p. 83.

[21]Ibid, p. 95.

[22]Ibid, p. 127.

Still loyal to Micheltorena, Barnett had ridden to the pueblo of Los Angeles, perhaps to encourage Pico in overthrowing Castro.)[23] Billy Baldridge and a friend, Wesley Bradley, were getting grindstones for a gristmill they were building at Joe Chiles' place and had camped on the west side of the Berryessas' Putah Creek, when they were hailed by Captain John Grigsby and a companion, William Elliott, who were traveling in Merritt's band.[24] The men had fanned out in order to communicate with as many American settlers as possible in the Napa Valley area. Baldridge and Bradley learned that a meeting was to be held at Bale's gristmill the following night. It would be the final rendezvous before an invasion.

John Grigsby, William Ide, Ezekiel Merritt and the others recruited about 20 men who lived or would soon live in the Napa Valley.[25] Besides Merritt and Grigsby, these may have included Sam, Andy and Ben Kelsey, John York and David Hudson, John Gibbs, Bartlett Vines, Peter Storm, Harvey Porterfield, Calvin Griffith, Pat McChristian, Thomas Knight, William Elliott, John Kelly, Granville Swift, Benjamin Dewell, William Hargrave, William "Le Gros" Fallon, Franklin T. Grigsby and William Todd. Nearly all of them were from the Grigsby-Ide party.[26] Since the total number of original revolutionaries was only 33, most of the group who stormed Sonoma could be considered Napa Valley pioneers.

Chiles, Baldridge, Wesley Bradley and John Fowler decided to join up with Fremont rather than join *los Osos* (the Bears) for the siege. Quite a few people in the valley decided to opt out of the initial fighting, among them Nathan Coombs; the ex-sailor Harrison Pierce and his boss Ralph Kilburn, Edward Bale and George Yount, to name a few. It may have seemed to these men that, while mounting a rebellion sounded like a lot of fun, Mariano Vallejo and the

---

[23]Ibid, p. 107.

[24]Palmer, pp. 391-92.

[25]Bancroft, p. 107.

[26]There is discussion among Bear Flag Revolt aficionados as to the accuracy of such roll calls.

Californios had actually been hospitable to the emigrants. They may also have feared for their lives. Prudently, perhaps, Nathan Coombs joined the Bears after the outcome was clear.

On Saturday night, June 13th, most of the American emigrants in Napa County collected at Bale's to discuss plans for the "conquest of California." They were a scruffy group. Their facilitator was Robert Semple, who, with Thomas Larkin, later helped to lay out the city of Benicia. Semple wrote that "almost the whole party was dressed in leather hunting-shirts, many of them very greasy...They were about as rough a looking set of men as one could well imagine."[27] Ezekiel Merritt was particularly dreadful. Henry L. Oak, who actually wrote most of the Bancroft histories, called him "a coarse-grained, loud-mouthed, unprincipled, whisky-drinking, quarrelsome fellow."[28]

Early on Sunday morning, June 14, the Bears took off through the woods toward Sonoma. They arrived just before dawn at Mariano Vallejo's house. They demanded entrance, rousting him from his bed and terrifying his wife. When he answered the door they immediately placed him under arrest, along with his brother Salvador and the Vallejos' French secretary, Victor Prudon. Because Vallejo could not speak fluent English nor the settlers Spanish, Jacob Leese was called in to interpret. Through Leese, Vallejo assured the Americans, truthfully, that he was very sympathetic to the US annexation of California, which he believed was imminent anyway via proper diplomatic channels (a belief that may have been enhanced by Leese, who knew the contents of Larkin's secret letter).

Few of the revolutionaries had actually met Mariano Vallejo. Some of them, like Granville Swift, disliked the Californios altogether. Ben Kelsey and Ezekiel Merritt had particular grudges: they were among the 14 ruffians who rode to Sonoma to rescue Bale after Bale shot at Salvador Vallejo and Cayetano Juarez in the summer of 1844.

For organizational purposes, the settlers appointed three men-- Merritt, Semple and William Knight (for whom is named Knight's

---

[27]Bancroft, XXII, pp.111-112 .

[28]Ibid, p. 738.

Landing on the Sacramento)--to stay inside Vallejo's house. Their assignment was to draw up the terms of his surrender and enumerate the group's demands. The remaining insurgents waited outdoors. Always the affable host, Vallejo offered his guests some *aguardiente,* brandy made of native Californian grapes. Thanks to the alcohol, the emotional stress of their actions and at least two nights with much riding and no sleep, the American negotiators were soon drunk.

Vallejo opened a barrel of wine for the group waiting outside. The results were similar. Eventually the drunken group outside grew tired of waiting and elected John Grigsby to go in and find out what was going on. He joined the brandy drinkers inside. Finally the now-staggering outsiders nominated Ide to enter the house and speed up the negotiations.

The pact facilitated by Leese and signed by Vallejo and the tipsy Bears featured assurances by the Americans that they would not harm them nor appropriate more property than was needed for their immediate wants. In turn, Vallejo promised that the Californios would not take up arms against the Americans.

Thinking that the negotiations were complete, Leese left; but when he returned a half-hour later, the agreement had exploded, and the Bears were arguing with the Californios and each other. William "Le Gros" Fallon was demanding horses; Ezekiel Merritt wanted to put Salvador Vallejo in leg irons; the rest were ransacking Vallejo's house for arms and ammunition. In the end Fallon supervised the theft of 60 horses from Leese's rancho, including two that were pets of his children, and Don Salvador was allowed to go unmanacled. The Bears "arrested" both Vallejo brothers and Victor Prudon. Grigsby, Merritt, Hargrave, Semple and William Knight escorted them to Fremont's camp as hostages, with Leese in tow as interpreter.[29] (Fremont eventually ordered that Leese be arrested, too.)

The Bears and their prisoners got as far as the rancho of Marcos and Manuel Vaca (now Vacaville) and camped for the night. They fell immediately into deep, alcohol-saturated sleep. Word of these

---

[29]Bancroft, p. 119.

events reached Cayetano Juarez. Juarez found them, and while the Bears snored, he and a small contingent of Californios crept up and offered to free the prisoners. One of Juarez's group was a barber and sometime saloon-keeper named Juan Padilla, who had a reputation for brutality.[30] Mariano Vallejo told Juarez not to release them, since he was certain the whole thing would be resolved quickly. (The presence of the dangerous Padilla may have been a factor in his decision. As it turned out, Padilla was to meet the Bears again.)

The fragrant, hungover Bears arrived at Fremont's camp with their elegant prisoners on June 16th. From the Bears' point of view, Fremont's reception of them seemed odd--Bancroft's Henry Oak described it as "reserved and mysterious."[31] That same day Fremont ordered them all to go to Sutter's, where the prisoners were to be jailed. He told Billy Baldridge and Joe Chiles to go to Sonoma as reinforcements for the captured fort.

Vallejo and company were locked in a bare room with no furniture other than a few benches.[32] They had no food or water until the next day, when they were given a pot of soup but no bowls or spoons. They were not allowed to speak with family or friends, and any mail they received was to be read by their captors first. The guards were ordered to treat them roughly and were reprimanded if they were too "soft" with them.

Jose Noriega, a friend of Vallejo's, came by to visit the prisoners and was thrown in jail too. Another friend, Vincente Peralta, suffered the same fate. The Vallejo family then sent Mariano's brother-in-law, Julio Carrillo, to find out what had happened to everyone. He, too, was jailed. Neither Noriega, Peralta nor Carrillo had come armed, nor were they likely to produce mayhem: Noriega was the grantee of a rancho in Contra Costa and Peralta was the son of a well-established family--his father had been with Anza when he discovered the Napa Valley.

---

[30]Idem.

[31]Ibid, p. 120.

[32]Ibid, p. 123.

Back in Sonoma, the Americans now held Vallejo's house and the former garrison. As one of their first acts, the ragtag army set about to design a flag. One eye-witness, a teenager, described the flag as

> a Star...with a grizzly bear in the center looking up at the star and under the words 'Republic of California.' On the lower border was a red stripe of flannel [sic] the whole was composed of a piece of white cotton and blackberry juice, there being no paint in the country.[33]

The problem with accurately portraying how the Bear Flag was made is that no two accounts of it agree, and there are almost as many accounts as there were Bears. The Napa papers , which went on in jingoistic pride about the Bear Flag Rebellion throughout the 1870's, has half-a-dozen conflicting stories about the Flag and its creation.

William Todd, who is usually given most of the credit for making the Bear Flag, wrote to Billy Baldridge in 1872 that

> one of the ladies at the garrison gave us a piece of brown domestic, and Mrs. Capt. John Sears gave us some strips of flannel about 4 inches wide. The domestic was new, but the flannel was said to have been part of a petticoat worn by Mrs. Sears across the mountains...I took a pen, and with ink drew the outline of the bear and star upon the white cotton cloth. Linseed oil and Venetian red were found in the garrison, and I painted the bear and star. To the best of my recollection, Peter Storm was asked to paint it, but he declined.[34]

Other accounts say, for example, that the flannel came from William Matthews' native American wife Chepa, that Mrs. Sears gave the "domestic," that Mrs. Kelsey gave worn-out cotton, that Mrs. Elliott gave new cotton and the flannel, that the white part came from a chemise belonging to Mrs. William Hudson, that Thomas Cowie and Benjamin Dewell made the whole thing themselves, that the white

---

[33]Madie Brown Emparan, *The Vallejos of California*, Gleeson Library Associates, Los Angeles, 1968, p. 204.

[34]*Napa Register*, 7-6-1872.

part was from a sheet, that Peter Storm painted the thing, that the material was taken from a sloop harbored at the mouth of the Napa River, that the red came from pokeberries and the black from lamp-black, that a chewed stick was the paintbrush, etc. etc.

The Bear Flagger Peter Storm carried what he claimed was the true Bear Flag (painted by him, he said) in Napa Valley parades for several decades, and there is a rumor that the flag lies buried with him in a grave somewhere in Napa City's Tulocay Cemetery.

The discrepant and often fiercely held claims of glory among the Bear Flaggers underline the fact that in general, they were a group of over stressed but courageous people who for the first time in their lives had stumbled onto what turned out to be a winning cause. They were lucky they weren't all annihilated like the Americans at The Alamo, to whom they likened themselves. The star in the Bear Flag was a reminder of the struggles of the Lone Star State and the Bears' sense of fraternity with them.

Having taken Sonoma and the Vallejos without firing a single shot, the Bears now had to contend with the consequences of success. The families they left at home were terrified of reprisals. Nancy Kelsey reported that shortly after Ben and his brothers left for Sonoma, she gathered the children (including another baby) and headed there through the woods as well, certain that if she remained in her Napa Valley cabin, she and her family would be hunted down and made to pay for the men's role in the revolt.

The Bear Flag story in the York family has Lucinda York gathering the hot coals from the fireplace so that Castro's army would think they were long-gone and not pursue them.[35] While she may actually have done this, there was no army per se in the Napa Valley, but a rumormonger may have come by with word of one, which would certainly have been enough to cause the family to flee. The York family was among the 200 or so American emigrants who drew toward the safety of Sonoma, often under cover of darkness, during the following week.

---

[35]McCormick, p. 7.

William Ide assumed command of the Bear Flaggers as "governor and commander-in-chief of the Independent Forces," and John Nash, illiterate but devoted to the cause, was named alcalde, or town judge. After Grigsby *et al* left with the prisoners, William Ide spent hours composing rhetoric with which he hoped to stir the troops and commemorate their achievement. In a manic fervor, he also posted sentinels and guards, set up rules of government, oversaw the taking of 30-40 Californios as prisoners, organized the men into divisions and established an accounting system for apportioning food to the ever-swelling numbers of Americans pouring into the compound.

Ide's reality orientation dimmed, and he began making references to a battle for the fort which never took place. He wrote a highly fictionalized and very bombastic statement of all he had accomplished, put it in a sealed envelope and told William Todd and another man to deliver it to Capt. John Montgomery, the highest ranking US naval officer in the vicinity. Embedded within the rhetoric was an urgent request for gunpowder. Before they could accomplish their mission, however, Todd and his companion were captured and taken to the rancho of the *Kaimus* Wappo, Camillo Ynita, in Olompali.

Ide also sent George Fowler (no relation to Bill) and Thomas Cowie off to the Russian River to pick up a keg of gunpowder from the rancho of Henry Delane Fitch, an American grantee with a holding near the present town of Healdsburg.[36] Foolishly, the two young men chose to follow the main road from Sonoma toward Santa Rosa. The fierce Juan Padilla, who had been with Juarez's midnight rescue contingent at Vaca's rancho, was now patrolling the area with two dozen angry men. With him was Ramon Carrillo, whose brother Julio was in jail with Vallejo. Padilla's men surrounded Cowie and Fowler, lassoed them, dragged them alive, and bound them each to a tree, the way real bears were sometimes abused before they were killed. Some renditions of the incident report that the men's tongues were cut out and their bodies mutilated. Carrillo,

---

[36]For more on Fitch, see Joan Parry Dutton, *They Left Their Mark*, James Stevenson, Fairfield, 1998.

however, testified later that "Four-finger Jack," a desperado aka Bernardino Garcia, killed them with his dagger while the Californios were deliberating what to do with them.

When Cowie and Fowler failed to return, a Bear named Samuel Gibson rode off with four men, got the gunpowder at Fitch's and defeated a small band of Californios. They brought back one of the band as a prisoner.

General Jose Castro finally learned of the uprising in Napa and Sonoma on June 17. He launched his defense by issuing a proclamation asking Californios to fight to defend their country. He promised protection to foreign settlers who did not participate in the revolt. A half-hearted response to his plea resulted in the recruitment of about 160 men.

Pico heard of the state of affairs a day or two later, and on June 22 he denounced Castro in what became known as the Los Angeles Declaration. Elias Barnett was one of the document's signatories. He quickly returned to Sonoma to participate in whatever action was left and perhaps to check on the well-being of his wife and family.

Castro divided his small army into three sections. One was led by Jose Antonio Carrillo, a relative of Ramon and Julio. The second was commanded by Manuel Castro, the civil prefect in Monterey, and the third was headed by Joaquin de la Torre, who took his contingent of 50-60 men across the San Pablo Bay on June 23 to reconnoiter. The plan was that if all went well, the three forces would unite and attack the Americans in Sonoma.

The actions and plans of the Californian army were no secret-- general proclamation was the favored means of communication, even though most of the population was illiterate--and several Americans galloped to Fremont with news of the impending strike. Fremont gathered his men for a march to Sonoma.

Sam Gibson's prisoner told the Bears what had happened to Fowler and Cowie and revealed the location of Todd. The horrified and enraged Bears sought revenge. They induced their prisoner to lead them to Santa Rosa to find Padilla and Carrillo. They just missed them at one campsite but followed the trail to Padilla's rancho in the Tomales section of Marin. They made camp not far from

Padilla, slept, and the next morning attacked, taking three or four men prisoner. After breakfast, and after the rest of Padilla's men escaped, they changed horses and headed toward the rancho of Camillo Ynita in Olompali to free Todd.

When they arrived the Californios were having their breakfast. The Bears were in the process of stealing the horses in Ynita's corral and were readying to attack the house when they realized they had stumbled onto a much larger force than they had anticipated. Somewhere along the way Padilla and Carrillo had joined forces with de la Torre's army!

The Bears dismounted and hid among the trees nearby, killing one Californio and wounding a few more. Cayetano Juarez's biographer, Vivian Juarez Rose, claims that Juarez negotiated Todd's release.[37]

The Californios fled, and Todd continued on to Yerba Buena deliver his message to Montgomery. Future Napa Valley resident William Fowler Sr. later commented that the Bears considered plundering Ynita's residence but refrained from doing so. The Bears could truthfully claim victory in the only real combat of the Bear Flag Revolt.

The victorious Bears returned to Sonoma to find that Fremont had just arrived with all his men. On the 26th both forces merged and set out again to find Padilla, Carrillo and de la Torre so they could finish them off. They spent the night of the 27th at the old mission in San Rafael.

The next morning, June 28 (a Sunday), word came to the Americans that a boat was making passage across the San Pablo Bay. On the way to intercept it, Fremont's Indian killer, Kit Carson, asked if they should take prisoners. Fremont replied that there was no room for prisoners. So when three passengers disembarked from the boat, Carson shot them dead from a range of about 50 yards. Two of the dead turned out to be twins, Francisco and Ramon de Haro, age 24, one of whom may have had a message for de le Torre regarding Castro's plan for crossing the San Pablo. The other was

---

[37]Viviene Juarez Rose, *The Past is Father of the Present*, Wheeler Printing, Vallejo, CA, 1974, p. 6.

their elderly uncle, Jose de los Reyes Berryessa, who wanted to accompany his nephews because of the dangerous atmosphere that existed and check on the fate of his son, Jose de los Santos Berryessa, the real alcalde of Sonoma and grantee of the *Mallocamas* rancho in Napa. The three dead men were stripped of their clothing, and Jose de los Santos was later forced to buy his dead father's serape for $25.[38]

Later that day Fremont's men captured a native who carried a message stating that the Californios were planning a mass attack on Sonoma the following morning. A letter to this effect was also "found" on the street back in Sonoma and given to Ide, who read it to the settlers. A state of acute anxiety resulted, prompting the women and children to huddle in Vallejo's house while the men prepared for a siege.

The pioneers primed the fort's cannon and aimed it at the road, waiting for Castro to attack. A cloud of dust kicked up, and someone prepared to light the fuse on the cannon. Just before the flame hit the fuse, the Bears realized that it was Fremont and not the Californios who were coming down the road. They missed shooting at their own men by fractions of a second.

The well-advertised secret attack on Sonoma failed to materialize, and Fremont saw that he had been tricked. He turned his troops around and chased back to where de la Torre's army had been, but de la Torre had already crossed over San Pablo Bay to rejoin the rest of the Californios.

Some writers at the time tried to cover up the brutality of Kit Carson's killings. A salty Boston trader named William Phelps, for example, happened to be in the area to collect money from some "debtors" in the Napa Valley when the war broke out. In his diary, which was published for public consumption back east, he wrote: "These men were armed & letters were found on them with orders from Castro to Torre to kill every foreigner he found--man woman & child. These three men were shot on the spot. One of them was a

---

[38]Bancroft, XXII, p. 172.

notorious killer."[39] In truth, the three men were unarmed civilians. Phelps may have been irate, because it was his launch that de la Torre stole to make his retreat.[40]

Fremont's company returned to Sonoma. They soon left again, however, this time to determine the state of things to the south, where the threat of Castro's army persisted. On July 1 Phelps ferried Fremont and his men to the abandoned ruins of an old fortress that once monitored the Bay, Castillo de San Joaquin. All that was left of Castle San Joaquin were a few old brass cannon--less than a dozen-- that had been made in Peru in the 17th Century and hadn't worked for decades. Symbolically, Fremont "spiked" the cannon by plugging the touch hole where the fuse would be connected.[41] Phelps later charged the US government $50,000 for transporting Fremont, of which he ultimately received $500.

The next day Fremont went to Yerba Buena to make some arrests in the name of the Bear Flag Party. His primary target was the English businessman William Hinckley, alcalde of Yerba Buena and a partner of Leese and Spear. Hinckley, however, had died on June 30. Apparently hoping the purge the pueblo of Englishmen, Fremont's Bears did manage to take as prisoner Robert Ridley, the British-born harbor master.[42]

While in Yerba Buena Fremont made what was probably his most significant contribution to the history of California: he renamed the entrance to Yerba Buena Cove "The Golden Gate."

Meanwhile, Phelps wrote, he and a passenger, Nathan Spear

arrived in the long creek Napa at noon & with the help of a

---

[39]William Dana Phelps, "The 1846 Journal of William Dana Phelps," in *Fremont's Private Navy*, Briton Cooper Busch, ed., Arthur H. Clark Co., Glendale, CA, 1987, p. 31.

[40]Phelps, p. 32.

[41]Ibid, p. 33.

[42]Fred B. Rogers, *Bear Flag Lieutenant*, California Historical Society, SF, 1951, p. 14.

fair wind & tide reached the landing place about 4 PM. Here we were soon pounced upon by a scouting party of Americans who charged upon us supposing our boat was from the enemy camp. These people informed us that Capt Fremont was to camp that night about 6 miles distant from the boat...[43]"

Phelps and Spear spent the night on blankets spread out "on the dry long grass on the high banks of the creeks,"[44] and left the next morning for Bale's. The Napa Valley was virtually empty, "most of the people absent & engaged in the war."[45]

Fremont returned to Sonoma for the 4th of July. True to the patriotic spirit of the time, the Americans hosted a huge celebration. Lt. Woodworth of the United States Navy read the text of the Declaration of Independence from a book that Billy Baldridge had salvaged on his trek across the continent.[46] The next day, Baldridge chaired a meeting to reorganize the Bears, much to William Ide's disappointment. John Bidwell was chosen as secretary. Fremont was made the de facto chief of the Bears' operation, with Marine Lieutenant Archibald Gillespie as his adjutant. The Bears elected John Grigsby, Granville Swift and William Ford as captains. Each Bear was given the opportunity to sign up with one or another of the three. For the most part, Fremont's men stayed with him.

On July 6th the Bears at Sonoma split up into sections, each with its own task. Grigsby's men stayed at Sonoma. Fremont headed to Sutter's Fort, and Swift and Ford led their contingents through the *Las Putas* rancho to round up whatever horses they could find and appropriate them for the Bears. They were unable to find any horses at all.

Billy Baldridge joined Swift's company and was elected orderly sergeant. He went to Sutter's to procure provisions for his group.

---

[43]Ibid, p. 39.

[44]Idem.

[45]Ibid, p. 40.

[46]Palmer, p. 392.

When he arrived, he was greeted with a closed, barricaded door--something unusual for New Helvetia. He banged on the door, and a native sentry who was guarding the place told him he could not enter. Suddenly John Sutter himself peered through a window in the door. Recognizing Baldridge, the wide-eyed Swiss opened the door and said, "I surrender to you! I held out as long as I could, but you were too strong for me!"[47]

Baldridge found himself confronted by the frightened Sutter, two large cannon, and several armed men who quickly threw down their weapons. New Helvetia, the second strategic target of the "revolution," fell to the surprised but worthy hands of Billy Baldridge without a shot, and Sutter's dreams of fathering a new country were shattered.

Meanwhile, Fremont's path led to the nexus of ranchos by the Napa River. Salvador Vallejo was in jail at Sutter's, and Higuera may have been hiding. Cayetano Juarez somehow managed to ingratiate himself with the Bears. For years afterward he carried a special pass signed by John Grigsby himself:

"Pass the bearer, Cayetano Juarez, to his rancho on his own business without molestation; also not to interrupt his property for he has signed the pledge. Sonoma, July 9, 1846"[48]

Fremont arranged for the shipment of some saddles and munitions, which he had hauled from Sonoma. The materiel was loaded on *The Mermaid*, for transport to Sacramento via the Napa River. The little crew enthusiastically made a Bear Flag replica from their shirts and flew it on the ship--the Bear Flag's second naval adventure.

Captain John Montgomery assigned Lt. John Misroon to accompany Todd back to Sonoma. Montgomery's teenage son went along, too. Misroon observed what was happening at the fort and returned to report all to Montgomery, including his son's description of the strange flag that now flew over Sonoma .

---

[47]Palmer, p. 393.

[48]*NCR* 10-2-1875.

Meanwhile the US Commander of the Pacific squadron, John D. Sloat, had been informed of the settlers' uprising. He had to decide whether to claim California for the United States (and risk making a fool of himself like Catesby Jones) or sail on and let the Bear Flag Revolt dissipate.

The official US agent, Thomas Oliver Larkin, was also surprised by the emigrants' revolt, and his confidante, Leese, was in Sutter's jail. Fremont's role in it all was probably unclear to everyone. On July 7, after much contemplation, Sloat reluctantly sailed into Monterey and raised the American flag. Two days later, Captain Montgomery did the same in Yerba Buena under Sloat's orders, as did Lt. Joseph Revere, a grandson of Paul Revere, in Sonoma. On July 11, 1846, John York and Sam Kelsey carried the US flag to Sutter's Fort to signify America's conquest of California,[49] and the Bear Flag Rebellion was over.

Most of the Bear Flaggers saw service in the Mexican War. Still dressed in their buckskins and moccasins, they formed a volunteer battalion under Fremont and went south in pursuit of Castro. Sloat was against allowing this motley assemblage to fight under the US flag, but he was exhausted and in ill health and turned his command over to Commodore Robert F. Stockton, who was much more aggressive and seemed delighted to employ them.

There was problem, though. Stockton was a naval officer, but Brigadier General Stephen W. Kearny and the US Army had fought their way up from New Mexico. Like Sloat, he did not want the services of Fremont, his grubby topographers or the Bears. A dispute ensued over who was in charge, Kearny or Stockton. Although he was a West Point graduate commissioned by the Army, Fremont opted to side with the Navy's Stockton and continued to command his hardscrabble heroes. Directly insubordinate, "The Pathfinder" was later court-martialed for this. His enemies--who were considerable, for there was much in Fremont's life about which they could be jealous--suspected him of entertaining visions of unlimited

---

[49] John W. York, personal correspondence to author.

power in remote California. (He did, in fact, run for US Senator, successfully, in 1850. He later made an unsuccessful bid for President.)

But someone more venomous than Fremont had slithered into Yerba Buena. He came by sea. Sam Brannan was born in Saco, Maine (between Portland and Kennebunkport) in 1819. He left his abusive, alcoholic father and traveled about in the east and midwest, spending time in New Orleans, Ohio and New York. He became a printer and went where there was work--in this case, the Mormon church. Recognizing his gift as a communicator, the Church nurtured him as one of their own and made him publisher of their newspaper in New York City. When the Mormons' prophet Joseph Smith was murdered by a Missouri mob in 1846, the Mormons realized that America held no reliable future for their organization. That year they put together a mass exodus to the west, where they hoped to establish a theocracy without interference from Americans. Brigham Young led those with possessions worth carrying on a wagon train. Brannan took his printing press and the less wealthy on a boat, the *Brooklyn*, around the Horn, with Oregon and then Salt Lake City as his destination.

Many of Brannan's followers believed in him implicitly, and many accorded him the same devotion as Brigham Young. Others, however, were put off by his ambitiousness. Fully aware of the failure of Mexico City to protect Alta California, Brannan saw an opportunity to establish himself and his ship full of followers as the major presence in Yerba Buena. He bought munitions and hoped to make an impressive entrance in San Francisco Bay the very week that the Bears and Fremont were chasing Castro and de le Torre!

They were an impressive sight when they landed. "Every man of them," wrote William Phelps, "is armed to the teeth with Rifles, six barrel pistols, and bowie knives."[50] With visions of empire of their own, Brannan and his Mormons were deeply disappointed to see the Stars and Stripes flying in Yerba Buena Cove. "Captain Montgomery

---

[50]Phelps, p. 43.

told me," wrote Phelps, "that he should watch them sharp and should put them down if they committed treason."[51]

There were 236 men, women and children aboard the *Brooklyn* and only about 150 people in Yerba Buena. When they disembarked, Brannan's Mormons dominated the city. Their influence was soon diluted, however, because "the saints" split into three groups: the San Francisco contingent, a group that chose to farm on acreage in the San Joaquin Valley and a third who went up the Sacramento to what became known as Mormon Island. Brannan remained in San Francisco and set up a newspaper on the second story of Nathan Spear's gristmill.[52] He first called it the *Star*, then the *California Star*.[53] He later moved it to a building of its own, on a lot he leased from Stephen Smith, the man with the steam engine who had employed Nathan Coombs.[54] Brannan would have an impact on the history of the west, but no place more strongly than in the Napa Valley.

Edwin Bryant and the Graysons crested the Sierra around August 30. They rested up near what is now Wheatland, at the rancho of William Johnson, a Boston sailor who plied the Sacramento on a flat-bottomed boat he co-owned with *Huichica's* Jacob Leese.[55] Yankee businessman that he was, Johnson sold the emigrants critically needed supplies at very high prices.[56] So exorbitant were the prices, in fact, that another Yankee businessman, the trader William Phelps, wrote that "the little cash they bring with them will soon be expended for

---

[51]Idem.

[52]Bean, p. 184.

[53]Its final name was the *Alta California*.

[54]Douglas S. Watson, "The Great Express Extra of the *California Star* of April 1, 1848," in *California Historical Society Quarterly*, XI, 1932, p. 130. Hoover (p. 361) says the lot was located at what is now 743 Washington St., SF.

[55] Jack and Richard Steed, *The Donner Party Rescue Site*, Graphic:Publishers, Santa Ana, 1991, p. 2.

[56]Daniel Rhoads, letter, in Steed, p. 26.

the necessities of life, for which they will be compelled to pay high prices." [57] Johnson also showed (or perhaps sold) them a copy of the first newspaper published in California--*The Californian*, edited by Bear Flagger Robert Semple, which predated Brannan's *Star*. In the two months after taking Sonoma, Semple had actually had time to set up a publishing company.

Throughout the next several weeks, other emigrants, triumphant and exhausted, emerged from the craggy peaks. They set up camps on Johnson's property and at the rancho of William Gordon and socialized. Some, like Jackson Grayson and Edwin Bryant, headed out to explore the area. ("Frank" Grayson stayed at Gordon's.) Lilburn Boggs, his wife, two daughters and seven sons continued to Sonoma where they were taken in by the newly freed Mariano Vallejo, who was amazingly hospitable after the insults he had endured during the Bear Flag revolt.

Not everyone was in such a hurry. A slower pace enabled the pioneers to experience and explore the beauty of their surroundings-- the adventure of a lifetime. John Bidwell had been a powerful advocate of drinking deeply of the American scenic offering. Those who viewed life not as a battle to be waged but as a banquet to be savored wanted to hasten less. In the Donner Party the two factions argued several times on the way to Fort Bridger, a rest station in the southwest corner of present-day Wyoming.[58]

The station masters at Bridger--mountain man Jim Bridger and his partner, Louis Vasquez--had lately employed Lansford Hastings, author of the national best seller, *The Emigrant's Guide to Oregon and California,* to lead a party west over a shortcut he had recently "discovered" that would, he said, cut 200 miles off the trip. The personnel at Fort Bridger were the ones who outfitted the pioneers with supplies for the most rigorous portion of the journey. They were considered the ultimate experts on the road west. When they

---

[57]Phelps, p. 72.

[58]See C.F. McGlashan, *History of the Donner Party*, Stanford University Press, 1968

promoted the Hastings Cutoff, the Donner Party listened.

Another seasoned tracker tried to talk the travelers out of taking the shortcut--indeed, out of going to California at all. Veteran mountain man Jim Clyman had been there and had stayed with the Kelseys in the Napa Valley. He told of sparse rain and failed crops and the "low quality" of the Americans already living there. Unable to dissuade the Russell, Smith and Boggs groups from heading for California, he urged them not to risk the untried Hastings Cut-off. He probably saved their lives.

Most of the other California-bound wagons of the Class of '46 chose to take the long way around, which led through Fort Hall. But Jacob Donner, impressed by Hastings' book and swayed more by Jim Bridger than Jim Clyman, opted for the Cut-Off. Three weeks down the road the Donner party found a note stuck in a split stick, informing them that the shortcut was, in fact, impassable.

It took a month and many deaths for the Donner party to reach the Salt Lake instead of the week that Hastings had advertised, and their provisions dwindled dangerously. After a dry, agonizing drive through the desert, the party finally drew near to what is now Reno around October 27.[59] They turned their livestock loose and ambled a few miles west for the next three days, eventually reaching what is now Truckee Meadows. Some believed that the livestock should have a chance to forage and fatten up in the mountain meadows just east of the Sierra's summit. This, they felt, would improve the animals' chances of surviving the arduous final portion of the trek. Coming to California with healthy cattle meant arriving rich.

Had any of the Donner party been fearful of portents they would have camped there and waited for Spring before trying to cross the mountains. Having endured scurvy, dysentery, deaths, violent factionalism and increasingly unfriendly encounters with the natives, their journey was already more fraught with disaster than that of any other wagon train so far. They saw huge gray clouds closing in on the elevations ahead of them, but it was still only the

---

[59]McGlashan, p. 56.

end of October, and the snows weren't expected to arrive in the Sierra until Thanksgiving. The party believed there was ample time.

There wasn't. Near present-day Truckee, the Donner party stalled in six inches of snow. The peaks ahead were buried in three feet of it. A lack of decisive leadership that had plagued them earlier took its toll, as some members of the wagon train dug out and pressed on down a steep hill, probably along a route roughly parallel to today's Northwoods Boulevard in Truckee, while others decided to stay put near what is now Alder Creek Road. The group that pressed on got as far as Donner Lake. A few tried vainly to scale the mountains. They followed a road of sorts that had been etched into the rocks by emigrants from the previous five years, but they lost the trail in the snow and ice and had to turn back.

The same storm slammed into the Napa Valley. It was October 31--Halloween--and Edwin Bryant, Jackson Grayson and a small group of companions were looking for the Kelseys' campsite in the Napa Valley. A few days earlier they had located Elias Barnett's rough cabin, but it was vacant.[60] In his journal Bryant wrote that the door to Barnett's place had been open, and some pigs were running around inside.[61] Corn and wheat had been harvested there earlier in the season. Bryant and company left the cabin and got lost. They saw the storm brewing and asked some natives to help them find Barnett's cabin again so they could stay dry.

Bryant described the storm that ravaged the Napa area on Halloween, 1846:

> It rained all day, and when we reached Barnett's (the empty house) about four o'clock, PM, the black masses of clouds which hung over the valley portended a storm so furious, that we thought it prudent to take shelter under a roof for the night. Securing our animals in one of the enclosures, we encamped in the deserted dwelling. The storm soon commenced, and raged and roared with

---

[60] Barnett was in Los Angeles with Pio Pico, and his family may have been in Sonoma.

[61] Perhaps the Bear Flaggers had left the door open after they rendezvoused there on the way to Sonoma.

a fierceness and strength rarely witnessed. The hogs and pigs came squealing about the door for admission; and the cattle and horses in the valley, terrified by the violence of the elemental battle, ran backwards and forwards, bellowing and snorting.[62]

But up in the Sierra there was no venison, and even making fire was a problem. A few days later the emigrants tried again to cross with the surviving livestock, but the path was lost beneath the snow and ice. The men and animals returned to their camps, and it was agreed that the following day they would abandon the animals and make the ascent on foot.[63] Time, however, had run out. That night another huge snowstorm swept in that continued for several days. It buried the livestock alive and sealed in the Donner party.

It was horrible for them. In a letter written from "Nappa Vallie California" in May of '47 little Virginia Reed described what it was like:

> we had to kill little cash the dog & eat him we ate his head and feet & hide & evry thing about him o my Dear Cousin you dont know what trubel is yet many a time we had on the last thing a cooking and did not know wher the next would come from but there was awl wais some way provided there was 15 in the cabon we was in and half of us had to lay a bed all the time thare was 10 starved to death while we ware there we was hadley abel to walk we lived on litle cash a week and after Mr Breen would cook his meat and boil the bones Two or three days at a time...[64]

Virginia Reed's father, John, had been exiled from the Donner party back in the desert because of an unfortunate incident where he killed a man. He and a companion made it to Sutter's fort and waited for the others. When they didn't show up, he knew the party was in

---

[62] Edwin Bryant, *What I Saw in California,* reprinted by Ross Haines, Inc., Minneapolis, 1967, p. 350.

[63] McGlashan, p. 65.

[64] Virginia Reed Murphy, in Morgan, *Overland*, p. 285.

trouble. He pleaded for volunteers to help rescue the troubled wagon train.

Instead, he himself was recruited to join in the war against Castro and the Mexican Republic, which was going full bore. He went to Sonoma and became attached to a militia group there where he struck a bargain: he could head back to the Sierra with supplies, provided he would enlist other volunteers for the Mexican War on the way. He made good on his promise to the US Army and recruited a dozen men to fight against the Californios, including Edwin Bryant and Jackson Grayson.

Reed met up with another Donner party member who had left the group to find help, and together they hauled a supply wagon that had been donated to them. At a place called "Bear Valley" they came across a husband and wife who had been stopped for several days by the first storm and then buried in the second. The couple had run out of food and were just finishing off the last of the family dog when Reed arrived, miraculously, with the wagon-load of food.

The snow continued, and Reed could make no further progress up the mountain. Before turning back, he secured the provisions on the supply wagon so that they could be used by anyone else going up or coming down from the mountain.

Meanwhile, up in the Sierra, small parties were sent out from the various cabins around Donner Lake to assault the summit. The refugees made snowshoes of rawhide, and the women dressed in pants,an occurrence so unusual for those times that it warranted mention in the survivors' diaries. The snow blinded them, and the effort of snowshoeing was exhausting to the point of paralysis. Food gave out, but the blizzards continued. No one spoke. In order to survive, the living had to eat parts of those among them who perished. The corpses' remains were apportioned so that relatives did not have to eat relatives.[65]

Finally, one of the women--Mary Graves--saw human footprints in the snow, and soon seven barely living, incoherent skeletons

---

[65]McGlashan, pp. 85-86.

staggered into an Indian camp. They looked so hideous that the native children who saw them ran and hid. The natives fed them pinole and acorn bread and nursed them while six of the seven lingered close to death. The seventh, William Eddy, was able to walk with assistance, and, supported by two natives, emerged from the mountains. It had been 32 days since he and the others had left Donner Lake.[66] On January 11, 1847, future Calistogan Harriett Ritchie opened the door of her makeshift cabin at Johnson's ranch, and the emaciated William Eddy fell inside.

Reasin P. Tucker was a tall, soft-spoken Virginian whose first wife had died and whose second wife refused to follow him west.[67] He had just crossed over with his three sons and the Ritchies, and was resting up near Johnson's ranch. Without hesitation, he, Harriett's husband Matthew D. Ritchie, and two other men sped to the Indian camp. They rescued the six who were languishing there.

Tucker and Ritchie slaughtered some of their own cattle while another emigrant tried to find men courageous enough to reascend the snowy peaks. It took two weeks. When the "First Relief Party" came together, Tucker was their captain.[68]   Driven on by the desperate desire to reunite with the family he had left behind, William Eddy also became one of the relief workers, leaving from Johnson's on February 5, with 16 year-old George Tucker, son of Reasin. It was raining, so it was very difficult to make much progress. The rain turned the ground to a sticky, soupy mud. George's horse gave out, so Eddy proceeded without him.[69]

George Tucker would have been a sophomore in Calistoga High School had this been happening today. He described what happened

---

[66]Ibid, pp. 109-110.

[67]See Barbara Neelands, "Reasin P. Tucker: The Quiet Pioneer," *Gleanings*, V, No. 2, Napa County Historical Society, March, 1989.

[68]Murphy, p. 40.

[69] Eddy didn't know that his daughter, Margaret, had died on February 4, or that his wife had followed her four days later.

next:

> My horse could only go in a slow walk, so I walked and led him
> to keep from freezing. The rain continued to increase in volume,
> and by dark it was coming down in torrents. It was very cold. The
> little stream began to rise, but I waded through, though sometimes
> it came up to my armpits. It was very dark, but I kept going on in
> hopes I would come in sight of the camp-fire. But the darkness
> increased, and it was very difficult to find the road. I would get
> down on my knees and feel for the road with my hands. Finally,
> about nine o'clock, it became so dark that I could not see a tree
> until I would run against it, and I was almost exhausted dragging
> my horse after me. I had lost the road several times, but found it
> again by feeling for the wagon-ruts. At last I came to where the
> road made a short turn around the point of a hill, and I went
> straight ahead until I got forty or fifty yards from the road. I
> crawled around for some time on my knees, but could not find it.
> I knew if the storm was raging in the morning as it was then, if I
> got very far from the road, I could not tell which was east, west,
> north or south, I might get lost and perish before the storm ceased,
> so I concluded to stay right there until morning. I had no blanket,
> and nothing on me but a very light coat and pair of pants...[70]

They planned for the first leg of the journey to end at Bear Valley,
where they would utilize the supply wagon that Reed had cached
earlier. When they reached this point eight days later, they
discovered that the cache had been ransacked by bears.[71] Ritchie,
Eddy and a few others turned back, but Reasin Tucker persevered,
promising to pay each man who stuck it out five dollars a day for his
efforts. The ones who endured were Tucker, Aquila Glover, John
Rhoads, Daniel Rhoads, R. Moultry, Joseph Sels (aka George or
Joseph Foster) and Ned Coffeymire (aka "Sailor Mike").[72]

---

[70] George Tucker, quoted in McGlashan, pp. 114-115.

[71] Murphy, p. 50.

[72] Daniel Rhoads letter to Bancroft in Morgan, Dale, *Overland in 1846: Diaries and Letters of the California-Oregon Trail,* Talisman Press, Georgetown, CA 1963.

On February 19th Reasin Tucker and his six stalwarts descended the gorge leading to Donner Lake. The snow at the summit they had just crossed was 30' high, and the little makeshift residences below were submerged in snow. Tucker saw the bodies of several dead emigrants on or near the surface. He shouted to arouse whoever might still be alive in the cabins and was greeted by the emaciated survivors.[73] Tucker decided not to tell them the full truth about the fate of the 15 Party members who had attempted to cross the mountains, for fear it would discourage them too much.

The rescue workers gave the survivors small amounts of food to eat, because large portions would have been fatal. The workers camped outside, not only to protect the food from being devoured by the starving emigrants, but also to protect themselves from having to look at them. (Nevertheless, one child got into the supplies and gorged himself to death.)

The next day, Tucker led a team of four men the seven or eight miles up to the other encampment by Alder Creek, finding a scene similar to that at the lakeside. Small amounts of food were again distributed. Both at Alder Creek and the lakeside, many of the people were too weak to make the difficult passage back to civilization. The problem was who to bring back and who to leave there, starving. The patriarch Jacob Donner was a case in point. He had contracted an infection in his hand and had taken to his bed. His own personal reserves became depleted. His wife, Tamsen, was still relatively healthy and had devoted herself to nursing him. She elected to remain with her husband while six at the Alder Creek camp (including two small Donner children) made the journey downhill to lakeside.

Everyone who left Alder Creek made it to Donner Lake. Now the question became, who could survive the 40-mile trek over the mountains to safety? In all, 23 of the stranded emigrants seemed intact enough to make the trip. One child was carried on the back of a relief worker, but two other children--Patty and Thomas Reed-- proved too feeble to continue, so one of the rescue party led the

---

[73]Murphy, p. 40.

children back to lakeside while their mother, Margaret Reed (wife of John Reed) traveled on to safety.

Phillipina Keseberg attempted the escape without her husband. Louis Keseberg, a German and future Calistogan, had come up lame during the exodus to Salt Lake and was unable to help the pioneers in their abortive attempt to scale the mountains weeks before. Their son had already died of starvation, and now their infant daughter, Ada, became the first casualty of Tucker's rescue party. An Englishman named Denton became the second a few days later.

On February 26, just beyond Bear Valley, Tucker's rescue crew crossed paths with the "Second Relief Party," headed by John Reed. After being turned back by the snow, Reed had decided to try again and petitioned Commodore Stockton for reinforcements. The Navy was unwilling to outfit Reed for a second rescue attempt, although many of Stockton's sailors donated money. Reed collected more money from the citizens of San Francisco and took a boat to Higuera's embarcadero at *Entre Napa* to recruit men willing to join him. He and his partner, a man named McCutcheon, found five volunteers in what was about to become Napa City and another two men and some horses at Yount's.[74] The Yankee trader William Phelps noted the Donner's situation in his diary and witnessed Reed soliciting help.[75]

Reed and McCutcheon then rode over the hill to Joe Chiles' rancho. Chiles donated a horse, a mule and two wagon covers to use as tents. Reed wrote in his diary that he and McCutcheon traveled "very Rough road"[76] to Berryessa Valley and found another volunteer. The company arrived at Sutter's Fort shortly thereafter, where they prepared a large supply of food. Reed and McCutcheon's "Second Relief Party" left Sutter's around the same time Tucker's

---

[74] Dale Morgan, ed. *Overland in 1846: Diaries and Letters of the California-Oregon Trail, Vol. I,* Talisman Press, Georgetown, CA, 1963, p. 342.

[75] Phelps, p. 72.

[76] Morgan, Loc. Cit.

"First Relief Party" started back down from the lakeside cabins. When the two parties crossed paths, Reed gave Tucker some badly needed food. Tucker and his 21 survivors continued west to Sutter's, and Reed and company followed Tucker's trail back to Donner Lake.

Reed's Relief consisted of Reed, William McCutcheon, Hiram Miller, the mountain man Britt Greenwood, Howard Oakley, John Turner, Matthew Dofar, Charles Stone, Charles Cady and Nicholas Clark.[77] They were greeted by the same sight of starvation that Tucker had seen two weeks earlier. Reed and his two children were reunited. Two days later he began guiding 17 walking skeletons back down the mountains.

Three of the Second Relief team, Charles Cady, Charles Stone and Nicholas Clark, (all Napans) went to the aid of the ailing Jacob Donner and the Alder Creek group. Clark had the good fortune of seeing bear cub tracks in the snow and followed them to a small cave. Afraid to enter the cave himself, he fired a random shot, hoping to scare the bear out. Nothing happened, and a day passed while he waited for the cub. Believing that if he failed to bring back any food the rescuers and the Donners would all starve, he finally mustered the courage to go inside, feel around and maybe find the cub, whom he could perhaps wrestle to the ground and kill. Gingerly, he entered the cave, only to have the snow at its entrance collapse beneath him. He tumbled down a small natural shaft and landed on a furry lump which turned out to be the cub. His random shot into the cave had killed it.[78]

While Nicholas Clark stalked the cub, a new storm was brewing. Tamsen Donner paid Cady and Stone $500 to rescue the three children still with her at Alder Creek. They left, and when Clark returned with the fresh meat Tamsen persuaded him to go down to the lake and make sure her children were safely on their way to the flatland.

At the lake, Clark found that Cady and Stone had abandoned the

[77]Murphy, p. 58.
[78]McGlashan, pp. 163-167.

Donner children at the Kesebergs' cabin. They were still there, without a parent to protect them, and Clark feared they would be killed.[79]

The blizzard came and dumped itself on everyone and proved to be one of the most severe of the season. Reed's "Second Relief" was just past the summit, perhaps in the Royal Gorge region, and the emaciated crew huddled together under blankets with nothing to eat and nothing to protect them from the snow other than the drifts themselves. Two of the refugees died, and one of them, a boy, became food for the rest.

Down below, the indefatigable William Eddy assembled a "Third Relief Party." By now everyone in the northern part of the state knew about the crisis in the mountains, and the young, the brave and the unattached wanted to be part of the action. Too out of shape to join in, George Yount got some glory by claiming that he had advance knowledge about the tragedy through a miraculous dream. The Navy was kinder to Eddy than it had been to Reed; they donated food and horses.

Napans William Thompson, Howard Oakley and John Stark joined Eddy. Perhaps troubled by a guilty conscience, Charles Stone went back too. Stark, Stone and Oakley tended to the survivors in Reed's "Second Relief," and the rest fought their way back to Donner Lake.[80] Of the 11 starving people in Reed's group, only two could walk unassisted.

Oakley and Stone left John Stark with the invalids and guided the others to safety. Stark knew that without food and warmth his charges would soon be dead. Strapping on his back the group's blankets and the little bit of food he had brought along for them, he single-handedly directed the remaining people down from the mountains, carrying all the children most of the way. Stark later commented that the starved children were so light they were easy to

---

[79]Ibid, p. 169.

[80]The volunteers were paid for their efforts. Stark got $117 for a total of 39 days' work. William Thompson received $50.

carry.[81]

Meanwhile, Eddy's contingent had found the cabins at Donner Lake. Several people were still alive, among them the German Louis Keseberg. It was only now that William Eddy learned that all of his family had died.

Jacob Donner died up at Alder Creek, and Tamsen came down to lakeside. When she arrived, Louis Keseberg was in the process of eating a corpse. Refusing to join him in this, Tamsen died of starvation and exposure shortly thereafter and was consumed by Keseberg too.[82] He also ate a child whom he was later accused of killing for that purpose.

When the "Fourth Relief" party came to Donner Lake in March under the leadership of the Napa Bear Flagger William "Le Gros" Fallon, the only living person there was Keseberg. The Fourth Relief confiscated the Donners' goods on Alder Creek. It was a haul of some worth, since the Donners had been wealthy. They were unable to find a large horde of gold and silver that was rumored to be there. After searching thoroughly they decided that Keseberg had stolen it. Fallon and the rest of the group threatened to lynch him if he failed to come forth with the treasure. Reluctantly, Keseberg turned over the Donner's gold and revealed that he had stashed $531 of the Donners' silver in the snow under a branch near their camp.

Keseberg was then accused of having killed Tamsen Donner for her money and/or her flesh. He professed innocence and said that he had promised Tamsen before she died that he would bring the money to her children if he survived the winter. The only member of the relief party who seemed willing to extend any kindness to him was Reasin Tucker, who was now a very seasoned Sierra-crosser.

Surrounded by the mutilated remains of all the victims at lakeside, Keseberg became the scapegoat for the Donner party. Given the spirit of the times, the fact he was a foreigner may have been an additional mark against him. Napans "Le Gros" Fallon and Ned Coffeymire

---

[81]McGlashan, p. 196-98.

[82]Lewis Keseberg, quoted in McGlashan, pp. 211-213.

later testified that Keseberg had "buckets of fresh blood" in his cabin. Keseberg sued them in a Napa Court for this slander and was awarded one dollar.[83]

Misfortune followed Keseberg for the rest of his life. He worked a while for Sutter, but his holdings were wiped out by a flood. Sam Brannan eventually employed him at a brewery in Calistoga, but the "Cannibal of the Sierra" lived in a world apart. In a final tragic twist, two daughters who were born to him and Phillipina after the ordeal suffered a form of pervasive mental retardation. They could only be cared for at home, and their condition upset the neighbors.[84]

The heroism of big John Stark, who single-handedly rescued the invalids of Reed's "Second Relief Party," did not go unnoticed by his peers. He won the heart of Matthew Ritchie's daughter, whom he soon wed. He was elected to the State Legislature in 1852. In 1855 he was appointed Sheriff of Napa County by the Board of Sessions and was voted into the post the following year, where he remained until 1861. He later became a judge. Stark's generosity remained with him the rest of his life. Over the years, while many of his associates turned their talents toward swindling the public, Stark donated more than $10,000 to help pay the taxes of his friends. He died of a heart attack in Calistoga on a hot day in 1874 while working in his hayfield.

Reasin Tucker, no less a hero but a quieter man, returned to Sutter's and was soon convinced by his son George to move to the Napa Valley. He planted crops and worked at Bale's lumber mill.

On October 20, 1849 Charles Cady, who promised but failed to bring the Donner children out of the mountains, was the defendant in one of the first legal cases tried in "Napa Valley, Territory of California." The crime was petty larceny and resulted in a hung jury, so he had to be retried. Charley Stone's questionable ethics caught up with him in 1849, as will be described later.

Among the Donner Party survivors, Mary Graves was taken to live with an American family in the pueblo of San Jose, while her

---

[83]McGlashan, p. 219.

[84]Ibid, p. 223.

sister Sarah Graves Fosdick waited for their other siblings, Ellen and Lovina, to emerge from the mountains. When they were ready to travel, Lovina went to San Jose too, while Ellen, Sarah and William were taken in by a family in Sonoma. All but Mary soon came to live in the Napa Valley; a city, Marysville, was named for Mary Graves.

William Eddy settled in San Francisco and became the area's first surveyor. He made detailed, accurate maps so others would not lose their way. He gave his name to a street in downtown San Francisco.

Harriett Pike, one of the living skeletons who followed Eddy to the Indian camp and scared the wits out of the Indian children because of her emaciation, fully recovered and married Michael Nye, the young man who traveled with Elias Barnett.

The Reed family--all of whom survived the ordeal--came to Yount's and stayed on his land as his guest. Virginia's second letter to her family back east, written from Yount's a few months later, reveals that healing had begun:

> we are all verry fleshey Ma waies 10040 pon and still a gaing I weigh 80 tel Henriet if she wants to get Married to come to Callifornia she can get a spanyard any time that Eliza is going to marrie a spanyard by the name of Armeho and Eliza weighs 10070...[85]

---

[85] From Virginia Reed's diary, quoted in *Overland,* p.288.

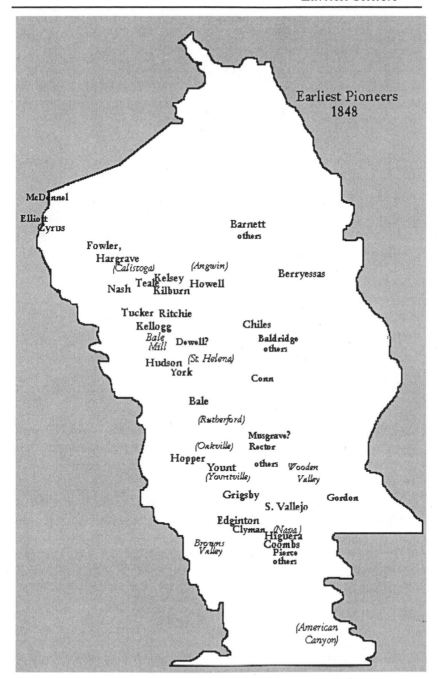

Earliest Pioneers
1848

McDonnel

Elliott
Cyrus

Barnett
others

Fowler,
Hargrave
(Calistoga)   *(Angwin)*
Teale Kelsey Howell
Nash   Kilburn   Berryessas

Tucker Ritchie
Kellogg
Bale Dowell?
Mill   Baldridge
Chiles   others
Hudson *(St. Helena)*
York
Conn

Bale

(Rutherford)

Musgrave?
(Oakville)   Rector
Hopper   others   *Wooden*
Yount   *Valley*
(Yountville)

Grigsby   Gordon
S. Vallejo
Edginton
Clyman *(Napa)*
Browns Higuera
Valley Coombs
Pierce
others

*(American
Canyon)*

109

Chapter Five

Earliest Settlers, 1848

N apa was rapidly becoming an American valley, as were its smaller, adjacent valleys, Franz, Snell, Pope, Conn, Berryessa, Chiles, Wooden, Capell, Browns and Congress.[1] It was also relatively industrialized. By the spring of 1848, four gristmills and two lumber mills were in use at various locations in what would soon be Napa County.

Mallocamas Grant

William Elliott, a Bear Flagger from the Grigsby-Ide party, squatted with his family in what would soon be called "Franz Valley," named for the man who lived there after him. He erected a small gristmill in the area. Later, the stones in it were removed and used in a similar mill in the Mark West Springs area of Santa Rosa. [2]

Elliott was a hunter and adventurer, leaving his wife Elizabeth and his seven children for long periods of time. During one of his explorations to the north Elliott discovered the geysers in what would later become Lake County but at the time was considered part of Napa County. (Lake split off to become its own entity in 1861, and the boundary between the two was further clarified in 1872.)

His family lived in a tent next to a huge oak tree that held an elaborate tree house. Bears prowled the area constantly, and whenever the family felt itself in danger they climbed into the tree

---

[1] The *Napa Register* (special supplement, 5-23-1998) also listsBear, Carneros, Cedar, Cherry, Elder, Foss, Gordon, Lovall, Mysterious, Soda, Spanish, and Wild Horse Valleys as Napa County place names.

[2] Elizabeth C.Wright, *Early Upper Napa Valley,* unpublished, Calistoga, 1924, p. 14.

house, which the bears, apparently, could not penetrate. Elliott's wife was good with a rifle and killed the bears from her perch in the tree.[3] One of the Elliott daughters married another Bear Flagger, Benjamin Dewell. They lived a few miles to the south, not far from the Bale Mill.

Enoch Cyrus was the patriarch of a large clan that also took up residence in the *Mallocamas* grant. Part of the same wagon train as the Tuckers, Kelloggs, Starks and Ritchies, the Cyruses just missed being snowed in with the Donner Party. They bought acreage from Jose de los Santos Berryessa about a mile north of what would be come Calistoga. Cyrus Creek still bears their name.

Carne Humana

The large Fowler and Hargrave families came down from Oregon. They settled into and improved upon the cabin that John York had built in Kortum Canyon and took jobs working at the sawmill for Bale's artisan, Ralph Kilburn. With their wages they were able to buy 6.5 square miles of land at $.50 an acre. With what would prove to be very acute foresight, Henry Fowler galloped to Mexico City to have the deed validated. Their land straddled both Berryessa's grant and Bale's, stretching part way up the flanks of Mt. St. Helena.[4] Hunters and mountain men like Britt and Caleb Greenwood camped there often, as did newcomers to the Valley while they found work and waited to see where the chips would fall.

Peter Storm, a Bear Flagger, was a semi-permanent guest there and at the Kilburns' and Cyrus's. He made himself useful doing odd jobs and fine woodworking. Storm was born in Norway in 1799 and ran away to sea at age 14. He jumped ship and kept himself alive by hunting. He was a teller of tall tales (or out-and-out lies). He was best known to his peers for claiming (probably falsely) to have made the true Bear Flag. He carried a Bear Flag with him in parades throughout the next three decades.

---

[3]Wright, p. 24.
[4]Mallett, p. 84.

The primary Napa Valley Wappo living site was in the hot springs area in the center of present-day Calistoga, particularly in the vicinity of the Calistoga Public Library. They continued their sweat lodge ceremonies, and white pioneers wrote that they were frightened by the noise that the natives made.[5]

Enoch Cyrus's daughter Francis married Henry Owsley, a farmer. She lived near the Fowlers while Henry worked for George Yount. With the money he earned he, like the Fowlers and Hargraves, bought acreage from Ralph Kilburn, the mill-builder. Owsley was elected Justice of the Peace several times in the 1860's and was a well-known personality in young St. Helena.[6]

Cyrus's other daughter, Mary, married William H. Nash, who had a team of oxen. Nash's team survived the trip west, and he used it to haul logs to Napa for the Kilburns. Thanks to his animals, Nash was able to make a profit before his neighbors did. A stash of peach pits that he brought along also survived. He planted them with great success. He harvested 100 peaches the first year and sold them for $1.00 each.[7] In 1857 the Napa newspaper reported that 43 of his peaches weighed 44 pounds.[8] He also imported walnuts from England and from a little town called, quaintly, "Walnut Creek." His place became known as "Walnut Grove."[9] Mary Nash whiled away the hours raising their 12 children, usually without William there to assist.

Ben and Nancy Kelsey built a cabin about a mile below present-day Calistoga, in the area around what is now Dunaweal Lane. Perhaps finding the region too domesticated for their tastes, they pulled up stakes and headed north to the Clear Lake region. Ralph Kilburn and his brother Wells built homes close together in the same location after the Kelseys left. Ralph acquired the land in payment for

---

[5] Wright, p. 2.

[6] Ibid, p. 23

[7] Ketteringham, p. 79.

[8] *NCR*, 8-29-57.

[9] Wright, Loc Cit.

his work for Bale constructing the sawmill and gristmill described earlier.[10] The Kilburns grew onions, and by 1852 they had about two acres of them planted. One year during the Gold Rush they made $8,000 selling onions in San Francisco: a huge sum for the time.

Maria Pope Kilburn, Ralph's very young wife, was said to keep a clean, comfortable home. John Russell Bartlett of the US and Mexican Boundary Commission traveled through the Napa Valley in 1852 and wrote in his journal that the good-looking Mrs. Kilburn seemed somewhat flustered that he and his party showed up for dinner, unannounced. Nevertheless she prepared them "a fine supper."[11] Kilburn became very involved in the development of Napa and later Benicia and spent large stretches of time away from home. Perhaps not surprisingly, the marriage ultimately ended in divorce.

Peter Teale and Benjamin Dewell and their families also squatted in this general area. Teale eventually moved to Alexander Valley in Sonoma County. The Dewells stayed longer: their eight children are listed in the roll call of the Napa Valley's first school.[12]

In the fall of 1848 George Tucker, age 18, returned from placer mining with enough gold to purchase 150 acres of farming land from Bale. He soon convinced his father, Reasin, and his brothers to join him in the Napa Valley. Reasin bought a section adjoining his son's: a gorgeous, wild place, densely timbered with live oak and crisscrossed with the trails of wild animals and cattle.[13] Today Tucker Road and the Tucker Farm Center are on it, as is much of Bothe State Park. The seller in the transaction was Pope Valley's Elias Barnett, who claimed that Bale gave him the tract in return for services rendered.[14] Barnett's apparent lie would prove disastrous to

---

[10]Ibid, p. 24.

[11] John Russell Bartlett, *Bartlett's Personal Narrative,* Vol II, Rio Grande Press, Chicago, 1965, p. 24.

[12]John Wichels, *Pioneer One-Room Schools of Napa County,* Napa County Historical Society, Napa, 1979, p. 1.

[13]Bryant, p. 349.

[14]Ketteringham, p. 80.

the Tuckers in the years to come.

Matthew D. and Harriett Ritchie and their family of six daughters remained close to the Tuckers after their rescue of the Donner party. They settled across from the Tuckers on land bordering the Napa River. The name of one of the creeks that runs through Bothe Park is "Ritchie Creek," named for them. Matthew commuted to Napa frequently after 1850 to serve as an associate judge. Another man with almost the same name, M.G. Richie, moved into the area around 1860. He was no relation.

Outgoing, dynamic Florentine Kellogg was trained as a mechanic. He brought tools and equipment with him on the overland trek: valuable commodities that served both him and the community he helped build. Bale met him when Kellogg was recuperating from the trip across the continent. The story goes that Bale asked Kellogg why he had come west. "To find a good climate and get cheap land," said Kellogg. Bale's reply was, "I think we can fit you out with both."[15] For his expert ironwork at the gristmill Bale paid him 600 acres of land, located one creek down from the Tuckers'. George Tucker married the Kelloggs' oldest daughter, Mary, reputed to be the prettiest young woman in the Valley. The same Bartlett who commended Mrs. Kilburn's hospitality gave a less positive review of the Kelloggs' place. "In the farm and arrangement of the buildings," he wrote, "a sad deficiency of taste was visible."[16]

Kellogg finished building the gristmill that Ralph Kilburn had started for Edward Bale. To increase the flow of water and thus the mill's power, Kellogg and his crew diverted water from "Mill Creek," a mountain spring that ran down "Spring Mountain," which was rich with such creeks. The diverted water gathered in a dam which they had built about a quarter of a mile to the west. Then they dug a ditch to carry the water from the dam to the mill and inserted a flume made of long, hollowed-out logs laid end to end. The flume conveyed the water from the ditch to the top of the mill wheel and poured out

---

[15] *SHS*, 3-31-1933.

[16] Bartlett, p. 24.

on it from above.[17] Gravity thus helped give the water additional force.[18]

The mill itself and the granary that was attached to it were made of lumber from the thick oak and redwood forest on Spring Mountain behind it. Kellogg, Harrison Pierce and their fellow workers had to saw and adze each piece by hand. The original millstones were also taken from the mountain and prepared by John Conn. The mill wheel turned huge wooden cogs that served as gears to move the millstones that ground the grain. With no white noise of traffic or electric appliances in the background, Bale's mill made an enormous racket in the otherwise quiet valley.[19] Harrison Pierce hung around a while and served as the first miller.

Kellogg's popularity with his peers won him an appointment as the County's first Coroner and as one of the three original County Supervisors. Perhaps Kellogg's most public-spirited act, however, was to build, at his own expense, a series of watering stations along the County Road from the Bale Mill to Napa City. Horses and oxen could refresh themselves at these oases.

Kellogg also donated property for the construction of the first schoolhouse in Napa County, the second Amercian school in the entire state.[20] William Nash, father of most of the school's children, did the actual construction. Situated under a fir tree, the school opened its gates in July of 1847. Sarah Graves Fosdick of the Donner Party was its first teacher. She lived near the school until around 1850 with another survivor, her sister Ellen Graves. Sarah married a neighbor, Silas Ritchie.[21] Silas may have been a nephew of Matthew and Harriett's, or possibly Matthew's brother--he was 45 when he wed Sarah. Like most pioneers, Sarah and Silas kept pigs. They built a roofed house to protect them from the bears. One night when Silas

---

[17]Lyman, *Memoirs*, p. 91.

[18]Verardo, p. 12.

[19]Idem.

[20]Hoover, p. 243.

[21]Wright, p. 24. Hanrahan says his name was William.

was gone, a piglet turned up missing, so Sarah and a friend who was spending the night went out to find it. They ran into a grizzly bear, who immediately started chasing the piglet. The women dashed inside, and the grizzly started chasing the piglet around and around the house. Every time the piglet ran past the door, Sarah tried to get it to come inside, but it was too frightened to respond. Eventually it tried to take a different route and ran across the yard, but the grizzly caught up to it and had pork for dinner.[22]

A third Graves survivor, Lovina, visited her sisters on July 3, 1848, her 14th birthday. When Lovina arrived, Ellen was at the home of friends, the Isaac Howell family, who built a cabin about 100 yards north of today's Deer Park Road/Silverado Trail junction, in the Crystal Springs area. To join Ellen, Lovina hitched a ride on the wagon of Yount's housekeeper, who was going that way. The rig had no seating. The driver sat on the coupling pole, and Lovina sat near the rear axle with her feet dangling out the back for the 10 rough, dusty miles. A young man came by while she was at the Howells: John Cyrus of the Calistoga family, who was then 17. They married in 1855.[23]

Later in 1848, Ellen Graves married Bill McDonnell,[24] who had been a team driver for Florentine Kellogg during the 1846 overland trip. Sister Lovina joined them on their honeymoon, which consisted of a trip on horseback to the pueblo of San Jose. An American family there had taken in Lovina after the Donner tragedy. They then proceeded to San Juan Bautista to see their remaining sister, Mary, who had also just gotten married. After ferrying across San Pablo Bay, Ellen, Bill and Lovina became lost, since there were no roads, let alone road maps. They spent the night by a freshwater stream, the San Pablo, which they followed to their destination.[25] They did not fear robbers. Having survived starvation, blizzards and

---

[22]Idem.

[23]Ibid, p.15.

[24] sometimes referred to as "McDonald."

[25]Wright, pp.16-17.

the death and mutilation of their parents and friends, the Graves girls probably feared (or felt) very little. A few years later, Ellen and Bill squatted in Knight's Valley, a picturesque area just to the north owned by and named for Bear Flagger Thomas Knight,[26] the gentleman whose locker exploded in the Sierra. There were no American settlers between them and Oregon. John Russell Bartlett met the McDonnells while traveling through the area and described Ellen as "a young woman of twenty, who must have some courage to settle down in this lonely spot."[27]

John York's family left their cabin in Kortum Canyon and sheltered in Sonoma while John fought in the Mexican War. When it ended he went to work for Bale splitting rails. He used his pay to buy land from his employer at $.50 an acre.[28] After a short stint in the gold fields, he augmented his purchase and eventually owned a narrow but substantial strip of land that extended from what is now Madrona Avenue in St. Helena to the boundary of today's Beringer Winery. The piece stretched all the way to Sonoma County, encompassing Spring Mountain.

David Hudson's first plot was just north of York's. Hudson partnered with York in gold mining, and with his profits he bought more land and extended his holdings east to the Napa River. David married a young woman he had met with Grigsby-Ide on the trip west, Frances Griffith, the daughter of a fellow Bear Flagger, Calvin C. Griffith. They raised seven children. The Hudsons outgrew their quarters and built a much more substantial a house in 1852 that still stands and is used as a kitchen and banqueting facility by the Beringer Winery.

David Hudson's brother William stayed in Sonoma for a few years and then joined John York and David by purchasing from Bale all the land from Sulphur Creek to Madrona Avenue (York's southern boundary). William Hudson's holdings paralleled York's and reached

---

[26]Dutton, pp. 157-158.

[27] Bartlett, p. 27.

[28]Wright, p. 13.

back to the Sonoma County line. If William still owned the land, his domain would include much of St. Helena's western residential area.

Edward Bale needed to keep selling off chunks of his huge land grant to cover his ever-increasing debts. By 1848 his realm had shrunk considerably but was still substantial. He apparanetly blew an excellent business opportunity in 1846. He and his long-term houseguest, Nathan Spear, had discovered a quicksilver deposit somewhere on his grant. Spear told the American consul, Thomas Larkin, that he himself owned it, and Larkin responded enthusiastically. "When together," Larkin wrote, "we can I am confident make agraingement [sic] to push the silver to the quick. I expect to see Iron flasks in August. If your mine is equal to the one at the Pueblo [New Almaden], that I have seen, I assure you we will arrange our business that you will be in any state of affluence you could wish in two or three years." Of Bale, Larkin added, "I plainly told him I could not depend on his word."[29]

Despite the fact that Larkin mistrusted Bale, he entered into a contract with the "Doctor" and Ralph Kilburn for a shipment of 40,000 clapboards, which would be hewn from the forest on the Valley hillside and brought to the embarcadero in Napa City. Larkin and Robert Semple hoped to use the lumber to build a planned city they would call "Benicia." Bale and Kilburn failed to make the delivery.

Bale and his wife Maria Soberanes had six fair-haired children, and their home was the oldest and best equipped in the valley. Maria enjoyed gardening and planted roses and flowering shrubs around the adobe. She grew grapes and had a large orchard of pears and peaches. Bale's daughter Carolina married the pioneer vintner, Charles Krug. Another, Isadora, wed Louis Bruck, a colleague of Krug's.

The Wappo population that camped near Bale's adobe gradually diminished and disappeared altogether by about 1885.

---

[29]George P. Hammond, ed., *The Larkin Papers*, V, University of California Press, Berkeley and LA, 1952, p. 131.

Rancho La Jota

George Yount was granted this rugged, forested terrain for the construction of a sawmill, and because of the mill's presence the area was heavily logged. The Wappo leader La Jota had operated there the decade before. La Jota and his men rustled large numbers of cattle from Yount, and in retaliation Yount and his men killed La Jota.

The Howell family settledat the mountain's foot. It was at the Howells' that the Donner Party's Lovina Graves was reunited with her sister Ellen. Others also started homes on Howell mountain, among them an Irishman named Moore, or More, who squatted in what is now Las Posadas Forest. Moore's wife was a very large woman. When she died her friends and family had a hard time getting her body into the coffin, and an even harder time getting the coffin down the 12 miles of rutted road to the cemetery. Moore's property was taken over by a man named Musso, who sold it for $1000 and a cow to the Morris family in the 1860's. Sally and Milton Morris were veteran pioneers, having been the first white couple to be married in what is now Kansas.[30]

Locoallomi Grant

Elias Barnett appears to have reassumed possession of the widow Pope's land grant after the Mexican War, which might have prompted his 14 year-old step-daughter, Maria, to run off with Ralph Kilburn. Relatives and descendents of Barnett moved to Pope Valley. Several other individuals were attracted to the Pope Valley area. They set up camps and cabins and worked felling trees and hauling wood. Although quite arid, much of the land was suitable for wheat farming, and the American squatters and land owners employed natives to work the fields.

(Conn Valley)

Between *Locoallomi* and its neighbor, *Catacula*, was land that almost became a grant. John Conn and John Ranchford were

---

[30] Edith Gregory, "Pioneers of Las Posadas," unpublished, Berkeley, 1938.

partners who in 1844 applied together for a grant of land that spanned acreage between Pope and Chiles Valleys. The morning after the Bear Flag revolt was officially over, however, Ranchford died, and the grant was never completed. John Conn had learned stone dressing in his native Ireland and prepared grinding stones for both Kellogg and Joe Chiles. Conn remained a bachelor for life and worked at Chiles' mill along with Billy Baldridge, who never married either. John was an alcoholic whose habit proved to be his undoing, and he died in a hospital of the complications thereof. John was joined in Conn Valley by his nephew, Connolly Conn, in the 1850's. Connolly became the patriarch of the family. He was known to locals for keeping a bullwhip by his saddle when he rode.

Rancho Catacula

True to his word, Joe Chiles set up his gristmill, with the help of Billy Baldridge, John Conn and a handful of others. The flour was packaged under the "Catacula" label. Later they built a distillery and began producing whiskey on a small scale. Joe Chiles was also true to the word he gave his children. In 1848 he made another trans-Sierra trek and returned with his sons, Kit and William, and his daughters, Fanny, Elizabeth and Mary. Fanny Chiles married a young man named Jerome C. Davis, and with Joe's help, started a town that would be the site of a university.

Donner Party rescuer William "Le Gros" Fallon also guided a party west in '48 and may have taken up residence near Chiles. It is likely that a number of other pioneers also squatted in this beautiful, remote valley, drawn there by the presence of the gristmill, as well as by the other Americans. Baldridge established a farm of his own near Oakville in 1851. He seems to have been beloved by many. The *Napa County Reporter* referred to him as "Uncle Billy," and his trips to Napa City were sometimes considered newsworthy events.

Las Putas

Like the Barnetts, the Berryessas used native labor for their ranching pursuits, but a special commission sent by the Department of Indian Affairs reported that the Berryessas acquired their help by kidnapping the natives. Furthermore, "they and certain Sonora Mexicans living with them are constantly in the practice of selling the young Indians, both male and female to whomsoever will purchase them."[31] Bill McDonnell and the Kelseys were implicated as Indian slavers. Years later, Knights Valley's Thomas Knight told the historian Bancroft that Ben and Sam Kelsey were arrested for enslaving natives, but "through some flaw in the law or informality" were never punished.[32]

Rancho Caymus

For reasons still unclear, George Yount called the community that began to form around him "Sebastopol." His daughter Frances and son-in-law, Bartlett Vines, also settled there, alongside the surviving natives who still camped nearby. The Vines' baby was the first white child to be born in Napa County.[33] A few years later Yount's granddaughter, Lillie, went to school in San Francisco and returned to marry Thomas Rutherford. As a wedding present, the Rutherfords received a large tract of land to the north of Yount's rancho, which is still called "Rutherford." Sebastopol was often referred to as "Yountville," and after Yount died the name became official.

Yount was perhaps the best known American in the Napa region. Nearly everyone of importance who passed through stopped to spend time with him. Many of the Donner Party survivors recuperated at Yount's, and other emigrees rented land from him. Freer spirits, like John Rector, simply squatted. One of his paying renters was old Jim Griffith, who evidently came with his wife, grown children and perhaps grandchildren. His sons were Bears who served with Fremont. Calvin Griffith, mentioned above, squatted in the

---

[31] Robert Heizer, ed. *The Destruction of the California Indians*, Lincoln and London: University of Nebraska Press, 1974, p.20.

[32] Knight's quotation taken from Heizer, *Destruction*, p. 247.

[33] But not the first American baby to be born in California. That honor went to a son of William Boggs, Guadalupe Vallejo Boggs, named for Mariano Vallejo.

Rutherford area. Calvin's daughter Frances married David Hudson and lived in what would soon be St. Helena; and there were Griffiths in a place called "Spring Valley," which later came to be known as "Meadowood."

Joe Chiles' old friend Charlie Hopper returned as captain of a wagon train in 1847. Yount gave him 650 acres for his "willingness to cooperate."[34] Apparently uncomfortable with accepting such a large gift from Yount, Hopper purchased it from him instead, thus acquiring a deed to the property. He bought and later sold and gave away other pieces of acreage in the area. Hopper continued to be highly esteemed by Napa County's early settlers.

Napa/Trancas

After the Bear Flag Revolt, but before the Mexican War ended, Salvador Vallejo sold Captain John Grigsby a 1.5 mile square of his *Napa/Trancas* rancho for $1100. The northern boundary was Yount's property, and the eastern was the Napa River.[35] A staunch conservative by today's standards, Captain John had little patience for free-loaders. When he found that a squatter had set up residence on his estate he chased him off at gunpoint.[36] Another Grigsby, Franklin, emigrated with John, and they were joined in 1852 by brothers Terrell, Jesse, John Melchisadeck ("Mels") and Achilles. The Grigsby family became involved in nearly every aspect of the County's subsequent development. Mels Grigsby settled on Cobb Mountain in in Lake County and played a formative roles in that

---

[34] Franklin Beard, p. 13.

[35] Grigsby sold a half-mile square in the northwest corner to another Bear Flagger, James Harbin. Harbin sold some to Henry Boggs, son of the former Missouri governor. Henry Boggs became an important figure in the history of Lake County. Groezinger built a winery there in 1870, thus providing the location for a shopping mall, "Vintage 1870," established more than a century later.

[36] Gregory, p. 439.

area's development.[37]

William Edginton (aka "Edington," and "Eddington") bought land from Salvador as well. He was a volunteer with Fremont who fought in the Bear Flag Revolt and then went off to the Yuba River, where he found enough gold to trade in his buckskins for three-piece suits. He married Captain John Grigsby's daughter Theresa. In 1850 the Edgintons built a house for his wife, six sons and two daughters, at the foot of Fourth Street in Napa. He puchased an entire city block at the eastern end of First Street and 1,000 acres of land in the country.

Another denizen of Salvador's kingdom was James Clyman, who served in the same regiment as Abraham Lincoln in the Black Hawk Indian War. He became a mountain man, or "surveyor," and chronicled his travels in a book that became a best seller in his time. It was Clyman who tried to dissuade the Donners and others in the 1846 emigration from coming to California. William Hargrave guided him through the Napa Valley in 1845, and in 1848 he led a wagon train west, with Napa as his final destination. Many of the people in the party were members of the McCombs family, most of whom settled in the Napa City area.[38] The next year Clyman married Hannah McCombs, who was many years younger than his hoary 57. It was the Valley's first wedding.[39] The Clymans lived on and then purchased land from William Edginton. They built a comfortable home and rambled no more.[40]

Salvador Vallejo sold Nathan Coombs a tract that Coombs dubbed "The Willows." County Records indicate that the transaction was formalized in 1850, but Nathan and Isabel may have lived there some time; there were no County records prior to that year. It lay to the

---

[37]Harriett Reinmiller, "A Brief History of the Grigsby Family of Lake and Napa Counties," NP, ND, pp. 1-3.

[38]Charles Camp, ed., *James Clyman, Frontiersman,* Champeog Press, Portland, 1960, p. 235.

[39]Ibid, p. 240.

[40]Ibid, p. 241.

northwest of what would become Napa City, near what is now Trubody Lane.[41]

Entre Napa

Development of the Napa City area hummed right along throughout the Mexican War. Nathan Coombs and John Grigsby helped Nicholas Higuera with some carpentry. Higuera found it convenient to pay them with land. Grigsby's new parcel lay along the Napa River at the head of the tidewater in what was a beanfield, and Coombs' new piece lay a little to the west.

Napa had a valuable asset. The salty Napa River turned sweet near where the embarcadero had been built (across from today's Napa Library), and river trade had been underway since at least 1841. Far more savvy about matters of business than the Bear Flag hero, Nathan Coombs traded lots with Grigsby. Immediately Coombs staked out a town site. The original Napa City as defined by Coombs went from what is now Brown Street to the River, and from Napa Creek to the foot of Main Street: a distance of about 600 yards. For a while people referred to it as "Coombsville."

Harrison Pierce, the sailor-turned-miller, was the first to buy a lot. He and Higuera teamed up to build Napa City's first commercial building. They hired William Nash from up valley to haul lumber harvested from Fowler's property and planed at Kilburn's sawmill. When their little 18' x 24' building was nearly complete and only the roof remained to be constructed, Pierce and Higuera discovered that they had misread Coombs' stakes (which were buried in the tall, wild oatgrass that grew everywhere) and had situated the thing in the middle of what was supposed to become Main Street. Rather than upset his master plan for Napa, the punctilious Coombs had them move it to the south side of Third Street, near the River.

While Pierce and Higuera were wrestling with blueprints and wild oats and the war with Mexico was winding down, something was afoot in the foothills of the Sierra. On January 24, 1848 Peter

---

[41]Gregory, p. 882.

NATHAN COOMBS.

Florentine Kellogg built watering stations along the County Road.

Wimmer, a sometime Napan who traveled in the same wagon train as the Tuckers and Ritchies, was helping his boss, James Marshall, erect a sawmill near Coloma on the south fork of the American River. He found a pea-sized lump of metal behind a rock in the stream bed.[42] Wimmer showed the lump to his boss, James Marshall, and Marshall brought it to his boss, John Sutter. They thought it might be valuable but weren't sure, so they performed a few tests on it. Among other things they took it to Wimmer's wife, a woman from Georgia who had some understanding of the properties of metals. She dropped the lump in a kettle of soapsuds, and the lye in the soap brought out its true nature.[32] Marshall, Sutter and the Wimmers decided to keep their find a secret, but word eventually got out, thanks in large part to Yerba Buena's clever Mormon leader, Sam Brannan, and the whole world soon rushed to California for gold.

---

[42]Mallett, p. 95 Some sources, like the *St. Helena Star* (3-22-1878), say that the gold was discovered by children playing in a stream.

[32]Ibid, p. 94.

Chapter Six

The Rush Years

As publisher of the *California Star*, Sam Brannan was in a position to both hear interesting news and spread it. Rumors of Marshall and Wimmer's discovery made their way to Yerba Buena. Brannan sent his editor, E. C. Kemble, up to New Helvetia to investigate. Kemble was greeted warmly by the naively gregarious John Sutter himself, who guided him to Marshall's sawmill. Kemble and his companions found a few grains by panning with an Indian basket--not enough to get rich on, but enough to confirm the presence of gold. He rode back to Yerba Buena and reported all to Brannan. [1]

Immediately, Brannan bought 1,000 acres near gold country and set up a chain of three well-stocked mercantile stores under the fictitious business name of "C.C. Smith & Company." When all was in place, he himself ran through the streets of Yerba Buena with his famous proclamation that gold had been discovered in the American River. He also printed a special "extra" edition of the *Star* with news of the discovery and organized an overland mule train to transport it to the Mississippi Valley. The mule train left on April Fool's day, 1848.[2] He organized a second train on June 20th with the same message. Then he waited, like a spider.

The flies came. Brannan sold supplies to the miners at incredibly high prices. In the three months between May 1 and July 10, 1848, he raked in $36,000 in gold from the sale of food and goods. To

---

[1]DeNevi, p. 123.

[2] Oscar Osburn Winthur, *Express and Stagecoach Days in California*, Stanford University Press, Palo Alto, 1936, p. 19.

126

preserve his position of influence, he managed to become the alcalde of the area, as well as the region's prosecuting attorney.[3]

In one of the most stupendous instances of synchronicity in history, the war between Mexico and the United States ended just nine days after gold was discovered. The 2,000+ American soldiers, sailors and officers who had come to fight in California were mustered out in various California ports with no passage back to the States.[4] Approximately 800 citizen-soldiers--healthy, adventurous young men with a fever for gold--were freed in Sonoma in August and September of '48. They were known as the "New York Volunteers," because they were recruited from various cities in New York State. Nearly all of them went directly to the Sierra foothills and "C.C. Smith's" mercantile store. Many New York Volunteers would come to live and/or work in the Napa Valley, including three of the most prominent: George Cornwell, John Frisbie and John Brackett.

Gold fever had a profound impact on the struggling pioneers in the Napa Valley. Harrison Pierce dropped his hammer, gathered some friends and on May 20, 1848 left for the chilly streams of the Sierra foothills, his building project standing in the grass without a roof . With him went a substantial portion of the men in the valley: William Nash, Ralph Kilburn, John Kelly,[5] Florentine Kellogg, Bill McDonnell, Benjamin Dewell, Hiram Acres and a Wappo named Guadalupe, who brought his wife.[6] They were beaten to the placer mines by young George Tucker, who found enough gold within a few weeks to return and buy land for himself and his father, as described above. William Hargrave and the Fowlers took out large

---

[3] H.H. Bancroft, *California Inter Pocula,* p. 608.

[4] Bancroft, V, p. 515.

[5] Bear Flagger John Kelly left the Sierra with plenty of gold in his pockets. He returned to his home state of New York, became a Tammany Hall boss and later a US Congressman.

[6] *NCR* 2-19-1876.

amounts of gold near Colusa.[7]

The Napa Bear Flagger Granville Swift turned up a small fortune in gold: so much, in fact, that he felt he could now court Mariano Vallejo's daughter Natalia.[8] She found him to be coarse, ill-educated and basically unattractive. She married instead Attila Haraszthy, the second son of the founder of the California wine industry.

Billy Baldridge went to the mines with Joe Chiles' brothers and nephew, but Joe himself stayed home,[9] tired, perhaps, from his latest round trip to Missouri. Joe partnered with his new son-in-law, Jerome Davis, to build and operate a rope ferry company across the Sacramento River. His daughter Elizabeth also got married (to Leonard Tully), and Joe served as midwife for both women when they bore his grandchildren.[10] His enterprises prospered, and he bought land in several places in the area, including a spread in Rutherford from Bartlett Vines, to which he moved. He remarried. Life was good.

John York and Dave Hudson brought their families with them to rough-and-tumble Coloma, where they worked a placer mine all summer and extracted about $1500 worth of gold, sometimes collecting as much as $125 in a day.[11] They also mined in the equally primitive Hangtown.[12] York played a trick on Hudson while they were mining that nearly cost him the friendship. A stranger had come by, and York asked him what kind of luck he'd had. The man showed him a large nugget. He agreed to let York borrow it for a while. York slipped it into Hudson's pan, and when Dave found it he screamed that they were rich. York returned the nugget to the stranger but waited a while before telling Hudson it was a joke.

---

[7]Mallett, p. 95

[8]Ibid, p. 93.

[9]Griffen, p. 76.

[10]Ibid, p. 77.

[11]*NCR* 6-15-1888

[12]John W. York, personal corresondence to the author.

Hudson didn't speak to York for two years.[13] The Yorks and the Hudsons returned to the Napa Valley (presumably in silence) with their profits and made the second, larger purchases of land from Bale mentioned above.

"Doctor" Edward Bale went to the mines, got sick, and returned home to *Carne Humana*. In his time and place, the diagnosis was grim. Bale had stomach cancer, and he died within months,[14] leaving his widow Maria to raise their six children and grapple with his debts. His associate Nathan Spear died less than a year later, and the quicksilver mine on Bale's rancho went undeveloped for two decades.

Bale's daughter Isadora inherited the gristmill. She married a German, Louis Bruck. Their son Bismarck would be an important player in young St. Helena's formative years.

Ben Kelsey and his brothers went to the gold digs and returned with a lot of money in a short time: so much, indeed, that Ben enjoyed a brief career as a loan shark.[15] Ben used the gold from his initial efforts as well as money invested by ex-Missouri Governor Lilburn Boggs to buy sheep and supplies for a second venture to the mines the following year. This time Kelsey was accompanied by William Boggs (one of the ex-governor's sons), Salvador Vallejo, Don Juan Casteneda (a Mexican politician and close friend of Salvador's), Albert Musgrave (a close friend of Hargrave and Fowler) and A. J. Cox, a scrappy New York Volunteer who came back to publish Napa's first newspaper.[16]

Also on the trip was Charley Stone, hero/villain of the Donner rescue. Stone and Ben's brother Andy Kelsey now lived at Clear Lake, still considered part of Napa County, near a large, permanent camp of Wappo. Charley and Andy brought 50 young, strong Wappo men with them to work the mines. After they arrived,

---

[13]McCormick, pp. 4-5.

[14] on October 9, 1849, at age 38 (Verardo, p. 12).

[15]Kelsey lent $25,000 to one of the Griffiths--Cal, probably--at 25% compound interest. Griffith repaid in full.

[16] and then went to Healdsburg to found the Healdsburg Review.

however, Stone and the Kelseys decided that instead of breaking their backs panning for gold like the others, they would simply sell the sheep they had brought. This earned them a profit but provided no work for the natives, who were elbowed off the gold-bearing streams by white miners. Stone, Kelsey and the others did not feel obliged to pay the Wappo or even feed them, since they weren't working, so the natives went hungry.[17]

The Wappo had to return home. This was a problem, however, because they had no food nor means of procuring it. Equally vexing to them was the fact that they had to cross over the territory of rival, hostile tribes. Nearly all of the native men died or were killed trying to get home. When their families learned of the young men's fate, they were both grief-stricken and enraged.[18]

This wasn't the first time the Wappo had been angry with them. When they first came to the area near Clear Lake, Kelsey and Stone forced the Wappo to build a large adobe for them. Reluctant workers were whipped and hung by their wrists from a tree for extended periods of time. With good reason, Kelsey and Stone feared retribution, and at one point they had to remove the Indians' bows and arrows from them.[19] A native friendly to the whites sent word to the settlers in Napa that the Wappo at Clear Lake were going on the warpath. William Boggs and other friends of the white men rode to Stone and Kelsey's to assess the situation. They found the adobe surrounded by angry Indians and frightened them away.[20]

In terms of interracial relations, the ex-governor's son William Boggs was no angel either. With the help of a native servant[21] he traded with other natives for gold and convinced them to show him

---

[17] Virginia Hanrahan, *Historical Napa Valley*, unpublished, Napa, 1948, pp. 94-95.

[18] Y. Beard, p. 29.

[19] Ibid, p. 93.

[20] Hugh Francis Boggs, untitled family history manuscript, p. 5. Also in Hanrahan.

[21] Ibid, p. 58.

where they had obtained it. He then captured two of their leaders and ransomed them for a young native boy, whom he brought back as a slave to Sonoma, where he was living at the time. The boy eventually escaped.

When Kelsey and Stone returned with their gold, they had no sympathy for the grieving Wappo and resumed their punitive posture against them. One morning when the two were eating breakfast, a Wappo woman who worked in their house (probably as a slave) unloaded their rifles and sent a signal to a war party that had secretly gathered outside. Andy Kelsey was killed instantly by an arrow. Stone ran upstairs and attempted to leap to freedom from a second-story window. He was captured and died from being bashed in the head by a rock.[22]

A few weeks later Andy Kelsey's brother Sam led 40 mounted vigilantes on a vengeance mission. They killed every native they could find in Napa County. Some of the pioneers, like the Cyrus family, tried to dissuade the posse, and when they failed, they helped feed the Wappo who hid from the wrath of Kelsey and friends.[23] The final retribution, however, was made by the US Army the next year.

In the Spring of 1850, General Persifor Smith sent a lieutenant to punish the Wappo and end what the Army believed to be their harassment of Americans in the area.[24] A contingent of armed, uniformed soldiers marched solemnly through Napa City, over Howell Mountain and through Pope and Coyote Valleys. A local Wappo ran ahead of them and was able to warn the native community in Clear Lake of what was coming their way. The Wappo quickly built rafts of tule and retreated to an island that was just out of the Army's artillery range.

The Army sent back for reinforcements. Two full companies of infantry then marched up and across the Valley, following the same path as the first group. They brought with them two whaleboats,

---

[22]Hanrahan, p. 95.

[23]Wright, p. 17.

[24]Anecdote is from Hanrahan, p. 96.

loaded to the gunnels with howitzers and ammunition. Local men and boys tagged along, wanting to join.

When they came to the shore at Clear Lake, part of the attack force proceeded to a place across from the island where the Wappo had gathered. The infantry made a show of trying to reach the natives with their weaponry, while the Indians taunted them from what they believed to be a safe distance. Meanwhile, the remaining part of the force launched the two whaleboats and crossed to the other side of the island. They surprised the Indians and killed every one of them, men, women and children. The Army abandoned the heavy equipment at the site and fanned out throughout the Lake area, killing every native they found. The incident came to be known as the "Bloody Island Massacre."

Ben and Nancy Kelsey never did become domesticated. They continued to have problems with native Americans. They set up a trading post on the upper Sacramento, but the Indians raided it while they were gone. They lived in Mendocino and ran into financial and legal trouble. Ben caught malaria, and the family, which now included seven children, decided to move south to Mexico and Texas, which they thought would be easier on his health. While they were there, however, Comanches attacked them and scalped one of their daughters. Little Mary Ellen Kelsey survived the scalping and the 17 lance wounds she received, but suffered post-traumatic stress disorder for the rest of her short life. She died five years later in Fresno. Ben and Nancy finally separated. He stayed in the Los Angeles area and is said to have become a maintenance worker for the city. (Another source says he became an itinerant preacher.) He was buried in the Rosedale Cemetery. Nancy made her way to northeast Santa Barbara County and lived by herself in a cabin in the hills. She raised chickens, rocked on her front porch and probably sipped whiskey from a jug: just as she would have, perhaps, had she never left Kentucky. Occasionally she administered herbal medicines to her far-flung neighbors. Her dieing request was to be buried in a real coffin next to her husband Ben. Her equally poverty-stricken neighbors scraped up the money to provide for the first wish but couldn't fulfill the second. She was laid to rest beneath a tree by a creekside.[25]

Not everyone who went gold panning came back rich. Harrison Pierce didn't like mining. He returned to Napa City and completed the carpentry project he had abandoned when gold fever struck. His "Empire Saloon" was the first public building in Napa. It did a brisk business right away.

Other buildings sprang up. Massachusetts-born Joseph Thompson, who had arrived on a whaler in '46, opened the first general store at the foot of Main Street. He then bought from Higuera more than 100 acres south of what is now Division Street. This large section was first known as "Thompson's Addition" and then referred to as "Napa Abajo", or "lower Napa."

A second store was erected soon afterward, on the sandy slip of land at the end of First Street between Napa Creek and Napa River. This one was part of a chain of three owned by Mariano Vallejo, the others being in Vallejo and Benicia. Vallejo went into partnership with a new son-in-law, Captain John Frisbie, a lawyer who came west with the New York Volunteers. They hired another Volunteer, George N. Cornwell, to run it. New York-born Cornwell prospered as a businessman and became prominent in Napa society.

Miners coming down from the Sierra found Napa to be a very suitable place to spend the winter, as well as their gold. Napa City was a mini version of San Francisco, and featured the same raucous mixture of nationalities, classes and personality types. Hundreds of shaggy-bearded men in blue- or red-checked shirts came to town with their pants tucked in their boots and knives and pistols under their belts. White-shirted gamblers with diamond tie-pins and broad-brimmed hats sought them out. Odd-looking, rough cabins of canvas and redwood shakes cropped up all over. Pierce's Empire Saloon expanded to become a boarding house, offering lodging for $1.00 a night and a meal of beef, hard bread and coffee, also $1.00.

Tourists could stay at the American Hotel, on the southwest corner of Main and Third, erected in 1850. The owner was Nathan

---

[25]Ault, pp. 32-41.

Coombs, who went into partnership with two others who were also destined to prosper: Lyman Chapman and Samuel Starr.[26] Another, more modest inn, the Valley House, was across the street and was actually built first. The next year two more hotels housed the ever-increasing flow of miners. James Harbin of Pope Valley built the Napa Hotel on the northeast corner of Main and First, and Joseph Mount built the Revere House, on Second Street. The Revere House was the largest building in town. Made of brick, it stood three stories high and was 60 x 60.

Every hotel had its barroom, and independent saloons like the Empire appeared all over town. The miners were a hard-drinking lot, and they wanted to have fun. To assist them in this pursuit, a number of establishments also offered prostitutes.

Since most of the structures in Napa were built of wood, brick was considered a mark of luxury. Lilburn Boggs built a private residence that predated the Revere House and was the first brick building in town. With much fanfare, Kit Carson laid the ceremonial first brick. Boggs moved to an estate north of Napa and sold the building to two businessmen, Thomas Earl and William James, in 1855. They converted it into a business. Called the "Earl Building," or "Earl's Brick Building," it housed a drug store, a saddle- and harness-maker and a barbershop that also sold cigars.

Gold dust and gold nuggets were the primary medium of exchange, and every merchant had a scale on his counter. Men arrived with bags of gold strung from their saddles. A historian for the Fowler family says the Fowler children were given sacks of gold nuggets to play with like blocks on rainy days, and that when Henry Fowler decided to transfer his wealth from one bank to another later in the century he had to do it in a wheelbarrow.[27]

Miners swapped gold dust for a night's lodging and the first bath in months, and the ones who wanted to settle down for good could

---

[26] Harry L. Gunn, *History of Napa County*, S.J. Clarke Publishing Co., Chicago, 1926, p. 300.

[27]Mallet, p. 97.

deposit their treasure in the town's first bank. James H. Goodman &
Company was established by two German New Yorkers, James and
George Goodman, who pooled the gold they took from the Sierra
foothills to start a financial house that played an important role in
Napa's economic life for decades.

The Goodman brothers knew how to make the unregulated
political system work for them. George was Napa County Treasurer
in the 1850's and augmented the bank's wealth, and thus his own, by
keeping the County's funds there. James became a partner with
William Bourn in the Spring Hill Water Company, which owned and
controlled the price of drinking water for San Francisco.

Little US currency was in circulation, but businesses in Napa City
accepted foreign currency. A French franc and an English shilling
passed for $.25, and a 5 franc piece was $1.00. An assay office in San
Francisco, Kellogg and Humbert, issued gold coins called "slugs" in
denominations of $5, $10, $20 and $50.[28]

Gambling was a popular pastime among the pioneer residents as
well as with the miners. Nathan Coombs was particularly fond of
this. Growing increasingly wealthy from his business investments, he
booked passage on a boat and went to Kentucky, where he purchased
several thoroughbred racehorses and returned with them, also by
sea.[29] The Fowlers, also thriving, imported horses as well, and
improved their cattle by mating their cows with Durham bulls.[30]

When the Mexican War ended, Napa County became part of a
huge area called the "District of Sonoma," which extended from San
Francisco Bay to the Oregon border, and from the Pacific Ocean to
the Sacramento River. Technically, the territory had been under
military rule since the moment the Bear Flaggers arrested the
Vallejos. The ardent but illiterate Bear Flagger John Nash was the
first alcalde--judge/civil officer--of the region. He cherished his

---

[28]Gunn, p. 301.

[29]Gregory, p. 882.

[30]Mallett, p. 88.

position and refused to relinquish it in August, 1849, when the District's voters chose a far more qualified man, ex-governor Lilburn Boggs, to succeed him. Nash was finally arrested for refusing to step down by a lieutenant in the US Army, William Tecumseh Sherman, who went on to greater things.

The military did not withdraw right away. General Persifor Smith commanded the American forces in the region and was responsible for the Bloody Island Massacre. The assignment then went to General Bennett Riley. With the approval of President Zachary Taylor, Riley issued a proclamation saying that all the Districts in the territory should organize civil governments for themselves so that they could prepare for statehood. Riley recommended that the pioneers elect delegates to draft a state constitution, which they would then submit to Congress.

Taylor sent out two emissaries, Thomas Butler King of Georgia and William Gwin of Mississippi, to assist the Californians in their preparations. Butler played a supportive role in the dramas that followed, but Gwin had a leading part. Gwin was not a Napan, but was certainly one of the most widely known public figures of his day.

A convention of delegates started work on a constitution for California on September 1, 1849 in Monterey, site of the capital when Alta California belonged to Mexico. Bear Flagger Robert Semple presided.[31] There were numerous extremely pressing issues needing immediate attention. A governor and his lieutenant had to be elected, as well as the rest of the governmental infrastructure for the soon-to-be State.

It took six weeks to draft the constitution. One of the touchiest issues in the document was that concerning slavery.[32] Would California be a slave state or a free state? The delegates decided to include in the constitution a clause prohibiting slavery: not because the pioneers had any particular scruples about human bondage, but

---

[31]Gunn, p. 278.

[32] Kenneth G. Goode, *California's Black Pioneers*. McNally and Loftin, Santa Barbara, 1973, pp. 45-49.

because the miners felt demeaned by the notion that slaves could do the work they themselves were doing. Moreover, California was chronically dry, and few of the earliest pioneers could envision the state as being suitable for agriculture. Napa was one of the very few districts where farming had even been attempted. The delegates, particularly Semple, seriously considered stipulating that all free blacks be banned from emigrating to California (Oregon had such a law) but in the end decided on a format that made it seem to align itself with the north. To do otherwise would have imperiled their admission into the Union.

The constitution and a slate of officers were put up for election, and the people voted on November 30, 1849. Napans cast their ballots at Pierce's Empire Saloon. Peter Burnett, captain of a wagon train that had brought several settlers to the Napa Valley, was elected California's first governor. William Gwin and John C. Fremont were the first US Senators from California. Barely bilingual Mariano Vallejo won the race for State Senator. Also elected were a lieutenant governor, state secretary, superior court with judges, prefects and sub-prefects, district judges, alcaldes, justices of the peace and town councils.

The newly elected California State Legislature met in San Jose from December 15, 1849, until May 1, 1851. California thus considered itself part of the Union nine months before it actually became one. (Admission Day was September 9, 1850.) While in San Jose, the Legislature voted to make Vallejo the permanent capital, and they met there in January, 1852. They then opted for Sacramento. A flood in Sacramento in May of 1852 caused an early adjournment.

Mariano Vallejo became fixated on the idea of having the legislature headquartered at the southern end of his Rancho Nacional Suscol. He not only lobbied vigorously for this, but also donated land for a capitol building, library and several other public structures. The State of California accepted his gracious offer, and when he proposed to call the future city "Eureka" to commemorate the gold miners, the legislature voted instead to name it "Vallejo," to commemorate him.

Bedbugs and the lack of amusement in Vallejo, as well as its distance from other pueblos, led the legislature to adjourn to San

Jose, not-so-coincidentally the home of Governor Burnett.[33] Vallejo soon had his way again, and in January of 1853 the legislature met in his new little city. Mariano's bliss only lasted a weekend. Excellent PR by the Sacramento contingent convinced the majority to pull up stakes once more, and the capital was installed "permanently" in Sacramento. Later in 1853 the seat of government was "permanently" established in Benicia, a city that had been laid out by the former American consul to Alta California, Thomas Larkin, with the help of Bear Flagger Robert Semple and Bale's former mill builder, Ralph Kilburn. A few months later--February 24, 1854--the final permanency was established, perhaps out of exhaustion, in Sacramento.

On February 8, 1850--seven months before statehood-- Napa became one of California's original 27 counties, and its boundaries were defined. The area that is now Lake County and the American Canyon area were included in this assessment. The boundary with Solano County was redefined in 1852. Lake County became a separate entity in 1861, and its border with Napa was adjusted in 1872.

Napa City, population 405 in 1850, was named the county seat, and steps were taken to provide for a courthouse in which to conduct business. Lumber and labor were extremely expensive. Since most of the population was transient--miners in for the season or squatters who owned no land and therefore were not part of the tax base--the least costly means of constructing a public building was to have it framed back East and shipped over by boat. This was done, and a duplicate was also framed and shipped for private use as a residence.

The finished product stood on the northwest corner of Coombs and Second Street, next to the Revere House on what had been, ironically, a yard for storing locally grown and planed lumber.[34] It was 20' x 30', with a 6'-wide corridor running the full length of the

---

[33]Bancroft, XXIII, p. 322.

[34]John Lawley was part owner of the lumber yard. Throughout the years he engaged in a number of different enterprises.

first floor and a 4'-wide corridor giving access to the four small rooms on the second floor. The courtroom was on the ground floor, and Napans also used it as a lecture hall, for church services, for parties and for other events requiring indoor space. The furniture was primitive. The three spectator benches were merely narrow wooden slabs placed on logs and arranged against three of the room's unpainted walls. The judge's stand was against the other wall, behind a desk that was positioned on a slightly elevated platform. There were no rugs, no cushions, no lights, not even candlelight.[35]

With so much money around, it is perhaps somewhat surprising that crime in Napa was rare, although public brawling was commonplace. The first recorded criminal case in the District began on October 20, 1849 and was presided over by the *alcalde*, Lilburn Boggs. The crime was "larceny," and the defendant appears to have been Charles L. Cady, the relief worker from the Donner party rescue. The case may have been concerned with the fact that Cady and the late Charley Stone were allegedly paid $500 by Tamsen Donner to bring their two children down from the Sierra, but left them with the group at lakeside, instead. The jurors were D.Q. Tucker, William Russell, John Brown, William Edginton, William Morgan and John Taylor.[36] They couldn't agree on a verdict, so another jury was appointed. Cady was eventually found guilty and disappeared from Napa County history.

One of the upper level rooms in the courthouse was the county jail. Prisoners were chained to the floor. For the most part the jail only housed petty offenders, the more serious criminals being incarcerated in Sonoma. An exception to this rule--and perhaps the cause for it--occurred in 1851. A man named Hamilton McCauley was tried and found guilty of murdering Justice of the Peace S.H. Sellers, and was sentenced to be hung. He was imprisoned in the Napa jail. McCauley's friends got him a reprieve from Governor McDougal at the last minute, and a messenger galloped back to Napa

---

[35]Palmer, p. 257.
[36]Ibid, p. 59.

with the news. The ferry master, however, was a supporter of the victim and would not allow the messenger to cross the Napa River. The rider was directed to go a mile and a half upstream to Salvador Vallejo's *trancas* and then come all the way back to Second Street. By the time he arrived at the Courthouse, McCauley had been lynched: hung by a rope from a rafter over his cell. Sheriff M.W. McKimmy, who happened to own the ferry, was locked in an adjoining cell. William Nash was spending the night at Angus Boggs' store. They were both questioned about the case, but no arrests were ever made. Nash served on the Coroner's jury for the case.[37]

Something similar happened in May of 1863. A Mexican, Manuel Vera, fired on two Anglos named Shefley and Preston. He was arrested and taken to a holding cell while bond was being arranged. Sixty armed men wearing masks burst into the jail, picked up the sheriff and carried him out, and shot the prisoner dead.[38]

In a reminiscence of days gone by, the *Napa Register* estimated that in 1852 Napa County had 2,110 people, including 1,330 Indians. Napa City's population dropped to 300, down 25% from the 1850 census. In contrast, the population of Stockton was more than 2,400 and growing fast. Two important factors checked Napa Valley's growth. First, Napa wasn't on the way to anywhere in particular. Indeed, from the beginning it was a good place to go to get away from it all. Second, a fatal flaw existed concerning who actually owned the land. The treaty of Guadalupe Hidalgo stipulated that land belonging to Californios at the end of the Mexican War would continue in their possession. The American pioneers, true to their ethnocentric roots, saw no reason to follow the customs of the culture they supplanted. They wanted to make the land their own. They wanted to put up fences and mark their boundaries. They wanted to buy and sell real estate and make a profit. These were concepts that were foreign to the Californios. The newly elected US Senator from California, William Gwin, introduced before Congress

---

[37]Menefee, pp. 32-33. The Coroner was Nash's neighbor, F. Kellogg.
[38]*NCR*, 5-9-1863.

a bill that would erase the Mexican Pastoral Period in one paragraph. This law

> gave the occupant title by possession, against Intrusion, provided the amount of land claimed did not exceed 160 acres, that it was marked out by boundaries easily traced, or had improvements thereon to the value of $100; but a neglect to occupy or cultivate for a period of three months should be considered an abandonment of the claim.[39]

Huge as they were, the Mexican land grants were casually defined pastures bestowed by a government more attuned to how the crow flies than a surveyor's compass (they didn't even have surveyors' compasses). Moreover, most of the grant holders--people like Jacob Leese and the Vallejos--had their principal haciendas near garrisons like Sonoma and only used their land as grazing space for the steer in their cattle-oriented economy.

Squatters on the huge land grants would thus be guaranteed the right to possess that upon which they could keep a toe hold, as in the children's game King of the Mountain. Absentee owners and people who obtained land from them could find their resources drained away in legal expenses trying to defend themselves from intruders. Gwin's Land Act of 1851 would provide for a board of three commissioners with a secretary and Spanish-speaking lawyer to hear the claims of squatters against the grantees whose land they wanted. The burden of proof would rest with the grantees, not the squatters, and squatters had the right to appeal cases all the way to the Supreme Court. Defending one's lands thus became an expensive legal problem that could culminate in a trip to Washington, DC. All lands for which the claims were rejected as not being precisely enough defined, or for which the grantees did not appear in defense, would be regarded as part of the "public domain" by this board, and in many cases squatters were given whatever they chose.[40]

Arguing vigorously against Gwin's bill was Thomas Hart Benton,

---

[39] Bancroft, XXXIII, p. 327.

[40] Ibid, p. 540.

the Senator from Missouri. Although he had strongly advocated the conquest of California, his daughter and son-in-law, the John Charles Fremonts, were now grantees elsewhere in the state; indeed, their grant was the only one that had gold on it. As such, they were very troubled by squatters. Arguing just as vigorously but less publically in favor of Gwin's bill was Sam Brannan, who would have a say in who was selected to the federal commission.[41] Gwin's bill passed, and the commissioners who would hear the cases were appointed immediately.

Early editions of the *Napa County Reporter* ran listings of the numerous land cases pending. George Yount seemed to have the lion's share of squatters. The pioneers John Rector and Andrew Musgrave were among Yount's opponents in these legal battles.

In time, nearly everyone who had received a land grant in the Napa Valley had part or all of it wrested away by squatters. A principal victim in the Land Act mess was Mariano Vallejo. After years of litigation he lost his claim to *Rancho Nacional Suscol* in a legal technicality that smacked of political chicanery.[42] He made wealthy men of his lawyers, William W. Chipman, Henry Alexander Gaston (of Napa) and his own son-in-law and business partner, James Frisbie.[43]

Another victim was Reasin Tucker, hero of the Donner party rescue. He could not prove that the piece he bought from Elias Barnett was legally ceded to Barnett. Barnett got to keep Tucker's money. After a long, costly battle, Tucker lost his home in 1872 and moved to Goleta.[44] His friend, the generous and community-minded Florentine Kellogg, left town the same year, selling out to an Episcopal priest, Rev. T.B. Lyman.

Jacob Leese lost *Huichica*. He was moderately successful as a gold miner, but the wily trapper-turned-businessman was no match for the

---

[41]Ibid, p. 634.

[42]Gregory, p. 80.

[43]Emparan, p. 106.

[44]Neelands, p. 7.

young Americans who rushed into the region. He lost his cozy connections with the local power brokers. William Hinckley and Nathan Spear were both dead by 1850, and Thomas Larkin had turned his finances over to Talbot Green, aka Paul Geddes, the embezzling bank clerk from the Bartleson-Bidwell party. (Green did well for Larkin and made him a fortune.[45]) Little Rosalia Leese, Yerba Buena's first baby, did not survive childhood. Leese himself moved to Monterey and then on to New York,[46] leaving behind his wife and their seven surviving children. Practically penniless, he finally returned to the city he co-founded and received shelter at the Old Peoples' Home on Francisco Street. The 1830's and '40's were made for the adventurous outdoorsman, but he was not prepared for the modern world. He was run over by a wagon on February 1, 1890 and died two years later, to the day.[47]

Salvador Vallejo sold off some of his *Napa/Trancas* and *Yajome* ranchos, and the remainder was simply stolen from him. Coombs and Grigsby paid good money for their "Salvador District" holdings, but John E. Brown claimed that he purchased "Brown's Valley" for a horse and buggy. Salvador lost the rest of his wealth and many of his personal possessions to legal fees. Nicholas Higuera sold his *Entre Napa* grant in sections. Most of his *Carneros* grant fell into the hands of a man named Julius Martin. Cayetano Juarez was able to hold on to *Tulocay,* although he gave a lot of it away in gifts to the City of Napa. Bale's widow Maria was victorious in the end but spent many years and a great deal of money in court.

Jose and Sisto Berryessa held onto their land grant, because they were permanent residents at *Las Putas* and thus could legally secure their property against squatters in theory if not in practice. Actually, their huge land grant swarmed with squatters, and over time the Berryessas had to sell much of their land to them to pay their debts. When Jose and Sisto died, the land commissioners rejected their heirs'

---

[45]Bancroft, XXI, p. 707.
[46]Michaelis, p. 72.
[47]Idem.

'claims to *Las Putas*,[48] although the heirs of William Pope in nearby *Locoallomi* were able to sell their shares of inherited land.[49]

Many Americans cashed in on the US litigation victory. Nathan Coombs, for example, applied for and received a post in the Surveyor's Office and helped himself and his father-in-law, William Gordon, to Ignacio Berryessa's rancho *Chimiles* in southeast Napa County. When Perry Fundlebruck attempted to squat in *Chimiles* and cut some wood there, Coombs had him arrested and sentenced to 30 days in jail.[50]

The uncertainty of the land situation resulted in "squatter wars" in several locations in Northern California, including the Napa Valley. This story from the *Napa County Reporter* reports on such an incident:

> On Saturday last, a homicide occurred at Suscol. Particulars were as follows: on the night previous a man named Joseph Elliott erected a shanty on lands occupied by one Finnelle, and was accompanied by a man named Cox, who went only as a witness. When Finnelle came and discovered the shanty the next morning, he returned to this house, and got a double-barrelled shot gun, with which he proceeded to the place where the building had been erected, and shot both Cox and Elliott, killing the former instantly, and severely, although not fatally, wounding the latter in the groin. Cox's brains were completely blown out. Neither of the two were armed. Sheriff Allen on receiving notice, immediately took steps for the arrest of Finnelle, but he had suddenly disappeared, and is still at large.[51]

Joseph Elliott may have been one of the many children of Bear Flagger William Elliott, who wanted something better than a tree-house to live in.

---

[48]Bancroft, XXIII, p. 540.

[49]Beales, p. 33.

[50]*NCR*, 9-20-1862.

[51] *NCR*, 1-31-1863

Suscol continued to develop as an entity all its own. Gravel roads from Sacramento to Petaluma and from Napa to Vallejo converged there. These roads had been established for centuries as passages for the native population, and there was probably some kind of ferry system long before the whites came. The *trancas* where Yount met Vallejo's troops for the Battle of Suscol was located near this point.

Travelers heading for Petaluma rode on what is now Stanly Lane. Edward Stanly, who ran unsuccessfully as California's first Republican candidate for governor, bought a large piece of Nicholas Higuera's *Carneros* rancho in 1856. He planted eucalyptus trees on his estate to serve as windbreaks to protect his crops.

A lucky 49'er named William Neely Thompson furnished lumber for Mariano Vallejo's ill-fated State Capitol building in Vallejo. Vallejo paid him for this with 320 acres of *Rancho Nacional Suscol*. Thompson bought an additional 300 acres and had himself a substantial, if swampy, ranch. In 1852 his brother Simpson joined him on the Napa estate, and Simpson saw potential in turning the virgin soil into a fruit orchard.[52] The Thompsons reclaimed the land by diverting and channeling Suscol Creek. In so doing, they uncovered remains from the Battle of Suscol. They found skulls and other skeletal parts of Wappo who had fallen in battle, as well as a cache of articles the natives evidently intended to unearth and take with them after fighting Vallejo.[53]

The Thompsons sent back East for saplings, which were transported by sea. Those that were packed in charcoal dried up and died, and those that were packed in wet moss rotted. But the saplings that were packed in dry moss arrived in good condition, and soon peaches and apples were flourishing south of Napa City. Within 10 years the orchards became so prolific that "Thompson's Gardens"

---

[52] Simpson Thompson came to California by sea. One of his fellow passengers was Sam Brannan, who was returning from a tour of the great spas of Europe.

[53] Palmer, p. 9.

were known throughout the west.[54] Because the water table was high, the Thompsons didn't have to irrigate, and they convinced others in the Valley that cultivation alone would yield a good crop. Because of the Thompsons, wrote the enthusiastic C.A. Menefee in 1873, "except in some of the Southern countries,...the practice of irrigation has almost disappeared."[55] The Thompsons also planted varietal grapes

British-born John Patchett cleared some acres a mile west of the court house near Clay and Calistoga Streets in Napa and planted a vineyard of mission grapes for winemaking. He hired a short, trim German named Charles Krug to make the wine. Krug was learning the craft in Sonoma under a close friend of Mariano Vallejo, Agoston Haraszthy. Before that, Krug had edited a German-language newspaper in San Francisco and had the distinguishing experience of blowing off the thumb of another editor in a duel. Krug probably had no idea he would eventually be revered as a founding father of Napa County's most important industry.

The Napa River was "a beautiful stream of clear water"[56] in Gold Rush days, its bed not muddy but made of rocks and gravel. The only time the river could be forded was at low tide; otherwise travelers were obliged to swim their horses across. Donner Party rescuer William Russell built the pioneers' first ferry across the river at the foot of Third Street. A second ferry was created in 1852 in Suscol, mainly for the new Petaluma-Sacramento stage, with a wharf to accommodate the traffic.[57]

---

[54] The Thompson name itself thrived in Napa County. Joseph P. Thompson purchased land from Higuera to build the first store in 1848; William Thompson was a Donner party hero; Isaac Thompson was an early farmer and vintner; Thomas H. Thompson, son of Simpson, was a Napa County supervisor during the Civil War; W.W. Thompson was an important Napa merchant in the 1870's and co-founded a large winery.

[55]Menefee, p. 78.

[56]Gunn, p. 333

[57]Ibid, p. 302.

The River was an important thoroughfare for commercial and private travel. The pioneers had utilized its properties as a sheltered yet ample waterway as far back as 1841. That year Rose, Davis and Reynolds, shipbuilders, built a schooner, the *Susanah*, and launched it from the same strip of land on which Vallejo and Frisbie later had their store. One of the builders, John Calvert Davis, sailed the little ship to Mazatlan and back the next year under the Mexican flag, and when he returned he married George Yount's younger daughter, Frances. Rose, Davis and Reynolds went on to build another small ship, the *Condresa*. In addition to the ships, they built a barge for carrying hides and tallow from the Higuera, Vallejo and Juarez ranchos (and later Coombs') and traded them for general merchandise all along the estuaries of the San Pablo Bay.

Sam Brannan ran a newsflash in the *California Star* in 1848 that a craft called the *Malek Adhel* had "explored" the Napa River and found it navigable. This wasn't really news at all, but may have been a publicity gimmick to arouse interest in the Napa area. The *Malek Adhel* had a history all its own. Originally a Mexican craft, it was seized at Mazatlan by the US warship Warren during the Mexican War. The Boston trader William Phelps bought it[58] and sold it, perhaps to Brannan, in '48 when he headed off to the gold mines. Interestingly, Brannan was also friendly with Nathan Spear and may have known about the quicksilver deposit on Bale's property. Was he getting ready to merchandise the Napa Valley in anticipation of another mining rush?

A tall, skinny man named Turner Baxter captained the first steamship running regularly from Napa to San Francisco. Christened the *Dolphin*, it was a small craft with a large smokestack, and it was powered by a locomotive engine. The ship was tiny, and the passengers had to arrange themselves in it carefully so it wouldn't tip

---

[58]Phelps, p. 14. Phelps claimed that the Warren "cut her out of the harbor at Mazatlan from under Battery & in the face of 700 soldiers within pistol shot..."

over.[59] He also established the Valley House hotel, Napa's first.

The steamship *Reindeer* began plying the waters of the Napa River in the summer of '52 and made tri-weekly runs from Central Wharf in San Francisco. Competition from another steamship, the *San Jose*, put the *Reindeer* out of business. The *San Jose* ran on the same schedule but left from a place called the Long Wharf in San Francisco. Two years later another steamer, the *Marion*, advertising itself as "elegant," also entered the Napa River trade. The Napa Steamboat Line began operating in 1856 and also followed a tri-weekly schedule. Its ship, the *Guadalupe*, was the preferred vessel for the wealthy San Franciscans who started partaking of the valley's salubrious resources.[60] In 1857 the sailing sloop *Kittorah*, under a Captain Strickland, advertised itself as being ready to accept grain and merchandise for transport.

During the next decade the *Anna Abernatha*, the *Sophia*, the *Vaquero*, the *Express No. 1*, the *Rambler*, the *C.M. Webber* and the *Paul Pry* also saw service. The *Paul Pry* could make the Napa-S.F. run in three hours--a feat which may have been its undoing, as it ran aground in 1862.[61]

Shipping and transport weren't the only activities on the waterfront. Ralph's brother Wells Kilburn went into partnership with Captain John Brackett of the New York Volunteers in purchasing a small ship, the *Josephine*, for $100.[62] They moored it in the Napa River and made a large cut in its hull for easy entrance. It became Napa's third store. For a while it also served as a residence for Brackett and his family.

In 1849 a rickety wooden bridge was erected in what was then the north part of the town, where Brown Street crosses Napa Creek, but

---

[59]Charles M. Loring, "A Resume of Early Steam Navigation on the Napa River," unpublished, undated manuscript, p. 2.

[60]Norton King, *Napa County: An Historical Overview*, Napa County Superintendant of Schools, Napa, 1967, p. 30.

[61]*NCR*, 12-27-1862.

[62] Brackett was a member of the first California legislature, 1849-50.

it collapsed when a drunken cart driver tipped over a load of hay on it, killing two horses. George Cornwell paid John Wooden (of Wooden Valley) $100 each for two 60' stringers with which to construct a replacement. This second bridge was carried away in a heavy rainstorm in 1850. The debris from the ruined bridge lodged downstream and created a dam that flooded the whole town.[63] They tried again the next year, with a bridge at the end of First Street that spanned the Napa River itself. John Howell came down from Howell Mountain to build a toll bridge over the river in 1851. The pioneers did not appreciate paying the stiff crossing toll.

Crossing the river in bad weather was risky business; but so was crossing the street. The streets of Napa City were unpaved and composed of the same silty, miry stuff that George Tucker encountered trying to rescue the Donner party. When it rained, the horse and cart traffic quickly whipped the dirt into muck so that it was impossible to cross Main Street or any other major byway. Someone finally got the idea of dumping bundles of hay in two places on Main Street, to be used as pedestrian crossings. A lot of hay had to be sunk into the mud before the bottom was reached. Crossings were thus constructed in front of the Napa Hotel on First and the American Hotel on Third. Even with the crossings, however, it was common for people to fall in the mud up to their waists: an event that increased in likelihood with the amount of alcohol ingested.[64]

Dry weather presented its own problems. The mud hardened into a concrety, rut-ridden mass that exploded in great clouds of dust when horses and wagons went by. Traveling anywhere was a teeth- and bone-rattling experience.

There was no sanitation department in Napa City, and the transient miners were unconcerned about niceties like the disposal of

---

[63]Ibid, p. 296.

[64]Campbell Augustus Menefee, *Historical and Descriptive Sketchbook of Napa, Sonoma, Lake, and Mendocino, 1873*, James D. Stevenson, Fairfield, 1994, p. 24.

litter. Moreover, everyone rode horseback, and the horses created litter of their own. An article in the *Napa County Reporter* reminisced that "it was a common sight to see more than one hundred horses tied to the fence on First Street on Saturday or Sunday, waiting to take their owners home at nightfall." Sometimes the riders would pass out at the bar or purchase female companionship for the night and leave the horses tied to the rail with nothing to eat or drink for 24 hours. The city streets were therefore acutely filthy, and the one beneficial effect of the winter mud was that the year's garbage sank into it and disappeared forever.

Public drunkenness was such an issue in Napa that Napans themselves nearly abolished the sale of alcohol in the county. In the election of 1855, Prohibition was a measure on the ballot. Napans just barely voted it down: NO 205, YES 198.[65]

John Trubody, who had crossed the plains in '47 with Charlie Hopper, left his family in San Francisco and commuted to Napa. He contracted with a German named Thomas Cordua to mow Napa's wild oats and ship it as hay to a haypress a few miles up the Sacramento.[66] Families were a rarity in Napa City's early years, for the excellent reason that there were no services at all. There were no schools, no parks or playgrounds, no library, no banks, no fire departments, no hospitals. There were hardly any women. Wisely, Trubody's family stayed at their residence on Powell Street in San Francisco until 1856. That year Napa acquired a real post office. Prior to then C.P. Briggs, who had fought with Fremont, had kept the mail in his stovepipe hat.[67] The first post office was located on East First Street, across the Napa River from the main part of town.

Soon the outskirts of the original Napa City were cleared of weeds and were suitable for building. With the money he made from

---

[65]Wallace, p. 105

[66]Gunn, p. 295.

[67]Joe Isola, "Through Rain and Sleet," *Late Harvest*, California Indigenous Arts Organization, 1984.

J. S. Peabody

Lilburn Boggs, once Governor of Missouri, came to California
with the 1846 emigration. Mariano Vallejo greeted him and his
large family with great hospitality. Boggs and at least three of
his sons, Angus, William and Henry, settled in Napa County.

Cordua, Trubody built a haypress himself, and then a warehouse on the Napa River to store the hay as well as the agricultural products that were coming down from the upper valley each week.[68]

One Sunday while still in San Francisco with his family, John Trubody heard the dynamic preaching of a Methodist minister, Asa White. White had recently come down from Oregon with his wife, three unmarried daughters and six married daughters and their husbands. They had encountered severe difficulties with the natives and narrowly escaped being massacred. White held services in a blue tent and provided music with an organ that had come west with the family. Trubody invited White to use the Powell Street property as his base of operations.[69] The damp San Francisco environment, however, bothered Asa White. Presumably through Trubody, he met Florentine Kellogg in 1852 and moved to the Napa Valley.

White was preceded in the Napa Valley by an itinerant Methodist minister, Rev. S.S. Simonds, who spent time in the county as early as 1851. A sect known as the Cumberland Presbyterians built a structure in which services were held. The Cumberland group faded away, so the Methodists used the building. Another Methodist, Rev. E. E. Hazen, built a parsonage in Napa City in 1853.

A Presbyterian minister named J.C. Herron came to town in 1853. It took two years to establish a congregation, possibly because Rev. Herron lived for some time up valley, at the home of Captain Matthew Ritchie. Captain Ritchie's daughter married the Donner Party rescuer John Stark, who was now the Sheriff, and the Presbyterians held their church services at the Courthouse. Rev. Herron and his flock parted ways when the latter voted to include

---

[68] Before Trubody's, another warehouse had stood on the south side of First Street , but it was carried away by the flood of 1850.

[69] Effa White Roberts and Mattie White Hutchison, "Father White and His Blue Tent," in *Second Annual Report of the Napa Historical Society,* February, 1951, p. 1.

music in the service.[70] His replacement was Rev. R.H. Veeder.[71] Rev. Veeder sought inspiration in the mountains bordering the west side of the valley. Perhaps his greatest achievement was to have one of them named for him. The Presbyterians purchased a lot of their own in 1857, and in 1858 they finished their church. They also ran a school, the first in Napa City. Several prominent Napans were on the Board of the Presbyterian church: among them Chancellor Hartson, James Lefferts, George Goodman, J. M. Mansfield and S. Wing.

An Episcopal Church was also constructed in 1858. The Rev. E. W. Hagar, an early priest of the parish, provided fodder for a scandal by being accused of illicit relations with ladies of the congregation. He was tried in an ecclesiastical court in Joliet, Illinois.[72]

The original St. John's Catholic Church was the third church built in 1858. Lots for the edifice were donated by the increasingly wealthy merchant, George N. Cornwell, and by the politically ambitious Presbyterian elder, Chancellor Hartson. The Catholic Church was noteworthy for its day because it was built of brick.

A.J. Cox, one of the group to go mining with the Kelsey brothers and Salvador Vallejo, founded the first newspaper in Napa, the *Napa County Reporter*, in 1856. Shortly after the paper began publishing, Cox was joined in the enterprise by R. T. Montgomery. The *Reporter* had only four columns and was printed with small, secondhand type, but it was a start. The paper was mostly advertising, which may have been irritating to its readers at the time. In addition to many of the enterprises listed above, advertisements ran for the Napa Bakery on Main Street; a fish and vegetable market; Goodman & Co ("A Cheap Cash Store"); Jacob Blumer's Lager and Beer Saloon; the "Yellow House" general store; and J.M. Dudley, an "agent of Wells Fargo Company's Express," who also sold books and stationery.

A "fine line" of four-horse carriages was advertised as ready to

---

[70]Palmer, p. 256.

[71]Idem.

[72] *NCR*, 5-16-1863.

transport travelers from the ferry landing at Suscol to Sulphur Springs in St. Helena, where a "new hotel will be opened on the 20th" of June, 1857. This particular fine line was owned by Nathan Coombs, who worked on improving the mediocre California stock. Meanwhile, the Kentucky thoroughbreds he had imported were bolstering his already considerable fortune by providing him with entrants in horse races, a very popular spectator sport in the 19th Century. In time Coombs bred four famous thoroughbreds: Eva Ashton, Strideway, Fleta and Lodi. Lodi was the most spectacular. In June of 1865 he ran in a race against an opponent named Norfolk on a track just south of San Francisco. The race was the subject of a satirical piece by Mark Twain, who noted that practically everyone in the city left work to watch the event.[73] Lodi lost, but got to spend his retirement years in comfort on a ranch north of St. Helena. A lane off of Highway 29 still bears his name.[74]

Another Napan who involved himself in transportation called himself Smith Brown. Brown had been a manufacturer back East whose projects ran aground for one reason or another. He came west for his health, both physical and financial. He established a stage line that ran between Sacramento, Sonoma, Petaluma, Napa and White Sulphur Springs, perhaps in partnership with Coombs. He operated the line from a depot at the Napa Hotel on the corner of First and Main. He made enough money to sell out at a profit in 1858. With the proceeds he bought a large tract of land from Juarez that included the land where Napa State Hospital now stands. He ran cattle and grew wheat there.

In 1858 a telegraph line was laid down between Napa and Vallejo, making it possible, finally, for news to travel faster than a man on a horseback.

By the mid 1850's the place euphemistically called Napa City was on its way to becoming a livable riverfront town: dirty, muddy and

---

[73]Bernard Taper, ed., *Mark Twain's San Francisco*, McGraw-Hill Book Co., New York, 1963, p. 91.

[74]Hanrahan, p. 117.

short on women, but livable. Down by the wharf, boats of various sizes and shapes were moored to the pilings, their lines knocking gently against their wooden masts. An old barge called the *Pilgrim* was anchored permanently at the foot of Third Street and became a regular fixture. Every day but Sunday a small side-wheeler deposited passengers at the landing where Division Street met the River. When it blew its whistle the natives who had come to town rushed to the riverbank to watch.

Where the river turned sweet, the town began. Rough-cut redwood buildings opened onto sidewalks that were gray with travel dust, and men wearing dirty white aprons did business with men in vests and baggy pants. Women were scarce.

The scene outside Napa City was bucolic. A gravel road laid out in 1851-52 ran from the landing at Suscol through the center of Napa City and continued northwest along what is now Pueblo Avenue.[75] It doglegged left near what is now the intersection of Redwood Road and Highway 29 and continued north. Its easterly parallel, the "Road to Conn Valley," (renamed the Silverado Trail) was later developed as an alternative route because it was higher and less prone to flooding.[76]

Landowners quickly put up redwood fences to mark off their property, and some dug trenches and earth walls with a newly invented mechanical ditch-digger to indicate boundary lines.[77] Farmers cleared out the wild oats and planted more substantial grains, mostly wheat and barley. Wild mustard had not yet found the valley, but other wildflowers popped up in the spring.

John Russell Bartlett described the area both in words and drawings for the US Government in 1852. He was swept away by the beauty of the place:

If this romantic valley were transferred to the older countries of

---

[75]Wichels, *Railroads,* p. 10.

[76]Ira Swett and Harry Aitken, Jr., *Napa Valley Route,* Glendale, CA, published by the authors, 1975, p. 16.

[77]Bartlett, p. 18.

Europe, it would be taken for the domain of a prince or nobleman. It answers to the idea one has of the old and highly cultivated parks of England, where taste and money have been lavished with an unsparing hand, through many generations. As one emerges from or enters each grove, he involuntarily expects some venerable castle or mansion to appear...[78]

Bartlett was especially impressed with the oak trees. He wrote that the Valley

is now studded with gigantic oaks, some of them evergreen...These magnificent oaks are found sometimes in long lines and again in clusters of twenty or thirty, forming beautiful groves; then again a space of ten or twenty acres will occur without a single tree...What is singular, and to me unaccountable in these groves of large trees is, that there are no young ones, none but the venerable and full-grown oaks...Nor is there any undergrowth of trees or shrubs...[79]

Clean-shaven John Trubody moved his family from their San Francisco home on Powell Street to a farm seven miles north of the hub of Napa City. With his sons he started the Trubody Ranch. The Trubodys planted 35 acres of blackberries. Their patch was the largest of its kind in California and flourished for decades. They later established a post office and a railroad depot. The post office and depot were referred to as "Trubody," and constituted a suburb of sorts. John's son William married a daughter of Terrell Grigsby and continued his father's work, and Dad retired to a home in Napa at 2021 First Street.[75] Perhaps inspired by Judge Edward Stanly, the Trubodys planted eucalyptus trees, some of which grew to massive proportions. A century later the California Department of Transportation preserved several of them in an island on Highway 29 north of Napa.

---

[78]Bartlett, p. 16

[79] Idem.

[75]Ernest Wichels, in *Solano Times-Herald*, 6-22-1969.

One of the Trubodys' neighbors was Joseph W. Osborne, a clipper ship Master from Massachusetts. When he saw that steamships would soon replace the speedy, beautiful sailing vessels in the China trade, the canny Osborne retired from the sea. He put up a little home on a spread of land in the Trubody district. He planted orchards, as well as flowering shrubs and a vineyard. He named his plantation "Oak Knoll" for a knob of hill that graced the property.

Osborne was dissatisfied with the quality of farm laborers available, so he advertised in the eastern press for workers. He employed New England farmers at Oak Knoll, many of them from Rhode Island, and paid them twice the going rate.[76] All went very well for Osborne until April of 1863, when a farm hand named Charles Brittain had trouble cashing his paycheck, due, evidently, to an error at the bank. Osborne promised to rectify the situation in a few days. Brittain went to San Francisco and purchased a revolver, and on the steamer coming back to Napa announced to his fellow passengers that if Osborne didn't have the problem solved he would shoot him. Brittain found his employer in the orchard, and, according to witnesses, an animated discussion ensued, during which Osborne picked up a rock and Brittain shot him dead. Brittain was found guilty of murder and was the first person in Napa County to be tried and legally executed for a crime.[77] As a 19th Century historian put it, "The drop fell at twenty minutes past three P.M., August 7th" in the yard at the Courthouse.[78]

Osborne's survivors moved to New York and sold Oak Knoll to R.B. Woodward, who operated the "What Cheer House" in San Francisco, a famous hotel in its day.[79] Woodward sent around the Horn for a ranch house, but soon after he erected it, the place burned

---

[76]Bartlett, p. 16.

[77]Palmer, p. 145.

[78]Ibid, p. 243.

[79] In St. Helena a copycat named Tonolla also erected a "What Cheer" saloon. There was also a "What Cheer" in the gold rush town of Columbia.

down. His second attempt at a home on Oak Knoll was much more successful. Woodward built a pillared mansion with towers, dormers, and gingerbread woodworking, set well back from the County Road at the end of a tree-lined drive.[80] He employed numerous servants and was able to provide his San Francisco friends with gracious hospitality reminiscent of the Old South.[81]

The area known as "Yount township" extended all the way across the Valley, from Solano to Sonoma, and included two population zones. Berryessa Valley was to the east. Among the pioneer families to set up cabins there were the Bottorf, Farnsworth and Ish families.[82] They were joined by Robert Hardin, John Adams, William Moore, Edward Cage and Andrew Wester, with their respective families. [83]

A rumor passed around that the Berryessas were hosts for a brief time to a bandit named "Joaquin:" perhaps, the story went, the legendary Joaquin Murietta, and that Joaquin killed a too-talkative American on the premises. Joaquin Murietta probably never existed, and if an Anglo had been killed at the Berryessas' the B.'s would have been lynched. But the story does suggest that the Berryessas may have felt a lot of animosity from the Americans (and vice versa, perhaps). It was their father, Jose de los Reyes, who was murdered by Kit Carson during the Bear Flag revolt.

The town of Monticello began to congeal in the 1860's after a man named Ezra Peacock built a house there. Other Monticello residents came, and by 1870 families named Finnell, Gillaspie, McCall, Marshall, Coleman, Smittle and Houghton moved in. The Berryessa population grew large enough to be a stopping-off place for the mail carrier, who came by buckboard in summer and on horseback in winter. He picked up the mail in Suisin and took a trail that went

---

[80]Oscar Lewis, *Here Lived the Californians*, Rinehart & Company, New York, 1957, p. 204.

[81]Maggie Turner, "The Oak Knoll Ranch," in *SHS*, 3-31-1933.

[82]Frank Owen, "Early Days at Zen Zen," in *First Annual Report of the Napa Historical Society*, May, 1949, p. 4.

[83]Idem.

beside Suisun Creek through *Chimiles* and Capell Valley. It continued more or less along what is now the Berryessa-Knoxville Road. The courier spent the night in the now-submerged little village of Monticello. A road connecting Berryessa with Napa was finally laid down in 1867.[84]

Sebastopol was the other population center in Yount township, although there were mini-settlements spread about in the area. It was renamed "Yountville" in May, 1867. At least one of the many sons of Lilburn Boggs moved there. Sebastopol/Yountville had two hotels-- the Sebastopol Exchange Hotel built in 1856 by David Wise and the White House Hotel built the same year by a man named Clayton.[85] There was also a blacksmith shop and a general store. Charlie Hopper owned a large spread, and Captain John Grigsby ranched there too, as described above. George Yount continued to be the grand old man of Sebastopol. In 1855 he married "the widow Geisweiler," in a ceremony that was performed at the Vallejos' in Sonoma by the Rev. T.B. Lyman, the Episcopal priest who eventually bought Florence Kellogg's place in St. Helena.[86]

The upper portion of the county was called "Hot Springs," and it included everything north of Sebastopol. Pope Valley, home of the Barnetts, was one little population nexus in this region. The Dealy, Duvall, Franklin, Hardman, Palmer, Wallace and Walters families were early settlers there.[87] There were enough people to start a little church, with the first service held June 5, 1853. A tiny town called "Wardner" existed there briefly.

An east/west road ambled down from Pope Valley. St. Helena's Pope Street and Howell Mountain Road were once parts of that passage. Eventually the Pope Valley road met the well-worn

---

[84]Owen, p. 4.

[85]Tillie Kanaga, *History of Napa County,* Oakland: Enquirer Print, 1901.

[86]Idem.

[87]Idem.

north/south road that began in Napa City and worked its crooked way up the valley. The Pope Valley route continued west along the banks of a warm spring the locals called "Sulphur Creek." It ended in a narrow, lush canyon canopied with soaring redwoods and gnarly oaks dripping in Spanish moss. Here a warm creek became very hot in places and smelled strongly of sulphur. Eight other sulphurous springs babbled nearby.

Almost spooky in its own shadows, the place was discovered by John York in 1848. He called it White Sulphur Springs. York sold it to David Hudson, but neither attempted to acquire a title to it, although they did put up a little "bath house" so that they could enjoy the warm springs. Hudson sold out to L.G. Lillie and Edward Evey. In 1852 Lillie and Evey opened a hotel with a restaurant there, and White Sulphur Springs became the first resort spa in California.[88]

On May 16, 1854,[89] an Englishman, J. Henry Still, in partnership with a Mr. Walters,[90] purchased 126 acres from Bale's widow. They tried first for a location farther south, near Maria Bale's adobe (on what is now Whitehall Lane) but Maria would not sell them the plot. Acreage adjacent to it was already in the hands of an Episcopal priest, Rev. John ver Mehr. Still and Walters' new holding was just north of the place where the route to Pope Valley met the path to White Sulphur Springs. The purchase price was $1041.25, or $8.25 an acre, representing a huge jump in the value of land since York and Hudson bought land for $.50 an acre from the Bales.[91] The piece ran roughly from what is now Spring Street in St. Helena to what is now

---

[88]Virginia Hanrahan, *Forgotten Spas of Napa County*, unpublished manuscript, nd, p.10.

[89]Leo H. Martin, letter to editor in the *SHS*, 3-17-1955.

[90] This is probably J. J. Walters, who settled in Pope Valley and eventually started Walters' Hot Springs.

[91] Still and Walters had first tried to purchase a plot of land near Bale's on what is now Whitehall Lane, but Maria Bale wouldn't sell.

Madrona Avenue[92] and was about 150' deep, abutting the property of William Hudson. Still erected a small wooden home with a section of it set up as a general store. A well was sunk.

Hoping to attract other merchants and thereby start a town, Still offered to donate nearby lots to anyone who would invest. John Scott Kister, a slim man with a long face, was the first to accept. Kister had arrived in the area in 1854 after harrowing experiences with the Pawnees. Not one to pass up a good offer, in 1855 he put up two businesses on the corner of what would be Main and Spring Streets: a shoe- and bootmaking enterprise and a fix-it shop, leasing Bale's mill to cut boards for the project. He also dug a well.

1856--a bad year for the economy in general--saw a building boom in St. Helena. Hiram Dixon and John Howell went into partnership in a blacksmith shop that year, and a consumptive named Robert Calderwood opened a wagon- and carriage-building trade. August Tainter and Charles C. Drew put up a small hotel near Kister's site, on the corner of the road to Pope Valley and what is now Main Street. They sold it soon afterward to Hiram Louderback. It burned down: a common fate for structures of that era. Another was built in its place by John Wolf. [93]Two more men, Christian Turkeldson and A. W. Elgin, established general stores. In 1858, David Fulton went into business as a saddle maker near Tainter's hotel. Had Fulton been alive and working today, the address of his business would have been 1230 Main Street.

A group of men playing horseshoes at Dixon and Howell's brought up the question of what they should call the little village that was forming around them. James Booker, one of the contestants in the game, suggested " St. Helena," which was the name that had been given to the local chapter of the Sons of Temperance, a fraternal organization that had taken root in the area in 1854. David and William Hudson were very active as founders of the chapter. It was

---

[92] The corner of Madrona and Main Street in St. Helena was the southeastern tip of John York's large, narrow tract.

[93]Gunn, p. 348.

a while before the name was used on official documents; well into the 1860's St. Helena was still referred to as "Hot Springs Township." Temperance did not stay fashionable in St. Helena for very long. A string of saloons and boarding houses soon went up.

Meanwhile, Lillie and Evey sold White Sulphur Springs to a San Francisco investment firm. The investors developed WSS as a private retreat, eventually expanding the hotel--the "Grapewine Cottage"-- to three stories and putting in a bowling alley among the redwoods. They opened it to the public in 1854. It burned down two years later. They built a replacement, but it too burned down, shortly after completion. The site was unlucky for them, so in 1861 they sold it. The buyer was a San Franciscan with prior hotel experience, Sven Alstrom.[94] Under Alstrom WSS reached a level of popularity with San Francisco society that was unequalled by any other resort of its day, not only because of its intriguing location, but also because Alstrom knew how to make extraordinary people feel comfortably human. A bevy of other spas went up in the Napa Valley after WSS, but York's discovery was the prototype.[95]

The presence of White Sulphur Springs changed the upper valley forever. It became the not-so-secret hideaway of scores of discerning San Franciscans, as well as many of the most famous luminaries of the 19th Century. Ambrose Bierce, Hubert Howe Bancroft, Bret Harte, Joaquin Miller, Lillie Hitchcock Coit and Leland Stanford were among the many who rested their auras for a while at WSS.[96]

Businessmen with money to spend liked to send their families up for the cold San Francisco summer. It took them a full day to make the trip, which began with an early morning steamship cruise from a wharf at the end of Market Street. The larger boats debarked at

---

[94] Alstrom was proprietor of the very fashionable Occidental Hotel and then joined the ultra-fashionable Lick House on Montgomery Street. The West's most gifted personages felt at home at Lick's hotel.

[95] Genevieve Sheffer, "History of White Sulphur Springs," unpublished manuscript, p. 2.

[96] Hanrahan, *Forgotten*, p. 1.

Suscol, where coaches like Nathan Coombs' "fine line" collected the travelers for the up-valley trip. The County of Napa accommodated the tourists by laying down a public thoroughfare along what is now Sulphur Springs Road.[97] Later, travelers coming to WSS by the Napa Valley Railroad debarked at Vineland Station where Sulphur Springs met the county road. Elegant coaches with fine horses met them and shuttled them across Sulphur Creek, continuing along what is now the western-most extension of Spring Street. Muddy, dusty St. Helena and the odoriferous Chinatown that grew up near the town's entrance could thus be by-passed completely. In order to facilitate the conducting of business while they were at WSS, several of the tourist regulars arranged to have a telegraph installed there. Only later was a wire run from the resort to the little township of St. Helena

The guests often came with their servants, their linen and their own china and were treated like the royalty which, in a way, they were. Some families were so devoted to their yearly pilgrimage that Alstrom leased them land on which they could build permanent, private cottages of their own.[98] A former WSS cottage stands at the corner of Madrone and Main Street in St. Helena.

One thing that distinguished the clientele at WSS was their exposure (or aspiration) to European tastes. Many recognized in the upper Napa Valley a certain similarity to the Mediterranean in climate and terrain. Quite a few of the guests were so taken by this that they eventually bought land nearby and put in vineyards, so that they could enjoy something America was so far unable to offer:wine.

From the very beginning "Hot Springs" had three centers of activity and in some ways, three identities. The best known of the personalities was the resort spot, the getaway for the city dweller who could afford to pay for fresh air and good food in a cottage in the woods or a summer house. "White Sulphur Springs" was a home away from home and a name to drop.

The second identity and center of activity was the little town just

---

[97]Sheffer, Loc. Cit.
[98]Sheffer, p. 5.

beyond the place where the coaches slipped into the woods and disappeared in the shadowy glade. St. Helena was a new beginning for ordinary folks, many of whom had come to California for their health. Consumption (tuberculosis) was the leading cause of death in St. Helena in the 19th Century, not because people acquired it there, but because they came hoping the unpolluted air would cure it.

The oldest center of activity was the Bale Mill, which Bale had willed to his daughter Isadora.[99] George Tucker wrote a vivid description of the labor that went into preparing grist for the mill:

> We raised our first crop of grain in Napa Valley in 1848, about 15 acres. We cut it with scythes, hauled it all up into piles--Spanish fashion--and built a fence around it. Then we drove in 30 or 40 Mustang horses, wild as deer, then got in there on horseback and with a long whip drove those horses around at top speed until the straw was pulverized as chaff. This was then thrown up with forks or shovels until the wind had blown away all the chaff and straw. Then before taking it to the Mill, the grain was put into big troughs with water and stirred until all the grit and dirt had settled to the bottom. The wheat was then taken out and spread in the sun to dry. It required two or three days to prepare a grist of ten bushels.[100]

WSS developer Leonard G. Lillie took over management of the mill in 1851. He put in a wheel nearly twice the size of the original and built a threshing machine that simplified the task but probably took some of the fun out of it.

The mill area was the meeting place for the established locals, who were mainly southerners from the Mississippi Valley. It had something for everyone. Its granary doubled as a social hall. The school house was within walking distance, as was a church and for some, the cemetery.

After a while the pioneers who met at the mill got used to the

---

[99]W.W. Lyman, *Memoirs*, p. 91.

[100] George Tucker, "Old Mill," unpublished, undated manuscript. Also in Verardo, pp. 19-20.

presence of the stores, but they had difficulty feeling comfortable with the elegant tourists. One local wrote about being seized with a desire to visit San Francisco after eyeing the fashionable summer folks at WSS. She had nothing appropriate to wear, however, and had to create a hoopskirt out of grapevines so she could pass as stylish.

In 1852 the Methodist minister whom John Trubody had befriended, Asa White, came to Hot Springs Township to preach from his blue tent as a guest of Florentine Kellogg. In the autumn of 1853 the pioneers built him a wooden church not far from Bale's gristmill and whitewashed the little (22' x 32') place's walls.[101] It was the first real church in the upper valley. The upper valley pioneers could only persuade the charismatic White to stay a short time, however, although he did return in 1873 to spend his final months.

The "White Church" (not unlike the "White Barn" of the late 20th century) remained a fixture in the locals' social and cultural heritage for many years. It saw several weddings in the 1850's. George Tucker, for example, married Mary Kellogg there. The White Church was non-denominational, but there was an unpleasant degree of friction in the congregation, because while the more influential pioneer families were Methodist (like the Kelloggs and the Ritchies), nearly everyone else was Baptist. Sporadic efforts had been made by some of the families to start a Baptist church as early as 1850, but for the most part they had to cross the mountains to Sonoma to get to services that were to their liking. They left on horseback very early on Sunday morning with their babies in their arms and older children sharing the saddle or on horses of their own. Eventually they started using Sarah Fosdick's schoolhouse for their meetings.

In 1857 the new hotel owner Hiram Louderback donated a lot to the Baptist Home Missionary Society, and the "Sharon Baptist Church" finally had a home of its own, on the corner of Church and Hunt streets. It was soon rechristened the "St. Helena Baptist Church." Many familiar names show up on the Baptist church's archives: the Cyrus, Owsley, York, Hudson and Nash families, along

---

[101]White, p. 1.

with the Rectors, Fultons and Louderbacks, were all involved in the Baptist church.[102]

As other settlers came, so did their denominations. Presbyterians laid a cornerstone for their church in 1860. WSS proprietor Sven Alstrom was an early participant. His daughter Sophie wed the pastor's son, John Mitchell. Pioneers Bill McDonnell, Peter Teale and John Howell were among the founders of the Methodist Church, erected in 1867. There was a small wooden Catholic Church on the corner of Oak and Spring Streets, but the Church owned much of the land on Oak Street and would have room to grow.

The planting, harvesting, threshing and milling of wheat dominated much of life throughout the 1850's and early '60's. Wheat quickly became Napa County's major crop, both in amount cultivated (34,600 acres in 1859) and dollars' profit. Pope Valley won fame for its special blue-colored variety. Because the Civil War interfered with planting and harvesting in other regions of the country, and because the Napa Valley was one of the few parts of California being farmed, Napa was considered a major "breadbasket" area.[103] Napa farmers claimed to be the first to put wheat in sacks rather than barrels.

Isadora Bale married a German vintner, Louis Bruck, and sold the Bale Mill in 1860. The new owners, Ralph Ellis and Edward Irwin, ran into problems almost immediately. The winter of 1860-61 was extremely cold. Water to the mill froze.[104] The winter of 1861-62 was the wettest on record. The Napa River flooded (as did most of the rivers in California), sweeping away cattle, hogs and fowl and a wooden boarding house/saloon called Lynch & Brother.[105] Homeowners in Napa City's "Cornwell's Addition"--a residential

---

[102]Palmer, p. 336.

[103] Another, larger farming region in California at the time was the San Joaquin valley, which produced more wheat than Napa County.

[104]Kerr, p. 75. Cattle froze, too, and ranchers were forced to strip the hides from the icy carcasses.

[105]*NCR*, 12-14-1861.

area near today's Fuller Park--awoke to find their neighborhood under water. The winter of '62-'63 started with an early freeze[106] and ended with a drought. What Bancroft called "the garden valley of California" encountered a major setback. The *Napa County Reporter* tried to be optimistic, predicting that without the rain the wheat harvest would be "very thin, but clean."[107] Ellis and Irwin enlarged the mill with a big overshot wheel and finally updated it with a steam engine so it no longer needed to depend on the unpredictable supply of water.[108]

Suddenly money, which seemed to flow in an unending golden stream in the 1850's, was scarce. Land exchanged hands frequently, as people sold out to pay their debts.

[106]*NCR*, 10-4-1862.

[107] *NCR*, 7-19-1862

[108]Verardo, p.25.

Chapter Seven

Victorian Valley

F ar as it was from Washington, DC and the crisis of conscience that was polarizing North and South, the Napa Valley was split on the questions of states' rights and slavery. St. Helena was hit particularly hard by this struggle, because so many of its leading citizens were originally southerners.

Throughout the 1850's the California legislature was solidly Democrat, although not necessarily pro-slavery. Some, like the Kelseys and William Boggs, enslaved young natives, but for the most part the gold miners did their own labor and resented those who would have slaves do the hard work they themselves were willing to do. In general, most folks despised abolitionists.

Nationally, the Democratic Party was itself was split in two. The moderate faction coalesced around Stephen Douglas, who did not believe in slavery but promoted the idea of "popular sovereignty." When Douglas won a bare majority in the 1860 Democratic convention, the Southern delegates walked out and nominated their own presidential candidate, John C. Breckenridge.

One of Breckenridge's staunchest supporters was California's Sen. William Gwin. Gwin was a former Congressman from Mississippi and a family friend of Andrew Jackson's. He was involved in Golden State politics from the very beginning–not always entirely honorably. He and his ally, California Governor John Weller, voted against measures to complete an overland mail route to California because it would compete with the Pacific Mail steamship line, in which Gwin held an interest. Gwin was put in charge of establishing a US mint in San Francisco. He used the money budgeted for the mint to start a government assay office, instead, where he charged the miners a 2.5%

fee on the gold he assayed.[1] When confronted with his failure to use the money as it was appropriated, he claimed that he intended to use the proceeds from the assaying office to build the mint.

Even more importantly for the Napa Valley, Gwin and Weller were behind the federal land reform act that separated the original grantees from their land grants. Only a small portion of Napa County's original settlers actually bought their land. The rest squatted, which made them appreciate the position taken by Gwin and Weller. The two further enhanced their popularity in the Napa area by advocating the idea of a "Pacific Republic." Gwin, Weller and others held the opinion, at least for a while, that California and Oregon should secede from the Union so that these states could decide upon their own policies regarding slaves. Another California congressman who is better remembered for similar views was John Burch, a contemporary of Gwin's. After the first volleys were fired at Fort Sumter, Burch won the hearts of the pioneers by calling on Californians to "raise aloft" the Bear Flag and revive the Republic of 1846.[2]

Gwin and Weller were part of a very influential group of ex-southerners who were referred to pejoratively as "The Chivalry," or "Shivs." These men and women comprised much of the old wealth in San Francisco:[3] the kind of people who could afford to spend summers at White Sulphur Springs in St. Helena. As a group, they were well educated, well traveled and well aware of their own blue-blooded ancestry. Their colorfully formal social gatherings were the envy of outsiders. They were ardent supporters of Jefferson Davis.

One of the most ardent was Lillie Hitchcock Coit. Her father, Dr. Charles Hitchcock, was the Medical Director of the Pacific Coast, but before his appointment in California he was a surgeon in the

---

[1] One-half percent would have covered the cost of assaying.

[2] Alvin M. Josephy, Jr., *The Civil War in the American West*, Alfed A. Knopf, NY, 1991, p. 234.

[3] Napa County's original southern pioneers were not ante bellum aristocrats, but good ol' boys of the Jacksonian variety.

Mexican War. He was credited with saving Jefferson Davis' leg when Davis was wounded in the battle against Santa Ana in Texas. Lillie's mother, Martha, was a cousin of the CSA's Secretary of State and a very close friend of Senator Gwin's wife.[4]

The Hitchcocks came to San Francisco when Lillie was about five, and by the time she was a teenager she had gained a reputation not only as a Southern belle but as something of an eccentric. She developed a fascination for fire engines and was actually invited to join "Knickerbocker Number 5," a San Francisco firehouse, as a volunteer fire fighter.[5]

Lillie was attractive, brilliant, headstrong and a spy for the Confederacy. Papers from the southern states were smuggled to her for translation into French and forwarded by ship to the French government.[6] Lillie herself traveled to Paris and became a favorite of Empress Eugenie, who insisted she be included in social events there, much to the disgust of the American consul, a Yankee. As a young woman Lillie spent her summers at White Sulphur Springs, where she found a friendly reception from the locals. William Boggs dined with her at her home. Her friend and biographer, Floride Green, writes that "she helped many a Southerner get away and join the Confederate Army."[7]

John Grigsby, co-leader of the Grigsby-Ide party and a driving force in the Bear Flag revolt, was one whom Firebelle Lillie might have helped. He left Napa County during the War and never came back. Captain Grigsby left behind a healthy number of relatives to carry on the family name.

Lillie and her family came so frequently to St. Helena that her

---

[4]Floride Green, *Some Personal Recollections of Lillie Hitchcock Coit,* Grabhorn Press, SF, 1935, p. 3.

[5] At first her parents sent her to the Napa Valley as punishment for chasing fire trucks, but it eventually occurred to them that exile to St. Helena was like throwing Br'er Rabbit into the brier patch.

[6]The Confederacy wanted France to help finance the war.

[7] Green, p. 23.

parents finally bought land from Florentine Kellogg and built a house in what is now Bothe State Park. Because the place was secluded, they called it "Lonely." Lonely was a wooden ranch-style home with wings constructed among the redwoods. Lillie secretly married a professional gambler named Howard Coit, to her parents' tremendous displeasure. She was briefly disowned for this characteristically rebellious gesture, but later she and her father reconciled. Her mother, however, could not accept Coit and apparently conducted subterfuges of her own that undermined Lillie's marriage.[8] They divorced.

Lillie built a bungalow in St. Helena on the Napa River where Three Palms Vineyards is today. She named it "Larkmead." It had a wide porch that went all the way around the house, and the interior was divided into four parts by two 20'-wide halls that intersected in the middle. She moved there with her mother, her French maid, her Chinese servants and her hunter. It was the scene of much social activity.

She matured into a large, deep-voiced woman who wore rings on her thumbs and all her fingers and refused to be bullied by anybody.[9] Perhaps to horrify her mother, she was known to don men's clothing, take her four-in-hand and go to the town of St. Helena, where she bellied up to the bar at the local hotel. She drank whiskey, smoked cigars and swore with the boys. A story circulated that she had gone on an overnight camping trip with five men.[10] Most of the stories about Lillie passed through the valley by word of mouth, but occasionally the newspaper tried to report on her doings (however coyly). The *Napa County Reporter*, for example, commented that at "Howard Coit's place a rattlesnake's head was 'bruised' by a lady's heel. After his demise rattles to the number of sixteen were counted

---

[8] Jourdan George Myers, *Tiburcio Parrott, the Man Who Built Miravalle-Falcon Crest*, published by the author, Deer Park, CA, 1987, p. 114.

[9] Lyman, *Memoirs*, p. 129.

[10] Myers, p. 117.

on his continuity."[11]

After Howard Coit died, Lillie discovered that her mother had conspired to wreck their marriage. She went into what appears to have been a deep depression. She stopped going to Larkmead but spent some time at Lonely. Larkmead fell into disrepair and was eventually looted by the locals. A contemporary of Lillie's noted that "Firebelle Lillie's" furniture could be seen in parlors up and down the valley.[12]

The Civil War was difficult for the Napa Valley. Home to whiskey-drinking pioneers as well as wine-sipping Shivs, there was a very strong Southern faction. The pro-Union *Napa County Reporter* was aware of the rebel sentiment and began publishing frightened warnings:

> There are plenty of such men among us who would blush to be detected in aiding such treasonable enterprises, but who would be among the first to drag California into the Jefferson Davis conspiracy if possible. There are plenty of such among us who will bear close watching in times present. The loyal citizens of the State should at once be organized and armed so far as to be able to quell any attempts at rebellion.[13]

An incident at Joe Chiles' place[14] in Rutherford might have helped spark some of the newspaper's anxiety. Someone hoisted a Confederate flag on Chiles' porch. Someone else asked Chiles to remove it, but Chiles said that since he hadn't put it there, he didn't have to remove it. Ben Shurtleff,[15] a Union supporter, called Chiles

---

[11]*NCR*, 8-1-1874

[12]Napa Valley Wine Library, *History of Napa Valley: Interviews and Reminiscences of Long-time Residents,* St. Helena, 1974. p. 200.

[13] 3-21-1863

[14] Joe's place at this time was on acreage he bought from Bartlett Vines in Rutherford.

[15] Dr. Benjamin Shurtleff--actually trained and licensed as a physician back east before arriving in California--made a lot of money gold mining before he came to Napa. He had been a Douglas Democrat before the

a rebel, and some of Chiles' friends knocked Shurtleff down.[16] A few years after the War Chiles moved his family to St. Helena, where Southerners were in abundance. He had two more children--Dixie and Henry Lee--built a home on land now occupied by the Native Sons' Hall and spent the rest of his life raising mules. Part of his home still stands and is used as the St. Helena Baptist church.[17]

Southern sympathizers had less support in Napa City. Union men formed three paramilitary organizations: an 80-man infantry, a cavalry and an artillery unit with two field guns. The groups performed at parades and other public functions. The presence of this armed guard did not, however, reassure the public, and as the War dragged on the fear of secessionists grew stronger. Some people thought that the Confederate Navy would land in San Francisco Bay and claim the state for the Confederacy. Southern privateers regularly cruised the Northwest coast to harass New England whalers. Others worried that England, France or even Russia would grab California while the rest of the nation was occupied with the war. In the spring of 1862 the telegraph to California was interrupted for two weeks, and Napans on both sides waited in silent dread for news. Guards were posted at the armory, ready to sound the Courthouse bell if trouble came.[18]

One night a Napan thought he saw some Copperheads (rebels) in the Yountville area, which abounded with them, engaging in field maneuvers with a large artillery gun. The Napa Guard was mobilized and stood at the ready for an imminent attack. Scouts sent to the "enemy camp" discovered that the gun was nothing more than a large stovepipe laid across the wheels and axle of a wagon.[19]

There never was a rebel insurrection in Napa County, but there

---

Civil War but came to admire and support President Lincoln. He eventually became the first director of the Napa Insane Asylum.

[16]Giffen, p. 91.

[17]Ibid, p. 94.

[18]Gregory, p. 343.

[19]Ibid, p. 344.

could have been. A potentially dangerous plot was aborted in San Francisco when a fast schooner, the *Chapman,* was seized by Union agents. It had aboard two brass cannons, 30 kegs of powder and a stockpile of rifles and pistols. Leather bags found aboard the ship came from a store in Napa City, Treadwell & Company. The *Chapman* incident was part of a large-scale plan involving some 200 men who were planning to cut the telegraph wires in many places between Sacramento and San Francisco and take Napa City. They would then seize the steamboat *Guadalupe* in the Napa River and use it to storm the Navy Yard at Mare Island and the arsenal at Benicia. With the munitions gathered from those places they would continue to Fort Alcatraz and Fort Point, which they would also capture. The *Chapman* would then head out to sea and take the other significant seaports in California, and California would secede from the Union.[20] Paranoid articles in the *Reporter* told of secret secessionist meetings being held all over Napa County by men who were fully armed.[21]

A pro-South newspaper, the *Napa Echo,*[22] was established and published in Napa City until the day Lincoln was assassinated. The *Echo* tried to counter the *Napa County Reporter*'s constant anti-South, anti-Democrat diatribes with jabs of its own. Both editors were named Montgomery, and each assailed the other in their editorials. Each had a different set of advertisers, and it is possible to deduce the probable political leanings of many county business people by the paper in which they advertised. The *Echo* also ran advertisements for magazines and pamphlets from New York, which, like San Francisco, had a solid pro-Confederacy element. There may not have been street addresses in those days, as it identified its office as being "in the Brick Building, Main Street near the Bridge, Up

---

[20]*NCR,* 3-21-1863.

[21]*NCR,* 4-4-1863.

[22] Given the pro-French leanings of the Confederacy, the paper may have taken its name from *Echo de la Pacifique,* the French-language newspaper available in the West at that time.

Stairs." The "Caucasian Shaving Saloon," one of its advertisers, could be found "west side of Main Street near Second."[23]

But while some Napa Valley people were red-hot Copperheads, most Californians rallied to the support of the Union as soon as Sumter fell. Many men dropped their previous party alliances and joined the Union party, whose only platform was the preservation of the Union. A Napa Congressman, Henry Edginton (or Edgerton), spoke eloquently at the state legislature on behalf of the Union party.

Few Napans felt called to go to arms for the nation. One who did was Nathan Coombs. Coombs joined the Union Army and was appointed Captain of the Washington Light Artillery Company in 1863. He paid for the passage back east out of his own pocket. He returned home to Napa, and in 1864 the former Democrat went to the Republican National Convention in Chicago with instructions to help elect Abraham Lincoln for a second term.

Another Napan, Chancellor Hartson, served the Union party from the safety of the California State Senate during the War years. As chairman of the judiciary committee he spearheaded the addition of an amendment to the state constitution outlawing treason, which was defined as open sympathy and support for the South. Hartson caught the eyes and captured the heart of many in his constituency for his get-tough stand. He capitalized on his good press and made a fortune in Napa County in the years to come in banking and in mining. Napans elected him to the State Assembly in 1879 and again in the following election.[24]

There were a few black families living in Napa around the time of the Civil War, but they seemed to have lived segregated from the rest of the community, mainly in a section of Pacific Street. In 1867 a group of African Methodists took over use of the Methodist church when that group built a new structure. When a new school was built for Napa's white children, the old school was sold to the blacks.

Education became important to Napans during the Civil War era.

---

[23] *Napa Echo,* 12-24-1864.

[24] Palmer, p. 478.

Two secondary schools were established in 1860: Napa Ladies' Seminary (near the corner of what are now Oak and Seminary Streets) and Napa Collegiate Institute, a co-ed school run by the Methodist church.

Perhaps inspired by the mayhem of a distant war, the Valley experienced a crime wave. Up at White Sulphur Springs, bandits victimized the old Bear Flagger Peter Storm, who was working as a bath attendant. In Napa City "Black Jack" Bowen captained a band of burglars who entered the home of John Patchett, the county's first serious vineyardist. They drugged Patchett and took off with many of his possessions. They then entered the pillared home of Napa's first major businessman, Thomas Earl, at 1221 Seminary Street, and were later found holed up in the hills behind the present-day Napa State Hospital, where the local artillery held its practice drills.[25]

Other than worrying about possible rebel raiders and chasing outlaws, however, folks in the Napa Valley during the Civil War years had little to entertain them:

> If a prize were to be awarded for the perfection of dullness, we should expect Napa City to be a prominent competitor. There has not been business done enough here in six weeks to break one Sabbath. (The) streets are generally almost deserted, but even if enlivened by the presence of a crowd, the dullness is only aggravated, as no man appears to do anything, or to have anything to do.[26]

There may have been more animals at large than people. A law passed in 1862 "outlawing cattle, mules, horses, goats, and hogs to run at large in the town of Napa City."[27] One consequence of the "perfection of dullness" was the failure of previously thriving Napa enterprises. Among those whose businesses the Goodman Bank foreclosed were pioneers Thomas Earl and William Edginton.[28]

---

[25]Hanrahan, p. 109.

[26] *NCR*, 3-21-1863.

[27] *NCR*, 8-2-1862.

[28]*NCR*, 6-7-1862.

While the good, bored citizens of the Napa Valley were getting married, grinding grain and fighting the Civil War in their own way, Sam Brannan was shrewdly weighing the merits of *Agua Caliente*, the scantily populated area north of St. Helena with the fumaroles and gurgling geysers. An important part of Brannan's formula for success was to combine business specualtion with power politics, while bilking the innocent. His life reveals many examples of this potent chemistry.

At first deemed the darling of the Mormons and Brigham Young's second-in-command, Brannan received tithes of up to 30% from the "saints" he brought over on the *Brooklyn*, with the idea that he money would be forwarded to Salt Lake City.[29] It never was. When the Mormons were afraid they would lose their farm in San Joaquin, he, as their leader, sold it for them-- and kept the proceeds. The Mormons turned away from him, angry and betrayed.

San Francisco's swelling population of gold-seekers greatly exceeded the new city's ability to enforce order. Anarchy reigned. Perhaps feeling flickers of guilt for his mistreatment of the people who had befriended him, Brannan became in 1851 the city's first hero by forming a "Committee of Vigilance," aka the *Vigilantes*, to protect and defend the populace from crooks. The Vigilantes were successful at scaring away some of the most unsavory elements, but their method of "lynch now, ask questions later" resulted in needless deaths. His popularity made him a shoe-in in the election for San Francisco's first City Council.

Seated with him on the Council was Thomas Larkin's personal business manager, Talbot Green, aka Paul Geddes, the embezzling bank clerk from Missouri. William Heath Davis, Nathan Spear's nephew, was also among the council members. Brannan and Green formed a partnership with Oak Knoll's J.W. Osborne to snatch up land in San Francisco at bargain-basement prices, particularly lots

---

[29]Kay Archuleta, *The Brannan Saga*, Illuminations Press, St. Helena, 1977, p. 39.

around the waterfront area.[30] Brannan and Green then sponsored measures to have the areas they bought reclaimed from the Bay with landfill. They even had wharves put up--all at taxpayers' expense. Another measure that this not-so-august body passed was to vote its members a $10,000 pay raise, an outrageous amount in those days. Green/Geddes' duplicitous past came to light when he tried to run for mayor. He was driven, almost literally, out of town.

Brannan entered into another partnership with J.W. Osborne and bought up all the tea in California at an auction. They sold it to the local tea cognoscenti and later to the myriads of Chinese men who streamed into the country to find luck in the gold fields.[31]

Another Napan who partnered with Brannan was James Estill, who represented Napa and Solano in the California State Senate in 1853. Brannan and Estill bought choice properties in Oahu and a sugar plantation on Kauaii and worked on a plan to annex the Islands as part of the United States, with themselves in commanding positions. Needless to say, they ran into opposition from Hawaiian King Kamehameha and were advised by the US to drop it.

Napa's Estill was a rogue in his own right. He gained notoriety for a bill he introduced in the state legislature that was more or less a reprise of Brannan and Green's landfill scam. His idea was to pour landfill into San Francisco Bay and reclaim the land, and then tax San Franciscans for the ground that emerged from the sea. Estill was close friends with then-Governor Bigler, and with his influence the bill nearly passed.[32] He was also in business with Mariano Vallejo. Estill and Vallejo contracted to house, feed and care for the State's convicts, for a fee. The prisoners provided their keepers with free labor, and they could rent them out. Convicts in California received extremely harsh treatment under Estill and Vallejo: so harsh that the usually

---

[30]Stellman, p. 104.

[31]Ibid, p. 101.

[32] The bill passed the State Assembly but tied in the Senate. The Lieutenant Governor broke the tie with a nay vote.

callous public actually complained.[33] When their contract expired in 1855 the legislature voted not to renew it. Estill was awarded the contract again, however, the next year.

Sam Brannan sailed back east and lobbied heavily for Senator William Gwin's Land Reform Act. The moment it passed he went to New York and convinced several banks to invest in his San Francisco properties, since he knew the titles he wanted would be secure. The banks gave him large sums at low interest rates. When he returned to San Francisco he was dinged with a bill for $6,370 in back taxes.[34] He refused to pay. What he did instead was use the banks' money to lend at the then-usurious rate of 12%. He also purchased land at ridiculously low prices from claimants who thought their titles were in peril. When word of the passage of Gwin's Land Reform Act hit the area he sold the pieces at high prices.[35]

Like Bale, Sam Brannan longed to be recognized as a Real Somebody, and his secret wish was to be accepted by "The Chivalry." He kept a servant and dressed in the cream-colored suits favored by Southern men.[36] Perhaps to attract the attention of Lillie Hitchcock and her circle, he sent away to Boston for an elaborate, fully outfitted fire engine. In partnership with another noted Southern blue blood, sometime Napan Volney Howard, he and several other "Shivs" founded a bank that issued private currency, "shinplasters," which had the effect of reducing by a third the value of everyone else's gold. Outwardly, however, Brannan passed himself off as a Union sympathizer--the politic thing to do. In reality, Brannan may have lacked the depth to grasp the nature of the issues in the Civil War.

Many people saw through him. As early as 1850, the Norwegian

---

[33]Bancroft, *Interpocula*, p.415.

[34]William H. Heintz, *San Francisco Mayors, 1850-1880*, Gilbert Richards Publications, Woodside, CA, 1975, p. 39.

[35]Archuleta, p. 39.

[36] He hedged his bets by contributing to the Union effort. This dampened his appeal to the largely southern aristocracy. Naming the main street of Calistoga "Lincoln" didn't help, either.

sailor/handyman Peter Storm stole one of Brannan's white dress shirts, upon which Storm painted a replica of the Bear Flag. Brannan, who could afford as many white shirts as he wanted, was furious. Later, when he had bought up acreage at the head of the Napa Valley, his pure-blooded merino sheep trampled his neighbors' fields. His cavalier reply to their complaints was "fence your farms."[37] A group of up-valley men murdered the shepherd[38] and drove the sheep over a cliff, killing them all. Brannan personally saw to it that a large group of young men were arrested for the crimes; but after a long trial, they were all acquitted.[39] His bad press with the people he felt did not count--the local citizenry and his wife and family--would prove to be, in the end, his undoing.

One man who may not have seen through Sam Brannan was Matthew Ritchie, who for several years was an associate judge in the Napa court. Brannan was his frequent guest.[40]

Fabulously wealthy by the standards of his time, Brannan toured Europe with his wife and children several times and eventually left his family there. During his European trips he spent time at the spas, which were very fashionable. Alert to the success of White Sulphur Springs, he decided to create a spa himself: a wonderland and mini sovereignty, where he could host the rich and famous and live the life of a European nobleman. The location of his spa would be among the *aguas calientes* at the foot of Mount St. Helena.

He found a consort with whom to share this dream, an actress who was a phony as he was. Lola Montez claimed to be a Bavarian baroness. She had already seduced some of the most powerful and gifted men of Brannan's day, among them Franz Liszt, Alexander Dumas and William Gwin.[41] Brannan was suitably impressed.

It took several years for Brannan to acquire the property that

---

[37]Archuleta, p. 42.

[38]Stellman, p. 173

[39]Hutchinson, p. 11.

[40]Stellman, p. 168.

[41]Ibid, p. 143.

became Calistoga. Some of it he won in lawsuits, but most of it he bought. The results of a Sheriff's Sale of land, signed by "J. S. Stark, Sheriff" were recorded in the *Napa County Record* in terms that referred to boulders and big trees as boundary markers. Besides this piece, Brannan purchased 1,000 acres from Matthew Ritchie for $10,000 in April of 1857 and additional land from Henry Edgerton (1859), Jose Santos Berryessa (1862) and Henry Fowler (1863).[42] Buying and building the resort cost him more than $500,000.

Although his Hot Springs Hotel opened for business in 1860, the resort itself staged its gala debut in 1862. Dandies from San Francisco and VIPs from all over chartered a steamer to Suscol, where they were met by coaches that bore them up the valley. While hosting one of his many inaugural parties, the alcohol-enhanced Brannan attempted to toast the new "Saratoga of California" and came out instead with the "Calistoga of Sarafornia." It was "Calistoga" from then on.

Calistoga was a kind of 19th Century up-scale theme park. While elsewhere in the United States a war was raging, travelers to Brannan's resort were greeted with sights of broad avenues graciously lined with shade trees and manicured gardens. There was a large general store, a swimming pool, a goldfish pond and a telegraph office. There were stables and a race track. Fanciful structures like a petrified wood fence and a "Druid Temple" dotted the grounds. In time Brannan added a brandy distillery operated by the Donner Party's Louis Keseberg, "The Cannibal of the Sierras;" a tea plantation and a grove of mulberries for the raising of silkworms. (The latter two experiments were funded by the California Department of Agriculture. They failed.)

A few entrepreneurs saw merit in starting businesses of their own in the "Calistoga of Sarafornia," unrelated to Brannan's enterprise. Woodward's grocery store and post office was the first independent establishment, followed by a general store and a saloon. G.B. Clifford established the Lodi Stables, named for Nathan Coombs' prize-

---

[42]Auchuleta, p. 40.

winning horse. Leonard G. Lillie, an early owner of White Sulphur Springs and millwright at the Bale Mill, built a home there, and Augustus Palmer became the town's first judge.[43]

Brannan believed that San Francisco would provide most of the patronage for his resort. He needed the cooperation of certain key people in Napa County in order to facilitate travel to his lovely but remote location. His first partner toward this end was Nathan Coombs. Coombs' horses powered the stage coach line, and Brannan joined him in the enterprise.[44] Passengers disembarking from the steamboats at the tiny but developing hamlet of Suscol would be met by Coombs and Brannan's six-in-hands: coaches drawn by six horses. They could rest and dine at the new Suscol House hotel (which in later days may have seen service as a brothel) or head directly up the valley. In addition to his usefulness as master of the connecting link between the steamboat landing and Calistoga, Coombs appealed to Brannan for political reasons, too. Coombs was elected to the State Senate as a Democrat and served from 1854-58, after which he ran for and won a position in the State Assembly. The perceptive Coombs probably saw the serpent in Brannan. After the stage line he managed to avoid further links with him.

Stage coaches were hot, dusty and uncomfortable. Brannan soon lobbied for something more modern--a railroad. If the citizens of Napa County could be persuaded to finance a steel trail to his front door, Brannan felt, all the better. After all, San Franciscans had paid for piers and landfill on his waterfront property.

In 1863 a group of San Franciscans teamed up, presumably under Brannan's direction, to build a railroad from Vallejo to Calistoga. The idea never got off the ground, perhaps due to the cost of the venture.[45] Shortly afterward Brannan persuaded the new State Senator

---

[43]Hanrahan, p. 40.

[44] Palmer, p. 95.

[45] John Wichels, "Railroads in Napa County: Why They Came and Why They Failed," Napa County Historical Society, Series 2, Number 3, p. 2.

from Napa, Chancellor Hartson, to introduce before the state legislature a bill authorizing Napa County supervisors to issue bonds for a railroad. A sum of $225,000 was proposed for a line to be laid between Suscol and Napa City. Napa County voters approved it in a special election.[46] The original Board of Directors consisted of Hartson himself, John Lawley, Charles Mayne, Alfred Cohen, James Goodman and a former Liverpudlian named A.Y. Easterby, who owned several Napa City businesses and served as president of the Railroad's board. The project came in well under cost (about $100,000). The first engine, suggestively called the *Calistoga*, pulled its cars into Napa on July 10, 1865 amidst great fanfare culminating in a banquet at the Revere House hotel, owned by Easterby.[47]

Brannan and Hartson were probably amazed and certainly disappointed to find that the people of Napa Valley were not interested in extending the line to the resort. Two special elections were held seeking a bond issue for their project, but it was soundly defeated both times. The Railroad Board then sued the County Board of Supervisors to release the monies that were left over from the Suscol-Napa City line. The Railroad won the first round of the suit in the lower court, but the Board of Supervisors appealed, and the California Supreme Court sided with the Supervisors.[48] Construction of the Napa Valley Railroad to Calistoga went on anyway, with hefty contributions from private individuals,[49] and in 1868 the 26.5 mile

---

[46]Ibid, p. 4.

[47]Ibid, p. 8.

[48] In February of 1866 County voters struck down a proposition to underwrite $5000 per mile from Napa to Calistoga, 892 to 415. The second election, on whether to donate to the Railroad the interest from the money not used in the initial bond issue, was held in September, and the measure was voted down 243 to 241. Clearly the public was not impressed with the Railroad.

[49] The original subscribers to the Railroad's stock were Charles Mayne, Alfred Cohen, Chancellor Hartson, Sam Brannan, W.R. Garrison, R.B. Woodward, H. Barriolet, Sven Alstrom, C.F. Lott, George Yount, James Graves, Thomas Knight, John Lawley, Smith

route from Napa City to Calistoga was completed.

That same year the state legislature passed a special act requiring Napa County to issue bonds for $30,000 to reimburse the local magnates who had paid for the line, and the people of Napa County were taxed--against their will and against their vote--for Brannan's iron carpet.[50] Some chroniclers of the time seemed mystified as to how this happened. Chancellor Hartson went down in local history as the emblem of probity and was not publicly suspected of harboring conflicts of interest. This adulation continued unabated even when, in 1876, the railroad's track was re-routed a few hundred yards to the west to pass over commercially important land that happened to be owned by Hartson and his friends William Chapman and the now rich Bear Flagger, William Fowler.[51]

Few people, however, actually prospered from the NVRR, and some suffered real hardships. Henry Boggs, son of Lilburn Boggs, was ordered by the court to convey a portion of his Yountville farmland to the Railroad so that the train could have a right of way through his property. He received $87.60 for this.[52] The Railroad cut in half the 90 acres of his neighbor, Thomas Fawver, and made sure he and his livestock couldn't cross from one side to the other by setting up fences along the tracks. Charlie Hopper remained on good terms with the magnates of the NVRR by quit-claiming a portion of his property to them.[53]

In 1866 the final link of the Napa Valley Railroad was laid down from Suscol to connect with the California Pacific Railroad at a little south county watering-place called Adelante, which thereafter was called "Napa Junction." Rendered somewhat redundant, the river town of Suscol fell into a decline. Perhaps to help rescue it, a local bill

---

Brown, A.Y. Easterby, J.H. Goodman, J.J. Lamdin, and Edward Stanly. Not all the subscribers were locals.

[50]Gregory, p. 146.

[51]Wichels, "Railroads," p. 6.

[52]Ibid, p. 10.

[53]Idem.

was passed allowing the Napa Wood Company to build a new, upgraded wharf there and collect tolls. But the Napa Valley was now part of the great steel network that connected just about everywhere with just about everywhere else in America.

The big black engines needed wood to burn and heat the water that made the steam that ran them. Whole forests were felled on the hillsides, and log piles lined the train tracks near the stations. Eucalyptus trees were imported from Australia, both for use as fuel and as ties.[54]

The train made scheduled stops, but it could be flagged down easily. There were several covered depots and other open-air platforms from which the train could be, sometimes rather literally, caught. After boarding the train at Suscol one could get off at Thompson Station (Thompson's Gardens) or at the depot in Napa on the road to Suscol just north of Fourth Street. The next stop was West Napa (aka the Union depot) on California Street. Traveling up the valley, there were depots and landings at Oak Knoll, Trubody's, Yountville, Oakville, Rutherford, Zinfandel (aka Bello and Pine Station), Thomann's winery, St. Helena, Krug's winery (aka Barro), Nash's Walnut Grove and Calistoga.

Calistoga was the jumping-off point for Billy Spiers' stage line, which ran up into Lake County via the Lawley Toll Road. The breakneck stage road would have provided the perfect backdrop for an old-time Western movie, and the stage coaches were, in fact, bothered by bandits from time to time. Clark Foss was the best known of Spiers' drivers. Stages left the railroad depot for the Oat Hill and Great Western mines, and the mining communities of Lakeport, Lower Lake, Sulphur Bank, Harbin Hot Springs, the Geysers and Kellogg, all in Lake County after the division in 1861. Mollie Lawley Patten sold the tickets at a toll house partway up Mt.

---

[54] As it turned out, they were a poor choice for fuel and railroad ties, but they continued to make moderately good windbreaks.

Partiers in Calistoga get ready to rumble.

A woman bicycles her way down Lincoln Avenue.

Rugged Lawley's Toll Road invited bandits.

Travelers bought their tickets at the Toll House.

St. Helena. They were expensive for their day.[55]

The toll road was an engineering feat built by an enterprising Napan, John Lawley, who also had an interest in the NVRR. Like the Goodman brothers, Lawley had a hand in most of the important business affairs in 19th century Napa County. He was part-owner of the lumberyard where Napa City built its original courthouse. In 1854 he opened Napa City's second grain storage facility, in competition with John Trubody. When the Berryessas went bankrupt trying to defend *Las Putas* against squatters, he bought 26,000 acres from them at $4 an acre, some of which he then subdivided and sold at a profit. He planted grain in the portion he retained and improved the road to facilitate its transport to his granary. He was the president of the Napa Valley Telegraph Company during the Civil War,[56] and a part-owner of the Phoenix quicksilver mine in Pope Valley.[57]

But the Napa Valley Railroad did not make the money its backers had hoped for. People in the Valley did not use it, and four months after its glorious completion it went into debt and then foreclosure.[58] The construction company to whom its unpaid bills were due was under contract with the California Pacific Railroad. The construction company sold the NVRR to California Pacific. Now, oddly, the NVRR did begin to prosper, and the decline that had begun in the town of Suscol took a steady turn for the worse. California Pacific sold the line to Southern Pacific in the 1870's. In the final analysis, it was the bigger fish like the Southern Pacific and California Pacific who came out the winners on the railroad. Little minnows like local investors and the taxpayers of Napa County ended up footing the bill.

In the early 1880's John Grigsby's brother Terrell tried to mimic

---

[55]See Ken Stanton, *Mount St. Helena & R.L. Stevenson State Park,* Illuminations Press, Calistoga, 1993.

[56]*NCR*, 5-16-1863.

[57]Stanton, pp. 44-45.

[58]Wichels, "Railroads," p. 6.

the railroad magnates and broke ground for a narrow gauge line that would go through Chiles and Pope Valleys out to Lake County. Naive about the chemistry of influencing legislation, he attempted to foot the bill himself. He went broke and the railroad was never built, although the County later used part of the route he had graded for a road.[59]

Despite its railroad connection and all its lavish appurtenances, Calistoga Hot Springs did not catch on with genteel San Franciscans, and Brannan was never welcomed into The Chivalry. White Sulphur Springs and, later, Aetna Springs and Napa Soda Springs attracted that group, while Calistoga was popular with what was often called the "sporting crowd"--an element with plenty of money but not necessarily the same level of respectability. This was probably the result of the character of Brannan himself. After bilking the Mormons, fleecing the gold miners and adding considerably to the general lawlessness of San Francisco with his Vigilantes, his publicly flaunted affair with Lola Montez was too much. Financial sleaziness was not especially condemned in Brannan's day, but publically flaunted sexual indiscretion was, and his wife Lisa divorced him.

The divorce sent him into a tailspin. He crash-landed in a scene that must have been reminiscent of his old Vigilante days. He had leased a small house to a man named Andy Snyder, who failed to pay his rent. Pumped up with alcohol and bad judgment, Brannan decided to confront Snyder. He gathered a small group of men and marched on Snyder's house. Snyder and two others fired on Brannan and his men, and when Brannan turned to run, Snyder shot him in the back. He survived but had to use a cane after that.

More than his spine, however, had been damaged. He began losing major parts of his dream. Lola left. He leased out his Hot Springs Resort to a real estate developer, George Schonewald, who had promoted the Del Monte holdings in Monterey. Calistoga suffered, too: Its school had to shut down in 1879 due to lack of funds. Brannan abandoned Calistoga, never to return, and died of a heart

---

[59] Chancellor Hartson and a partner considered building a line to Monticello over the same route but decided against it.

attack while on a cruise ship off the coast of Mexico around 1880. With him may have gone much of what was truly colorful about 19th Century Calistoga. A reporter for the young *Napa Register* put it this way:

> Reaching Calistoga in due time (that is, railroad time), that quiet burg was found nestling as usual among the picturesque hills and mountains which environ it. It nestled all the afternoon; and it was still nestling at 5 o'clock when I left.[60]

The distribution of wealth in the Napa Valley fluctuated wildly throughout the 19th Century. Established Californios like the Vallejos and Jacob Leese lost their holdings to lawyers and squatters; dreamers like Sam Brannan and Terrell Grigsby saw fortunes slip away. Lucky pioneers like the Yorks, Hudsons and Fowlers and others who shepherded their resources lived well. The imprudent-- Granville Swift and the Kelseys, for example--went broke. Honest businessmen like Nathan Coombs, George Cornwell and the Thompsons enjoyed a modest prosperity that coincided with the general well-being of the community. No one was as rich as they wanted to be.

Dreams of unlimited wealth prompted the Napa Valley "Gold and Silver Rush" of 1857. Someone had found metal on the flanks of Mt. St. Helena and brought it to the most educated person he knew, a Napa dentist named W.W. Stillwagon. Stillwagon sent the sample to an assayer in San Francisco, and the assayer pronounced it rich in gold and silver. Word spread very quickly, and soon Mt. St. Helena was crawling with prospectors, one of whom found another interesting rock and brought it, too, to Stillwagon. This piece was cinnabar.

Both the *Napa County Reporter* and the *St. Helena Star* were guilty

---

[60] *Napa Register*, 6-17-76. In fairness to Calistoga, it should be pointed out that the *Register* was at that time jingoistic about Napa City being the pre-eminent town in the county. It reported little about the grape harvest, which was already important at that time, and referred only to grain as "the crop."

of leaping to sensationalist conclusions about people striking it rich. It started up again in February, 1861 when the *NCR* reported that J. Bell and Charles Barrows of Conn Valley found "fine specimens of shot and scale gold...on the surface and down four and five feet from the surface." Once more, prospectors scoured the hills of Napa County.

It was not until 1872 that a real, richly bearing silver mine was found. The claimant for the "Calistoga Gold and Silver Mine" was Sam Brannan's nephew, Alexander Badlam, whose daytime job was managing Brannan's Hot Springs resort and working at Brannan's bank. He received the patent for a section on the southeast side of Mt. St. Helena he called the "Monitor Ledge." A booming mining town appeared around it almost instantly, named "Borlandville," after the new mine's president, Archie Borland. The mine and its boomtown were soon bestowed a far more glamorous name: "Silverado," immortalized a few years later by the writer Robert Louis Stevenson. Archie Borland's miners erected a stamp mill in 1874 to assist in recovering the ore, but just when it looked as if Silverado might rival the Comstock, the vein disappeared, and the men were unable to relocate it. After a year of fruitless search the mine and the instant town that supported it were abandoned.[61]

The Monitor proved to be just one of three ore-bearing ledges. The local newspapers reported silver strikes everywhere. An 1874 issue of the *St. Helena Star* told of David Hudson striking it rich near the Napa/Lake County boundary. The principals of the "Uella" Mine that resulted were David Hudson, Rodney Hudson, Egbert Hudson, William McCormick, W.T. Whitton, N.P. Banks and David Brown. The Langley and Bourn Mine was another enthusiastically greeted mining operation, conveniently located almost within the city limits of St. Helena in the hills behind White Sulphur Springs resort. It might also have been known as the "Esther" mine. One hundred fifty men were employed there. They worked two 10-hour shifts and dug a tunnel 110' long, but the mine turned out to be rich in iron, not

---

[61]Anne Issler, "Silverado," *First Annual Report of the Napa County Historical Society*, May, 1949, p. 4.

silver.[62]

The best of the silver troves was the Palisades Mine, located just north of Calistoga. The Palisades yielded nearly $2,000,000 in silver, gold, copper and lead. But silver mining, although more romantic, never came close to realizing the profit that was made in cinnabar. The blood-red mineral, also called "quicksilver" or "mercury," was in great demand in the mining industry because of its use in recovering other precious metals. The precious metals leave whatever other minerals they are associated with and cling to quicksilver. When the quicksilver is boiled away the gold or silver remains. Miners also used cinnabar in the manufacture of the caps they exploded to blow away boulders. Ship builders added cinnabar to the paint they used on ship bottoms as extra protection against marine wear. Scientists called it "mercury" and used it in pressure-sensitive instruments, and lighthouse engineers learned that they could float the revolving lenses of their beacons in it.[63]

Bill McDonnell, husband of Donner party survivor Ellen Graves, was credited with bringing the first marketable quantity of cinnabar to Napa. According to the *Napa County Reporter* (2-16-1861) the 50-lb mass "was retorted... in an old kettle, merely for experiment."

For almost half a century (1863 thru 1903) Napa County was California's second-largest producer. The most prolific lodes were in a band that ran from Berryessa to Calistoga, where rocks that were laid down beneath the sea during the time of the dinosaurs were punctured by volcanic material of a more recent period. One of the biggest was the Phoenix Mine in Pope Valley, discovered by John Newman in 1861 after a fire swept through the hills and cleared the underbrush.[64] Sixteen Napa and St. Helena businessmen teamed up to prospect for more of the dark red ore, and by the 1870's 45 men,

---

[62]Sheffer, p. 5.

[63]Walter Bradley, "Quicksilver Resources of California," *California State Mining Bulletin #78*, Sacramento, 1918, p. 9.

[64]Y.M. Hardin, "Early History of Pope Valley," unpublished, undated manuscript, p. 2.

among them many Chinese laborers, were drawing out the red rock. Four other mines were dug nearby--the Silver Bow, Red Hill, Starr, Pope and Washington. George Fellows discovered yet another quicksilver trove, but this one, the Aetna Springs mine--kept filling with hot water and had to be closed down. Chancellor Hartson turned it into a hot springs resort in 1877. In 1890 a San Franciscan, Len Owens, bought the place and invited his friend, the architect Bernard Maybeck, to design some of the resort's structures. Owens put in a golf course, reputed to be the first in California. Grover Cleveland, the first Presidential golfer, played there.

The Pope Valley mines made profits for some of their shareholders, but they were small compared with others in the county. The Oat Hill mine near the Lake County boundary was a good money maker, yielding about $5,000,000 over a period of 40 years.[65] The richest of the mines was the Redington, which brought in $17,000,000 worth of cinnabar.[66] Originally called the X.L.C.R., this proved to be one of the largest producers in the state. It was found more or less by accident in 1860, when a group of Napans were scouring the area in search of silver. The original trustees leased their interests to a mining firm named Knox & Osborn, and the town that flourished around it became known as Knoxville. Quicksilver deposits were also found near Oakville, where the mineral often occurred near the surface mixed with yellow clay. The Bella and the Union were two of the mines in the hills west of Oakville.

Many familiar names show up among the teams of men who searched for the red rocks: Billy Baldridge, Jesse Barnett and Henry Fowler; Reasin Tucker and John Stark; George Cornwell, R.T. Montgomery, W.W. Stillwagon, George Goodman and A.Y. Easterby were among those who found cinnabar worth mining. The real money was to be made not in locating the ore, however, but in becoming a trustee of the group that organized to run the mine. This corporate model was different from the way things were done during

---

[65]Bradley, p. 76.

[66]Idem.

Quicksilver miners in Knoxville at work in the carpenter shop, above, and at the furnace, below. The smoke was toxic, and the mines were extremely dangerous.

President Grover Cleveland was among the many who golfed, dined and relaxed at Pope Valley's Aetna Springs. The dining room and social hall still stand at the turn of the 21st Century.

the Gold Rush, when men like York and Hudson partnered up to find what they could behind rocks and in their sluices. The trustees of the Phoenix Mine in 1872, for example, were Napans whose ventures in quicksilver helped consolidate their wealth: John Lawley, Chancellor Hartson, C.B. Seeley, J.F. Lamdin, George Fellows and Robert Crouch.The dentist Stillwagon was the principal partner of two mines in Pope Valley. Many of the elegant Victorian homes in Napa were built with profits from mining, and some of them still stand. George Goodman was able to build a mansion for his family at 1120 Oak Street in 1872. The austere-looking Italianate house at 833 Franklin St. belonged to Robert Sterling, a mining partner who went on to become a director of what was then called the Napa State Asylum.

The mineral resource that provided the most visible and enduring yield for residents of Napa County was neither the silver nor the cinnabar, but the superior, fine-grained volcanic rock that occurs throughout the region. Of all the forces in nature, volcanism has impacted Napa Valley the most dramatically. The surrounding hills and mountains are often referred to as the "Sonoma Volcanics." Volcanic rock resists erosion particularly well; it remains long after stones of other types have broken down, turned to sand and soil and washed away. Volcanic debris therefore tends to lie on or near the surface.

For the most part, Napa County's hills and mountains rose during a phase in earth's history that occurred between 50 and 20 million years ago. The valley floor was still mostly underwater then, but volcanic islands punctuated the shallow seas in places. Mt. Veeder, near the Sonoma county line parallel to Oakville, is a remnant of that age.[67]

Volcanic forces blasted and flowed and created what must have been at times a hellish environment. One pyroclastic event, for example, spewed fireballs so hot they melted the ground they landed on, forming the Wappos' weapon mine, Glass Mountain. The

---

[67]Laurie Marcus, "Creation," *Late Harvest*, p. 5.

nodules of rock that the fireballs formed are a black obsidian known as "bottle rock."

By about 2 million years ago, most of the islands had eroded away. Volcanic activity gradually abated, and the Napa Valley dropped down along a line that ran parallel to the mountains on its eastern boundary. The Valley emptied of water as the Ice Age froze the Sierra Nevada's liquid assets, and the land rose a little, both from lack of hydraulic pressure and continuing tectonic activity. Volcanic energy geared up again briefly. An eruption somewhere near Mount St. Helena caused an avalanche of mud and ash that swallowed a redwood forest and all the flora and fauna in it. "Petrified Forest" just west of Calistoga was rediscovered a million years later by a human--something that didn't even exist when the trees were alive. During the Ice Age, rapid uplifts and landslides molded the Napa Valley into its present contours.

Remnants from many epochs in the earth's long history exist in various parts of Napa County. In Chiles Valley and under Lake Berryessa, for example, the soil features quantities of sandstone and shale that are as much as 300,000,000 years old. There might have been significant deposits of oil in those regions had the strata not undergone such damage in the continent's drift to the present.

There are large deposits of limestone around St. Helena. Limestone is calcium carbonate that is precipitated as aquatic organisms dissolve. Given enough pressure it could turn to marble in an eon or two, but for now some of the limestone deposits find use as caves for the storage of wine. Limestone often occurs near soil that is adobe: hardpan clay with poor drainage that is brick in summer and slimy mud when it rains.

Spring and Diamond Mountains between St. Helena and Calistoga have outcroppings of ancient rock folded together with "recently" deposited volcanic matter, as if a giant eggbeater had spun through the hillsides. Geologic forces have been extremely active there.

Families from northern Italy and the Italian part of Switzerland emigrated to the Napa Valley in relatively large numbers between 1860 and 1910, where plenty of work was available for quarrymen and stonemasons. They were accustomed to working with rock; it was a primary building material in their Alpine homeland. Volcanic rock on the surface is pitted and discolored by contact with the elements. Like the cheese from their native countries, it hardened upon contact with the atmosphere. Beneath the earth, however, the quarrymen found Napa County lava to be smooth and soft enough to cut with a saw or an axe. Whether in solid masses on the hillsides, in hardened floes of consolidated ash or in clumps of boulders in the valley, it was tough enough for heavy construction, yet so beautiful it could be used in the interior of elegant homes.

The quarrymen discovered that Napa County's volcanic rock varies in color from the blue of basalt to the creamy white of rhyolite, depending on the minerals with which the lava interacted when it was molten. They also found red, gray and brown volcanic rock, all of it finely grained.

The rocks of many of the bridges in Napa County were quarried from the same deposits as many of the wineries and other buildings in the area. The reddish rocks that built the "Hunt Block" at 1302-4 Main Street in St. Helena, for example, all came from a quarry two miles north of town on Sanitarium Road.[57] The rocks forming old St. Helena High School--now Vintage Hall--were born at the Moffat Quarry near the reservoir on Spring Mountain Road. Napa City's Brown Street Bridge, which kept getting washed away when it was built of wood, was finally made permanent with rock hewn at Wing's Quarry four miles northeast of Napa. The rocks from that site also went into the creation of four other bridges in Napa County. In all, almost 100 stone bridges were built in Napa and its adjacent valleys, many of them by Wing and a partner, a Scot named R.H. Pithie.[58]

The largest quarry of all is still in operation: 500 or more acres on Vallejo's old Rancho Nacional Suscol, about two miles south of Napa. The basalt rock that is quarried there was once the cone of a

---

[57]Hanrahan, p. 6.
[58]Ibid., p. 85.

submarine volcano. The Basalt Company[59] was the first to derive large profits from this huge deposit.

In many instances the stone structures that stand ivy-covered in the side valleys of Napa County were really just barns and family storage cellars; the fact that they were made of stone gives them an appearance more stately than their actual use might suggest. The stone buildings on Railroad Avenue and Church Street in St. Helena attest to this. 1215 Church Street was nothing more than a bonded warehouse built by the local Wine Association in 1878. 1345-47 Railroad Avenue, which has housed numerous restaurants over the years, was originally a foundry that specialized in making presses and other wine-related machinery.

Rock that stood in the path of natural springs found itself ground into gravel. Much of the gravel that once lined the bed of Sulphur Creek in St. Helena was scooped up and poured into the mud of Napa City to form the foundation of its street system. In turn, the gravel that once formed the bed of the Napa River was dredged out and sold to builders in the Bay Area, spoiling the River's natural clarity forever.

Mining was hard. Cinnabar mining was exceedingly unpleasant and especially dangerous. The mines were hot, and cave-ins could occur, as could death or injury from errant explosives. The fumes from processing it were toxic and attacked tooth enamel. The Swiss and Northern Italians avoided such work. With the supply of natives increasingly diminished, the mine owners looked to a new pool of laborers to do the dirty work: the Chinese.

Sam Brannan made a point of getting word to the Chinese that a fortune was waiting in the hills of California. His motive was strictly business: The greater the population, the more money he stood to make. With its history of famine, flood and economic uncertainty, China was in some ways analogous to the American midwest, and for many, both were excellent places to leave. Chinese men came to California in tremendous numbers and drank Brannan's tea. Most of

---

[59]now Syar Corporation.

them came from the Canton area.

Like the overland pioneers, it was the first to arrive who saw the most success. Also like the pioneers, the most powerful and best educated didn't bother with mining at all, but set themselves up in San Francisco as businessmen. One of their primary endeavors was to organize future emigrations. The "Chinese Six Companies," a select committee formed from six districts in China, established itself in the heart of San Francisco and controlled the lives of nearly every Chinese man, woman and child who came to California for decades.

A Chinese man who wanted to try his luck in the "Flowery Country" (China's nickname for the Golden State) contacted the appropriate representative from one of the Six Companies in Hong Kong or Canton and would usually agree to an "assisted passage" arrangement. This meant he gave personal collateral of $40 in return for sponsorship by the company and could thereby travel to California, probably on one of the ships of the Pacific Mail Steamship Company, owned in part by William Gwin.[60] He contracted to work one year for the sponsoring Chinese company, turning over whatever profits he made. After that his company would return him to China as a failure, with nothing to show for his year. Or, he could stay on and try to make it on his own. Either way he always maintained an affiliation with his company and continued as a dues-paying member all his life.[61] Eventually he would return to China. If he died in America, the company would agree to ship back his bones, as it was inconceivable for a Chinese man's bones to rest anywhere but in China. It didn't matter much to most Chinese where the bones of their dead women rested; there was philosophical debate among Chinese scholars as to whether women even had souls.

Sometimes the hopeful miner didn't have the $40 collateral, so he was free to mortgage his wife or children to the company. The company could sell the mortgage on his family members, but this did

---

[60] Alexander McLeod, *Pigtails and Gold Dust*, Caxton Printers, Coldwell, ID, 1947, p.8.

[61] Ibid, p. 77.

not mean that they were actually slaves.[62] Slave trading was engaged in by the companies, however, in the form of young women who were utilized as sex objects by those who could afford them. It happened to be a feature of the Chinese society that women had no rights whatsoever,[63] and the presence of the Six Companies allowed the Chinese to transplant their culture more or less intact.

The American 49ers regarded the Chinese men with immediate contempt. They were all that the ethnocentric, rough-and-ready Americans hated: foreign, not particularly good with a gun, not Protestant, polygamous and different looking. Even their manner of dress seemed odd. It was the custom among Chinese men to shave the front part of their heads and arrange the back of their hair in a queue, or pigtail, which the men wore as a badge of honor. They dressed alike in dark, loose-fitting blouses and matching pants that came above the ankle. Accustomed to wearing slippers or sandals and not leather shoes, they often bought boots that were several sizes too big.[64] They shaded themselves from the hot sun by working under conical hats made of straw or split bamboo. They drank tea and ate rice shipped in from China. They had a cultural more of walking single file wherever they went,[65] and rather than laying claim to their portion in life as "rugged individuals," they were communal in their approach--group members who found some safety, perhaps, in banding as strangers in a strange land.

By 1852 more than 18,000 Chinese men had come to California, some to farm or work in San Francisco, but most to pan for gold.[66] The Americans attempted to drive them out with force, at times succeeding. Their numbers had nearly doubled by 1860, however, and grew steadily throughout most of the Victorian period, despite discriminatory laws intended to harass them.

---

[62]Ibid, p. 174.

[63]Idem.

[64]Ibid, p. 45.

[65]Ibid, p. 29.

[66]Ibid, p. 63.

California State Legislators made themselves popular with their constituencies by passing laws legalizing discrimination against the Chinese. The California legislature of 1850 saw them as a good resource for funds and levied the "Foreign Miner's Tax of 1850," which charged a tax of $20 per month for each foreign-born man who wanted to work the placer mines.[67] The only "foreigners" who had to succumb to this sting were Chinese and Mexicans (the latter, of course, being less foreign to the soil than the Americans who taxed them). A pre-existing statute that forbade blacks and native Americans from testifying against whites in court proceedings was modified to include the Chinese.[68] Thus they had no way to defend themselves within the legal system. In 1858 the legislature voted to make it illegal for any Chinese or Mongolian to enter the state unless driven ashore by foul weather or unavoidable accident. The law provided for a heavy fine and imprisonment but was disregarded. It was followed, however, by laws written at the federal level to specifically exclude Chinese immigrants and to deny Chinese the right to become United States citizens.

As the rivers became stingier with gold and the Americans more formidable in their resistance, the Chinese moved to other pursuits. The building of the transcontinental railroad provided employment for many. In the fall of 1865 there were 3,000 Chinese men on Central Pacific's payroll, and when the railroad was completed in May of 1869 there were 11,000. Four-fifths of the CP's employment roster were Orientals.

Chinese men came to the Napa Valley to work in the quicksilver mines, help lay the Napa Valley Railroad and labor in the vineyards and wine storing caves that were being developed by another immigrant group, the Germans. Of a total of 5,521 American citizens living in Napa County in 1860, only 17 were Chinese, virtually all of them employed as domestics. Ten years later there were 263, many of these involved in agriculture. By 1880 the number of Chinese

---

[67]Idem.

[68]Ibid, p. 62.

documented as living in Napa County had grown to 905 out of a total population of 13,235.[69]

Some of the Chinese laborers set up encampments at the mines. The others congregated in Chinatowns in St. Helena, Calistoga, Rutherford and Napa. Chinatown in St. Helena started on the west side of Main Street on the banks of Sulphur Creek and grew to provide home for as many as 600 Chinese. Guarding the entrance to the town like a smoky dragon, it was the first thing a visitor would see. It was, evidently, an eyesore as well as an odoriferous experience, as described in this hate-mongering article in the *St. Helena Star*:

> Chinatown, with its miserable hovels, crowded with filthy and diseased heathens, its dens of infamy, and its reeking cesspools, is located on Main Street--the first object which attracts the eye of the stranger on entering St. Helena. Its tumble-down and smoke be-grimmed (sic) shanties are in themselves a sight which detracts materially from St. Helena's reputation for neatness and good order and depreciates the value of adjoining properties.[70]

Unmindful of the fact that they themselves, by their ethnocentrism, were contributing to the poverty that the Chinese suffered, the citizens of St. Helena formed an "anti-Coolie league." They named a street for Denis Kearney, who formed the Chinese-hating "Workingman's Party."They shamed the Alameda man who owned the land on which Chinatown was situated into selling it. The buyers were Frank Sciaroni and Felix Salmina, two local Swiss immigrants, who became the slumlords, so to speak, of St. Helena.

The Calistoga press also railed against the Chinese, calling them "the great curse of our state."[71] Two hundred of Calistoga's Chinese

---

[69] Thomas W. Chinn, editor, *A History of the Chinese in California*, Chinese Historical Society of America, San Francisco, 1969, p. 21.

[70] *SHS*, 12-4-1885.

[71] *The Weekly Calistogan*, 4-22-1876. J.H. Upton's newspaper only lasted a couple of years but was resurrected later.

congregated south of Lincoln Avenue, behind the railroad depot.[72] Many others lived at the cinnabar mines in squalid outdoor camps shared with pigs and ducks, potentially tomorrow's meal.[73] Their living environment was actually not too diferent from that of the 49ers in the Sierra foothills. Their social circumstances were very different, however, for while the Caucasian gold-panners were individuals free to boom or bust on their own initiative, the Chinese were at the mercy of their bosses in an acutely hostile culture. Even the native Americans looked down on them.

The Chinatown in Napa began on the tiny isthmus between Napa Creek and the Napa River and spread east. While smaller than St. Helena's or Calistoga's, Napa City's Chinatown may have been more appealing to the locals, because it appeared more orderly: It consisted of neat rows of low wooden buildings separated by a walkway.

The Joss House, actually a Taoist temple, served as the men's spiritual and social center. Napa City's Joss House was two stories tall and featured an impressive altar. Nothing evoked the feeling of their native homeland more than the temple, where the air was pungent with the scent of punk, sandalwood candles and the warm peanut oil that fueled the glass lanterns. Pictures of deities hung on the walls, along with strips of spirit-friendly red paper. Tea and food offerings were always close at hand to satisfy gods both benevolent and maleficent.[74]

The men came as individuals to worship, petition and consult their gods. A gong stood at the entrance. The arriving worshiper struck it to awaken the deity he wished to consult. He approached its statue or picture, lit candles, bowed reverently, spoke its name and burnt money or some other offering that had a prayer inscribed on it, the smoke being a vehicle to convey the words to the spirit world.

---

[72]Narrative of John Ghisolfo, in *History of Napa Valley: Interviews and Reminiscences of Long-time Residents,* Napa Valley Landmarks, Inc., St. Helena, 1974, p. 68.

[73]Goss, p. 66.

[74]McLeod, p. 294.

The deity delivered its answer to the worshiper through wooden blocks or numbered joss sticks. The worshiper dropped the blocks or shook the sticks until one or more fell out. The pattern of the fallen blocks and the numbers on the fallen joss sticks represented the god's response. The priest or deacon who served in the Joss House interpreted the results.[75]

In addition to their membership at the Joss Houses, many men also belonged to secret fraternities that were analogous to Masonic lodges and wore badges indicating their affiliation during public occasions.

The Chinatowns operated as worlds unto themselves. They had their own mercantile stores, herbalists, candle and incense stores and cobblers. The opium pipe repairer also had a little shop of sorts. There was a Chinese band in Napa that wore red uniforms and was ready to perform at funerals and Chinese New Year festivals.

A well-defined class system existed within the communities, probably based on the status the pioneer's family enjoyed or suffered back in Canton. Most emigrants brought with them scrolls delineating their lineage so that they could assume the correct position in California. The most influential man in the large St. Helena settlement was known as "Ginger".

What money the Chinese pioneers did have they often spent in gambling. Three forms of gambling were very popular: fantan games, simple dice games and a daily lottery, all of which were illegal. A fantan game required a large pile of buttons or coins (called chin), a small bowl, and a flat square numbered one through four on each of the four vertical sides. The croupier used the bowl to scoop up a portion of the chin. He then reduced the chin pile by fours, using a chopstick. The object of the game was to guess how many chin would remain at the last reduction. Like in roulette, the better anted up before the scoop, placing his bet in front of the number of his choice. He had a 25% chance of winning, and the house always took

---

[75]Nancy Wey, "A History of Chinese Americans in California,"in *Ethnic Historic Site Survey for California*, Office of Historic Preservation, Sacramento, 1988, p. 107.

its portion from the winnings. In her book *The Life and Death of a Quicksilver Mine*, Helen Goss noted that in the games she observed as a little girl, the croupier--a professional gambler--could rig the outcome by deftly capping a chin or two under his immensely long fingernail.[76]

Napa County's Chinese numbers games were probably similar if not identical to one that ran twice a day in San Francisco's Chinatown. The San Francisco lottery used as its matrix an ancient poem of 1,000 lines with eight words each. In the entire poem no word is repeated, so each of the words could be numbered. The bettor would buy a ticket with 10 lines from the poem and mark 10 or more characters. (The lines used would vary from day to day.) The lottery keeper took the 10 lines he had selected, cut apart each of its 80 words and rolled them into small balls. He mixed them up, divided them into four groups of 20 each and took five from each pile. The resulting 20 characters were the winning numbers for that lottery. Bettors checked in at their numbers seller to determine how much they won, or, much more likely, lost. Five matches returned the amount that had been gambled, six resulted in a profit of 10 times the original stake, seven 200 times, eight 1000 times and nine 2000 times.[77]

Professional gamblers came to Napa County each week, often bringing prostitutes with them as further incentives for the men to part with the pittance they earned. The prostitutes, like the gamblers, were under contract with their representative company. Caucasian men also used the prostitutes.

A further distraction was the smoking of opium, which was done in dens devoted to the purpose. Opium pipes, or "smoking pistols," were often made of hollow bamboo and had ivory mouthpieces. Opium smoking was extremely addictive and often resulted in the habitue suffering poverty so profound that when he died his estate

---

[76]Helen Rocca Goss, *The Life and Death of a Quicksilver Mine*, Historical Society of California, LA, 1958, p. 79.

[77]McLeod, pp. 168-69.

lacked the $10 necessary for the permit to have his bones shipped back to China.[78]

With wages averaging about $1 a day, it was very difficult for the men to accumulate much money. Besides sending dues to their sponsoring companies and their families back home, laboring men had to give a portion of their earnings to the contractor who connected them with their jobs. Wah Chung, San Sing and Fook Lee were labor contractors in St. Helena. Yung Him worked out of Rutherford. The labor bosses did their best to develop good relations with the grape and hops growers as well as with the quicksilver miners, construction companies and quarries. All of these industries needed to employ strong backs, but, consistent with the racial prejudice of the times, there were constant complaints in the local newspapers that the Orientals took jobs from whites.

One of the most visible enterprises in which the Chinese engaged was the laundry business. Napans could take their dirty clothes to Sam Kee at 58 North Main in Napa. In Calistoga the Chinese laundryman was Kong Sam Kee, and the labor contractor Yung Him in Rutherford also took in wash. St. Helena, with the biggest Chinese population, had the largest selection of laundries. There was Wah Sing Jim's on the corner of Church and "Pope Valley Street," Mow Hing Charlie's on Oak Avenue, and Ah Guy on Main Street.

Another industry in which the Napa Valley's Chinese population became involved was the manufacturing of cigars. In a direct insult to the Orientals, a Caucasian group in St. Helena started the "White Labor Cigar Company," which refused employment to Chinese. There were also laundries that advertised themselves as being "White Labor" businesses, including one in Napa City run by an African American family. "White labor" really meant "no Chinese work here".

Anti-Chinese laws affected the quicksilver industry, which depended on Chinese laborers to do the most dangerous work. St. Helena's Tiburcio Parrott, president of the Sulphur Bank Mining

---

[78]Goss, p. 80.

Company in Lake County, decided to challenge the constitutionality of anti-Chinese legislation by hiring Chinese workers. He won his case and probably saved the cinnabar industry, but may not have ingratiated himself with his xenophobic neighbors.

In 1860 the State of California officially prohibited Chinese children from attending California public schools. Six years later the law was softened to provide for Chinese enrollment as long as white parents did not object. Some Chinese children attended school in Napa, but apparently not in St. Helena. It was the presence of this law that led to the publication of several hate-filled editorials like this one in the *St. Helena Star*:

> The subject of using our public school evenings for the purpose of teaching the Chinese has called forth considerable comment and no little indignation on the part of many of our citizens. It is an established fact that the "Johns" were never known to contribute a cent toward anything of this character, and it looks rather unreasonable to admit them the same privileges that are enjoyed by the children of parties who stood taxation for the school...[79]

Periodically in St. Helena white boys amused themselves by throwing sticks and stones at the Chinese. The St. Helena Police Department did not appear to expend significant energy in apprehending the culprits, nor did the *St. Helena Star* use ink in the victims' defense. On the contrary, the local paper was outspoken in its hatred. One publisher, De Witt Lawrence, may have contributed more to the persecution of the Chinese than any other person in Napa County. He stoked the fires of the Americans' xenophobia with articles like this:

The Tallow Colored--
Rat-eaters of the celestial empire, we noticed while in Napa, are investing largely in revolvers. They evince a determination to fight

---

[79] *SHS*, 11-12-1874

their way to the Fowery (sic) Kingdom.[80]

Lawrence may not have been dealing from a complete deck. He left town in 1876 and in 1880 became newsworthy himself by arriving at the office of the *Democratic Herald* in Oakland with a pistol, ready to wreak vengeance for an article with which he disagreed. He had to be restrained.[81] The new *Star* publisher, Charles Gardner, opposed Kearneyism.

Napa Valley's old pioneer families could not bring themselves to tolerate the Chinese, although they provided the labor that built many of the stone structures, prepared the soil, built the Napa Valley Railroad, worked as domestic help and harvested the crops. Some of the larger employers argued in favor of their presence as a cheap and hard-working source of seasonal help, but the Chinese Exclusion Act of 1892 and other discriminatory laws put the final seal on further immigration. Nearly all the Chinese who tried to make a life for themselves in the Napa Valley left.

The Chinese had competition from another large laboring group that came emigrated to the Napa Valley in the 1870's: Italians and Italian Swiss, people from the European mountains. They worked in the cinnabar mines as foremen and supervisors. They also did hauling and teamster work and did not appear to encounter opposition in this from the Chinese. Coming as they did from Lombardy and Ticino--mountainous regions that used rocks and stones as their primary building material--they often took jobs as stone cutters and stonemasons.

Many of these pioneers left their rocky Alpine villages with the same hope of riches that the Orientals had. The emigration of the Rossi family to the Napa Valley in the 1870's was a good example.[82]

---

[80] *SHS*, 12-10-1874

[81] *SHS*, 6-4-1880.

[82] Information regarding the Rossi/Lagorio/ Cavagnaro family is from Bruna Maccantelli Haegele, "Family Tree and Heritage," unpublished,

Frank and Ricotto Rossi were brothers from a large family in Italy. They came to America around 1850 to mine for gold but found very little. They also tried mining in Alaska, also apparently unsuccessfully. Frank eventually went to San Francisco and set up a hotel, the "Campi D'Olio," on the "Barbary Coast." It offered liquor, lodging and ladies for a hefty price to miners willing to pay. (It also offered crooked card dealers, fist-fights, knifings and the occasional rolling and robbing of its guests.) Ricotto, more reserved, came to Napa as a laborer, working in Napa City and Yountville.

Frank and Ricotto wrote letters to their family back home, extolling the opportunity to build a satisfying life in the Golden State. The Rossis' two sisters, Nicoletta and Giuseppina, ages 17 and 15, read these enthusiastically. Neither girl was especially successful in Italy. Nicoletta was born with fingers missing and may have had difficulty finding suitors. Giuseppina, blind in one eye from an accident, had just married a bad-tempered young alcoholic named Sisto, against her parents' wishes. With Sisto's urging the three undertook the long passage to California.

Since Rossi's Barbary Coast hotel was profitable but not the kind of place to send one's sister, the three came to Napa County, where Ricotto could watch over them and help integrate them into the Italian community that was beginning to form. Giuseppina and Sisto opened a boarding house and cheap hotel in St. Helena; Nicoletta lived with Ricotto in a rented house in Napa City. Within months (perhaps weeks) she married a paisano named Charles Baracca.

Life was not easy for either of the Rossi girls. Giuseppina had 15 male boarders for whom she cooked and cleaned. Her only friend was a Wappo woman who helped with the chores and taught her to smoke cigars. The behaviors that earned Sisto his bad reputation in Italy intensified in St. Helena. He drank heavily, beat Giuseppina and engaged in frequent brawls. In one of these fights he killed a man and was sent to San Quentin. Giuseppina divorced him and married one of her boarders, Nicola Mangini. She sold the boarding house as

---

unnumbered manuscript, courtesy of Richard Cavagnaro.

soon as she could. The Mangini's had a son, but he died in infancy. Heartsick, the couple moved to Napa to be near the rest of Giuseppina's family. There they had a daughter, Uriglia.

Nicoletta Rossi had two children by Baracca,[83] but he died, leaving her with no means of support: a disaster in those days, when there were no social welfare programs. Her brother Ricotto quickly introduced her to another Italian, surnamed Lagorio, who married her. Lagorio was a good catch and probably the best thing that ever happened to Nicoletta. He was the proprietor of a trading post that did commerce with the few remaining Wappo and Wintu in Napa and Lake Counties. She had two children by him, Richie and Nellie.

Nellie Lagorio and Uriglia Magini--cousins and best friends--grew up in what had been Cayetano Juarez's *Tulucay* grant and was now East Napa, Napa City's "Little Italy." The Italians shared the location with the Chinese, who had outgrown their sandy beach between Napa Creek and the Napa River. Anglo-Saxon Napans generally held the new Italian immigrants in low regard; in return, the Italians frequently picked on their pigtailed neighbors.

Leo and Dave Cavagnaro were brothers who were probably born in the gold country town of Camanche. They came before the bench more than once in Napa City for beating up Chinese Napans. Their father was the proprietor of the Brooklyn Hotel in East Napa, where Italian-speaking newcomers to Napa could find a warm welcome and enter the network of laborers. But their father died of pneumonia before reaching age 30, and the boys' mother remarried. Handsome, strong and ambitious, the Cavagnaro boys worked as stonemasons and were well liked in East Napa by everyone but, presumably, the Chinese. They courted "the cousins;" Leo married Uriglia and Dave married Nellie.

Dave and Nellie Cavagnaro took over the Indian Trading Post, and when the native population declined to the point that trading was no longer a viable business, Dave ran the Brooklyn Hotel and engaged in other enterprises, as well. He lived in the old post, which

---

[83] Charlie and Julius Baracca

The very polluted Napa River, once a beautiful stream of clear water, was the major commercial artery in the 1800's.

By the late 1880's, moderate-sized factories lined the banks of the Napa River. Beside the Sawyer Tannery, above, there were McBain & Co (also tanners), Bachelder Manufacturing (wood products), Vernon Flour Mills, Stoddard Wool Mills, A.Hatt & Co., a tile company, a cream of tartar producer and an assortment of smaller enterprises. The Uncle Sam and Migliavacca Wineries were also on the River.

came to be known as "Dave's Place." Dave Cavagnaro would become one of Napa City's most influential men in the first half of the 20th century.

Rich or poor, Italian immigrant or Missouri pioneer, most non-Oriental families could find a relatively quiet but pleasant life in Napa City in the 1880's. There were few big factories to foul the air; nor were there rowdy cowboys hot and thirsty from the long trail. A half day's steamship trip from the city and off the beaten track, Napa City was regarded as the gateway to the Napa Valley. By the 1880's it offered 11 hotels and more than enough saloons. It also had its own Opera House for live theater on the second floor of the Napa Hotel, corner of First and Main. The Republican Party held rallies there. The opening of George Crowey's opera house was a big event, because the city had been without such a place for several years. Jess Grigsby had built the city's first public hall in 1871, but it burned down after an explosion in 1874. It had offered a dance hall, a lecture room with a stage and a roller skating rink.

Fourth of July parades were annual extravaganzas, and the Centennial celebration in 1876 was particularly spectacular.[84] Many of the original Bear Flaggers were still alive. William Hargrave carried the American Flag and marched down the street with an entourage of pioneers, including James Clyman, whom the local paper claimed had lived in the Valley for 35 years (about 28 would have been more accurate). Thirteen floats with a pretty young woman on each represented the 13 colonies. Another float displayed a complete 9'x16' log cabin, and a boat with a crew also paraded down the street, remembering, apparently, the Bloody Island Massacre, which was still considered a positive thing. The parade was followed by a fancy dinner and a ball.

The gentle Napa River had been the jumping-off point for the city's early development. It became severely polluted. B.F. Sawyer's Tannery was the largest industrial operation on the west bank. It

---

[84]*NCR*, 7-8-1876.

processed pelts and sheepskins, and it dumped its waste--some of it extremely toxic--into the river. A foreman at Sawyer's, E. Manasse, patented a method for making high quality glove leather from sheepskin. The company profited greatly from his discovery, and so did Manasse, who became an owner of the business.

Albert Hatt, a German, built a brick warehouse for storing wood and coal in 1884 near the foot of Main Street. It was the place residents went to supply their coal-burning heaters and stoves. William Stoddard's Napa City Mills (aka Napa Milling) was next door to Hatt's. It went out of business in 1886 and became a storage facility for Uncle Sam's Wine Cellars, then Napa's biggest winery.

Most of Napa's manufacturing concerns were on the east bank of the river, and East Napa was a small city in itself. The Napa City Tannery--also known as McBain & Co.--was located at Pearl and McKinstry and, like Sawyer's, dumped its effluent into the river. The Napa Glue Works were just north of McBain's and used the same means of septic disposal. Vernon flour mills were to the south on what is now the County Corporation Yard on Water Street. They had a loading wharf of their own. Other manufacturing enterprises in East Napa were the Napa Cream of Tartar Works, which processed this by-product of winemaking; the Napa Drain Tile Factory, making tiles from clay quarried nearby; and the Bachelder Manufacturing Company. Bachelder's made windmills, fruit boxes and other wood products. Albert Boggs, grandson of Lilburn, teamed up with another Napan, Lee James, to run the James & Boggs lumber company on Fourth Street.

An exotic blend of sewages thus poured into the river. An enterprising rock-and-gravel company then contracted to scoop out the stones from the river's bed to sell as street paving in San Francisco, effectively removing the means nature had provided for the river to self-cleanse. For all intents and purposes, the saltwater section of the Napa River died, or at least went comatose.

In 1877 Napa City saw another death. Its brave, tough and sometimes difficult founder, Nathan Coombs, died of a fever that year at the age of 51. The whole county turned out for his funeral, which included a procession of 50 old-time pioneers. It was the

Main Street Napa City, facing south from Pearl (above) and north from Second (below).

The Napa Hotel, seen here from two perspectives, stood on the corner of First and Main Streets in Napa City for decades. Pedestrians could cross the muddy streets on crosswalks made of cobblestone.

biggest event of its kind the Valley had ever known.[85] His 24 year-old son Frank had just opened a law firm and would carry on the family fame.

Life went on elsewhere, however. Main Street continued to grow as the mercantile center of Napa. Brown Street, really just a half block to the west, was also part of Napa's original "downtown." There were businesses on Third, Second, First, Pearl and Clinton, which was called "Stuart Street" in the 1880's. The eastern extension of First Street was home to a string of boarding houses and simple, wood-frame single-family dwellings. There were modest residences beyond Stuart/Clinton Street.

Second Street was the "bank block." Chancellor Hartson retired from politics and helped establish the Bank of Napa 1871, which occupied the corner of Main and Second. Hartson himself built a mansion on the northwest corner of Coombs and Third St., where he could eye the comings and goings at the Court House with an unimpeded view.

Many other affluent Napans had residences on Coombs, Randolph, Franklin, School and Church, from as far south as Palmer Street. Because the soil was so miry during the winter and the roads so rutted and dusty the rest of the year, commuting more than a few blocks was a hardship. Homes on Cedar and Wilson Streets were considered farm houses. The mountain man James Clyman felt right at home in his residence all the way out at 2344 Redwood Road.

St. Helena's White Sulphur Springs grew shabby as the years passed. Its popular proprietor Sven Alstrom went on to other pursuits, and it continued to encounter disastrous fires and floods. It closed for several years in the 1880's but reopened in 1892 under Col. Sandford Johnson with a library, reading room, piano and dining room for 250.[86] The cabins were equipped with indoor plumbing. Johnson died two years after the grand opening, however, and his

---

[85]Hanrahan, p. 58.
[86]Sheffer, p. 16.

widow attempted to run it. It changed hands a number of times in the 20th century, but never again drew the brightest social luminaries.

Other small resorts, like Inglewood, Starr's, Angwin's, Toland's and Walters' came and went in various parts of the valley. At the turn of the 20th Century Berryessa Valley, whose 36,000 acres were given mostly to grain and cattle-raising, had a pleasant getaway called "Samuel's Soda Springs."[87] Despite its flashy beginning and the railroad that was built at taxpayers' expense to its front door, Calistoga never really took hold with the trend setters. Nevertheless,"taking the waters" continued to be a popular pastime among Californians. The elite among them found a new favorite hideaway eight miles northeast of Napa City: Napa Soda Springs.

The 27 springs of mineral-rich cold water that gave Napa Soda Springs its name were discovered by Amos Buckman in 1855, although native Wintu people had camped there regularly before him. Several other people tried to lay claim to the property after Buckman, and in 1862 the small frame structure he built there burned down in a suspicious fire. He retaliated by burning down his neighbor's house. Greed, envy and unceasing legal and illegal hassles crippled attempts to develop the beautiful property until 1872, when Col. John P. Jackson bought the 1000-acre estate and started investing in its potential.

The results were stunning. So luxurious and well manicured was the resort that some called it "The Emerald Gem of the West;" others less approving of lavish displays of wealth and taste called it "Jackson's Folly." Visitors could bowl, play tennis or billiards and swim in the 150' pool that was 4' deep on one end and 10' on the other. Guests could hunt, fish in the stocked streams and ride fine horses from the stables. The less athletic were free to stroll among the olive and almond trees, eat citrus from the grove and apples from the orchard or walk to romantic settings on the property that bore such names as "Fern Glade," "Lovers' Retreat" and "Dripping Rock."

Perhaps the most memorable feature at Soda Springs was the

---

[87]*Napa Daily Journal*, 4-23-99.

"Rotunda." This architectural feat was a 75' high circular building made of Napa Valley stone topped by a glass cupola. The Rotunda was the centerpiece of the most spacious hotel at the spa. Guests stayed in fine rooms built around the sides of the Rotunda. Those on the second story could look over the inside balcony down to the immense lobby below, which was carpeted with Oriental rugs and strewn here and there with bear skins.

Guests could also stay at a hotel there called the "Castle." True to its name, it was a stone building with crenelated parapets and a hexagonal turret. There was a clubhouse with huge Corinthian columns that made it look like a Roman temple; a large separate dining hall, a hothouse and a bath house. Several fanciful pagodas were tucked among the glades. NSS could handle about 200 guests and provided employment for many Napans. A way was found to carbonate and bottle the water from Napa Soda Springs so it could be sold commercially.[88] The bottling plant continued as a money-making enterprise well into the 20th Century.

To get there, one needed to pass through the splendid country estate of General John Miller on the eastern rim of what had once been Salvador Vallejo's *Yajome*. Miller was a native of Indiana who lived in Napa County in the 1850's. He practiced law and served briefly as Napa County treasurer and then as Collector of the Port of San Francisco. He went back to Indiana and had just been elected to the state senate there when the Civil War broke out. He resigned and joined the Union Army, where he fought heroically. He returned to politics and was elected to the US Senate in 1880. Miller profited from the land grant crisis. He positioned himself to acquire part of Rancho *Yajome* and built a villa that he named "La Vergne," after one of the Civil War battles he had won. La Vergne was surrounded by acres of lawn and was often open to Jackson's guests at Napa Soda Springs. Ironically, it is General Miller's old estate, not Jackson's, that is used today as a resort. The villa remains, and its grassy lawns have been converted into the fairways and greens of today's Silverado

---

[88] Credit for perfecting this process was given to Charles Allen, an old Napan who had served as a delegate to the Union Party in 1862.

Country Club. Napa Soda Springs, on the other hand, crumbles away, its gothic ruins looking even more gothic among the overgrown vines off of Soda Canyon Road.

The great Scottish writer Robert Louis Stevenson was one who sought health in the Napa Valley. He fell in love with a friend of the Woodward family of Oak Knoll, Fanny Osbourn, and married her in Oakland in 1880. The trip to California exhausted the consumptive Stevenson, and to restore himself, he and Fanny went not to a posh Valley resort, but to the abandoned mine town of Borlandville on Mount St. Helena, which he called "Silverado." He described the adventure in *The Silverado Squatters*, basing his characters on real-life people he met along the way. In so doing, he brought the Valley to the attention of his world-wide readership.

The Valley's clean air and quiet ambience attracted the attention of other vulnerable people. In the late 1870's the San Francisco chapter of the "Grand Army of the Republic," a fraternal society of Civil War veterans from the Union side, recognized a need for a residential facility for their old and wounded heroes.[89] In combination with a veterans' group from the Mexican War (who were numerous in the Napa Valley) they raised enough money to purchase 910 acres in the Yountville area upon which they could build an old soldiers' home. After several fund drives they were able to erect a hospital and administrative facility, and in 1884, 42 disabled war veterans could call Yountville their home. The number of patients outgrew the place's resources very quickly. The beleaguered staff tried raising hogs, poultry and cattle to defray costs, but demand for space kept growing. In two years the number of inmates had tripled. The Veterans' Home struggled with overwhelming financial burderns until 1897, when it gave its grounds and buildings, *gratis*, to the State of California. More than 800 war veterans lived there when the State took it over.

People with health problems of an entirely different sort also had a refuge in the Napa Valley. Napa Insane Asylum, whose name was

---

[89]Norton King, *Napa County--An Historical Overview*, Napa County Superintendant of Schools, 1973, pp. 85-87.

Pioneer Chancellor Hartson organized the Republican Party in Napa City and was elected to both the state Senate and Assembly. He was instrumental in the creation of the Napa Valley Railroad, co-owned a cinnabar mine and, with fellow pioneers Cayetano Juarez and Henry Fowler, owned the Palace Hotel. He also founded and presided over the Bank of Napa, above.

Chancellor Hartson, businessman-politician, was the moving force behind the creation of the Napa Insane Asylum.

changed in recent years to Napa State Hospital, was Chancellor Hartson's most enduring gift to Napa County. He lobbied energetically to have the facility placed in Napa and became president of its board of directors.

The original Asylum was a four-story palace with a central spire and a high tower on each end. The building possessed gables and dormers and arches and turrets enough to inspire terror in the healthiest of minds. The doctors lived in fine mansions built on the approaching avenue. Originally built to serve 500 inmates, it exceeded its capacity in three years and was expanded three times between 1875 and 1881. Thirty-three patients somehow managed to escape during the institution's first six years in business, and of the 2955 admitted during that time, 458 died--approximately one in six. Patient confidentiality was not a concept known to Californians. The local newspaper listed the names of those who were committed to the Asylum.

The Asylum was the first of its kind in California. In order to derive a model for treating the mentally ill, Governor Haight appointed a committee of three to investigate the delivery of mental health services in Europe. One of the three was Dr. G. A. Shurtleff, a relative of the Asylum's first medical director, Dr. Benjamin Shurtleff. Californians tended to associate intellectual and cultural attainments with England, France and Germany. Psychiatric illnesses were as misunderstood there as they were in America, however, and the model that was imported was one that was mostly medieval in its approach. Americans regarded the mentally ill with fear and judgmentalism, as they had the Chinese and the Indians. The ornately gloomy Asylum that stood on the road to the city became a receptacle for the darkest projections of passers-by. Even Napans seemed uncomfortable with the institution's presence: the local newspapers wrote about screams and other sounds issuing from the Asylum. To some, "going to Napa" came to be synonymous not with taking the waters or touring the wineries, but with being "put away."

Chapter Eight

Napa Valley Wines

Many Germans, Swiss Germans and French people emigrated to the Napa Valley in the second half of the 19th Century. On the whole they came not as laborers, but as entrepreneurs who saw something in the Valley that resembled their homeland. Following the Civil War and during the early 1870's, several hundred European immigrants settled here, and many started wineries.

Charles Krug was the first to make winemaking his profession. Born Karl Krug in Prussia in 1825, he was a political radical, writing articles promoting the overthrow of the Prussian Parliament. For this he served a prison term. After his release in 1852 he fled to San Francisco, where he founded the West Coast's first German newspaper and once again wrote diatribes against Parliament. After a dramatic duel with a rival editor[1] he tried farming in Sonoma, planting, among other things, grapevines. His neighbors were Col. Agostin Haraszthy and his wife, the Countess Eleanora. Haraszthy taught Krug what he knew of viticulture. Krug and the Hungarian Colonel also entered a joint venture refining gold and silver. The project didn't last long and may have ended disastrously. Haraszthy and "two others" were accused of malfeasance as melters and refiners, according to a dirt-digging article in the pro-Union *Napa County Reporter* during the Civil War.[2] Krug and Haraszthy, both sympathetic to the Confederacy, remained friends.

In 1858 Napa's John Patchett invited Krug to make wine from the

---

[1]*Wine Library*, IV, p. 6.
[2]*NCR*, 3-9-1861.

mission grapes on his property. Krug helped Patchett produce 2,000 gallons, using a cider press. The exact site of Patchett's first crush has been lost to history, but the press itself gained some celebrity and was displayed for years at the winery Krug eventually established.

The next year Louis Bruck--another German--asked Krug for assistance in making wine from his crop of mission grapes. Bruck married Edward Bale's daughter Isadora and received as dowry Bale's gristmill. Perhaps in the process of working for Bruck, Charles Krug met Bale's other daughter, Carolina. He married her in 1860. Carolina's ample dowry consisted of 540 acres and the site of the Bale sawmill on the Napa River. Also in 1859 Krug expanded his resume by helping George Yount make 5,000 gallons of wine.[3]

Encouraged, perhaps, by his success in crushing other peoples' harvests, Krug planted 23 acres in mission grapes and built a small winery of his own near the old Bale sawmill. While waiting for his vines to bear adequately, he continued helping his neighbors. In 1861 he crushed mission grapes from the vines of Hudson, York, Tucker and Owsley.

Henry A. Pellet, a Swiss watchmaker from the canton of Vaud, took over Krug's post as manager of Patchett's winery. Pellet was among the first residents of Napa City and was mentioned on the city's census in 1855. He claimed to have been a boyhood friend of the pioneering paleontologist Louis Agassiz, and like Krug he was an important influence on the wine industry during its infancy.

Sam Brannan was aware of the wine-producing potential of the Napa Valley. He collected sample vines during an 1857 European trip and may have planted them on the farm of Matthew Ritchie, which he acquired that year. Perhaps influenced by Brannan, the fledgling wine industry received a small tax break from the federal government in 1859. A tariff was passed in 1861 that imposed a tax of $.50 per gallon on imports, including imported wine. This small impetus gave further encouragement to valley vintners and prompted this

---

[3]*Wine Library,* IV, p. 7.

prophetic but not entirely complimentary comment by the *Napa County Reporter*:

> The demand is greater than we can supply for some years to come, and if we will but furnish them with a good article, our wines will obtain such a custom that they cannot afterwards be driven out. The great increase in our vineyards during the last four years will not prove profitless: good wine will be made by millions of gallons.[4]

Others also planted varietal grapes, for use not in wine but as table grapes and raisins.

The American who had the greatest effect on Napa County's initial development as a wine region was Dr. George Belden Crane. Unlike some frontier docs like John Marsh and probably Bale, Crane really was a doctor: He received his MD from the State University of New York before coming west. Crane married "Frank" Grayson, the widow of the wealthy 1846 emigrant Andrew Jackson Grayson. Crane arrived in St. Helena in 1859 and built a house on the County Road, set well back and shaded with trees. He used Chinese laborers to clear away a large rectangle of scrub and gravel that was bounded in the south by what is now Sulphur Springs Avenue and to the north by Sulphur Creek. He was ridiculed by his neighbors for attempting to work the gravelly soil, which was so poor for most agriculture that it wasn't worth fencing.[5] He knew what he was doing, however. Encouraged by Haraszthy, he planted grapes specifically intended for wine: *Vitis vinifera,* the kind that European vintners had cultivated for centuries. He built a small wine cellar six feet deep (which may also have drawn wry humor) that stood about 16' x 24'. His first crush was in 1862, when he made about 500 gallons. The vines were not in full bearing until 1867.[6]

The winery outgrew itself very quickly, and Crane lured Henry

---

[4] *NCR*, 3-30-1861

[5] Gunn, p. 338.

[6] *NCR*, 1-3-1879.

Pellet away from Patchett to help him build and run a bigger place. With Pellet he increased his output. While the Civil War raged he shipped 14,000 gallons of wine around the Horn and went along with the shipment as his own agent to market it to New Yorkers. He wasn't able to sell enough wine to cover the cost of the trip, but he managed to break even by exchanging gold for greenbacks. The Napa newspapers wrote disparagingly of the dollars that entered the county with Crane's return, because gold, not paper, was the favored medium of exchange.

Crane's Swiss assistant, Pellet, was very popular. Described by peers as having a "kindly, earnest nature,"[7] Pellet was elected president of St. Helena's Board of Trustees when the city was incorporated in 1876. Pellet left Crane to start his own winery nearby with D.B. Carver, a fellow politician. Carver started out with a general store,[8] served as the St. Helena's first city treasurer and eventually established a bank in St. Helena, the Carver National Bank. The winery was called "Pellet & Carver."[9]

Dr. Crane understood the Valley's geological and social resources very well. His wife had traveled in prominent circles, and Crane himself was acquainted with the European-influenced families who summered at White Sulphur Springs resort, which was only a mile or so to the west of their home.

Crane expanded again after Pellet left, with the help of a winemaking friend named Rudolph Lemme.[10] He now had a building three stories high and 72' square. In time his landowning spanned both sides of the County Road. Like Charles Krug, he was father to the careers of several men who were active in the industry's earliest years. He hired Frank Sciaroni, an Italian Swiss, to replace Pellet as his cellar master. Sciaroni went on to start a winery and sherry house

---

[7] Frona Eunice Wait, *Wines and Vines of California*, Howell-North Books, Berkeley, 1973 (originally published in 1889), p. 101.

[8] *SHS*, 3-8-1878.

[9] *SHS*, 8-25-1876.

[10] *SHS* 7-4-1885.

of his own on the corner of Highway 29 and Charter Oak Avenue. Sciaroni also became part-owner of the property across the street from his sherry house--the site of St. Helena's Chinatown.

Crane and Sciaroni helped a Portuguese man, John Ramos, develop another sherry house in 1878.[11] The Ramos Sherry House, at 1468 Railroad Avenue, was adjacent to a structure that had a history all its own--Johnson's Depot Saloon, aka the Pink Saloon. The second story of the saloon was a house of prostitution.

Crane, Pellet, Krug and Haraszthy had similar interests and political viewpoints. All four favored States' Rights. During the Civil War Crane actually started a political party, the Independent Conservative Party, and ran as its candidate for the State Assembly. He lost.[12] Krug was a fervent radical during his youth, as described above. He was ethnocentric, refusing to hire Chinese to work at his winery. His brother-in-law by marriage, Louis Bruck, was a delegate from Napa at the Union convention in 1862.[13] Haraszthy was a delegate to the Secessionist party .[14]

Haraszthy suffered from unusually bad luck. After a series of what were described as "financial misadventures" by a sympathetic biographer,[15] he left his winery enterprises to his sons in 1868 and departed for Nicaragua. There he established a sugar plantation and distillery. It was said that he fell from a branch while crossing a jungle river and was devoured by an alligator.[16]

Crane and his friends had educated palates and were more aware than their contemporaries that the locally growing mission grapes

---

[11] *Wine Library*, p. 30.

[12] *NCR*, 8-15-1863

[13] *NCR*, 6-21-1862. Ralph Ellis, to whom Bruck sold the mill, was a fellow Unionist and represented "Hot Springs Township" at the convention.

[14] *NCR* 9-6-1862

[15] Harold H. Price, "Buena Vista," *The Vine in Early California*, III, The Book Club of California, San Francisco, 1955.

[16] Idem

did not produce a very palatable wine. The little black grape had been introduced by the Spanish, who made small quantities of a crude wine by crushing the berries with their bare feet.[17] Mission grape juice was very high in sugar, and the wine that resulted was correspondingly high in alcohol and packed a punch. Whiskey-loving local pioneers might have enjoyed it, and so might have the newly rich miners who were settling in San Francisco and the Bay Area. Unfortunately, Valley vintners shipped the product back east, where more sophisticated drinkers tasted and usually rejected Napa's offerings. Fully aware of the business consequences of making a poor first impression, the visionary Crane wrote articles in the local newspaper urging others to plant *Vitis vinifera*. Some of his readers responded, especially when they began to taste the results of Crane's experimentation.

Just as prospectors had run to the hills to stake quicksilver claims, landowners now rushed to plant grapes.Foolishly, however, most of the local farmers were very reluctant to plant European vines, despite Crane's pleas. The Valley grew green with mission grapes. The results were discouraging. Moreover, because the novice vintners didn't understand the first thing about winemaking, every kind of contamination that could occur during the vinification process did. San Francisco banks that had loaned money to help farmers venture into viticulture were disappointed with the results and reluctant to lend again when the growers wanted to replant with European stock. Scores of wineries were started in the 1870's, and most vanished. Many left behind clues to their existence, however, in the form of rock walls artfully prepared by Alpino laborers.

Up the hill beyond Brown's Valley and straddling the Sonoma County line, a Tennessee-born pioneer named Nicholas Carriger had planted vines as early as 1849.[18] By 1873 he had four cellars with a

---

[17] Sometimes they covered the grapes with hides to keep their feet from getting stained by the grape juice.

[18] Carriger came with the Boggs party in 1846. His father died on the journey, and one of his nine children was born en route. He was a Bear Flagger and served as a mail carrier between Sonoma and San Rafael

total capacity of 40,000 gallons and a distillery a few hundred yards away.[19] Carriger's estate seemed baronial. From the porch of his southern-style mansion he could see Mt. Diablo, unobscured by smog, as well as the small city of Vallejo.

A mountain man[20] named William Winter acquired (probably by squatting) a large parcel composed of a portion of both the *Carneros* and *Huichica* ranchos in the 1850's. He planted mission grapes and later experimented with European varietals. He called his stone winery "Huichica." James Simonton bought the land from him in the 1870's and built the "Talcoa" winery, which produced 25,000 gallons in 1879. The partnership of two Frenchmen, Michael Debret and Pierre Priet took over the winery in 1885 and elaborated on the existing structure, transforming it into a castle.[21]

John and Theodore Sigrist employed 30 men at their facility in Brown's Valley and made large quantities of brandy as well as wine. They had a cooperage on their property, where they assembled casks that were made in New York.[22] Their neighbor, Herr Buhman, had a smaller place. His 50,000 bearing vines were planted on the 100 acres he owned on both sides of Brown's Valley Creek.[23]

In Napa City a German named Van Bever teamed up with W.W.Thompson to form the Van Bever & Thompson Winery. At first they stored their wine in the warehouse of NVRR magnate A.Y. Easterby on the Napa River; then they built a building of their own called Uncle Sam Winery, a huge operation that bought and crushed grapes from local farmers. Eventually Uncle Sam's made at least a

---

during the Mexican War. Most of his estate was in what is now Sonoma County.

[19]*NCR*, 3-15-1873

[20]Haynes, p. 81.

[21] which is, at the turn of the 21st century, the residence of the art collector, Rene di Rosa.

[22]*NCR* 3-15-1873.

[23]Idem.

dozen varieties.[24] Uncle Sam's produced 250,000 gallons of wine in 1878, none of it particularly noteworthy except, perhaps, to editors of the local newspapers, who wrote about it glowingly. In its time it was the largest winery in the Napa Valley. Perhaps out of necessity, there was a vinegar factory next door.[25] A Frenchman, Charles Carpy, bought Uncle Sam's before 1890,[26] in partnership with C. Anderson, and may have improved on the quality of the offering.

Unlike most of his contemporaries, Giacomo Migliavacca actually had training as a winemaker, learning the craft from his father in Italy.[27] He came to Napa City in 1866 and soon started crushing grapes, although at first his main business was a grocery store on Main Street. He built a brick winery in Napa City on the river at Fifth and Main (site of the present-day Public Library) and another facility in Rutherford. He transformed the grocery store into a major commercial building on the northwest corner of Brown and First Streets. The Migliavacca Building occupied 37,000 square feet and was designed by a local architect named Luther Turton, whose creative genius lent character to several important commercial structures in Napa City and St. Helena.[28] Migliavacca's prosperity continued when he joined the Bank of Italy-cum-Bank of America. Privy to inside information, he invested heavily--and profitably--in Napa City real estate, and by the turn of the century he was able to build his family a mansion on Fourth Street.

The career of Bartolomeo Semorile was similar to Migliavacca's, but on a smaller scale. He, too, was both a grocer and a vintner, and Luther Turton designed his grocery store, as well. The Semorile family lived on the second story, above the store, which was located on the eastern end of First Street. Semorile was best known for his

---

[24]*NCR*, 1-25-1873.

[25]Palmer, p. 226.

[26]Idem.

[27]Ibid., p. 524.

[28]Kathleen Kernberger, "The Migliavacca Building," unpublished manuscript, 6-15-1973, pp 1-3.

special apricot brandy, which commanded high prices back east.[29]

Gotthelp Barth was also a producer of alcoholic beverages who worked within Napa City limits. Barth brewed beer, and for this purpose he bought a building from Philip Pfeiffer, a Bavarian, which was located on the corner of Clinton and Main Streets in Napa. In 1881 Barth bought the Sigrist brothers' winery, Dry Creek.[30] He sold his Napa building back to Philip Pfeiffer that same year. Pfeiffer converted it into a saloon. Since then it has done service as a Chinese laundry (Sam Kee's), a butcher shop and a delicatessen.

Jose Mateus (aka Joseph Matthews), the scion of a Portuguese winemaking family, used his considerable masonry skills in 1878 to construct the Lisbon Cellar on Brown Street,[31] which produced the amber-colored dessert wine, madeira.

East of town, the Hagen brothers owned vineyards and a medium-sized winery called "Cedar Knoll." Dr. J.A. Pettengill's "White Rock Winery," adjacent to Napa Soda Springs, was so-named because Pettengill cut the white lava rocks of which it was built from a quarry on his property, using nothing but a sharp axe.[32] He produced a minimal amount of wine (2000 gallons), just enough to qualify as a real winery in the list of producers published by the *St. Helena Star* in 1879.

Young George Tucker matured to become an enterprising businessman/farmer. In 1866 he and a partner, George Burrage, started Vine Cliff Vineyard, located three miles northeast of Yountville. Vine Cliff pressed grapes from the 65,000 vines that the two Georges planted on the rocky hillsides surrounding it. Their

---

[29]Charles Hall Page & Associates, *The Semorile and Winship Buildings*, SF: NP, 1976, p. 7. Next door to Semorile's, on the corner of Main and First Streets, was another Turton structure, the Winship Building, home to drug stores and professional offices throughout much of its long life. When it was first built it sported a tower.

[30]*NCR*, 3-25-1881.

[31]Haynes, p. 76.

[32]Palmer, p. 226.

wine cellar was four stories high, constructed of lumber on a story of cement. The adjoining cellar was built into the hillside, and during harvest grapes were hauled up onto the hill and brought over to the roof of the winery. The crusher, worked by two men, could process about a ton of grapes a day. Besides being among the first to start a winery, George Tucker was a pioneer in experimenting with cooperage. He influenced his peers by using redwood casks to age his wines.[33]

Terrell Grigsby learned to make wine at Vine Cliff and in 1878 built a large winery himself about a mile southeast of Yountville. He employed Chinese laborers to build it. This drew the wrath of an unknown antagonist, who burned the place down and left a note saying that if Grigsby continued this practice, other things would also be torched. Perhaps as a sop to the anti-orientals, he rebuilt and called his new place the "Occidental," and by 1880 he was producing 55,000 gallons of wine. Grigsby's Occidental was a very large three-story structure built of stone that was quarried from a lava deposit nearby. A small brandy distillery was linked to the winery by a short railroad whose rolling stock consisted of one handcar. The entire operation fell into the hands of Chancellor Hartson's Bank of Napa when Grigsby's ill-advised scheme to build a narrow-gauge railroad to Pope Valley failed. Occidental's stone walls stood quietly for scores of years until it was reborn as the Regusci Winery in 1998.

The quarry that provided the rocks for Occidental's walls belonged to Peter Gambetta and Frank Salmina, two Swiss who raised dairy cows on their 718 acres in the Yountville area. Inspired by Tucker and Burrage, Salmina planted vineyards too, manufacturing 15,000 gallons in 1878.[34] In 1893 Salmina took advantage of a drop in land values up valley and bought Larkmead Winery south of Calistoga.

A very prolific early vintner was Gottlieb Groezinger, who bought up land from the pioneer Henry Boggs in Yountville. By 1873 the big, affable German was producing 160,000 gallons of wine, about

---

[33]*NCR*, 1-25-1873.

[34]*NCR*, 1-3-1879.

100,000 of it from local mission grapes and the rest from foreign rootstock.[35] His winery (which became part of the Vintage 1870 shopping mall) was the most prominent feature of the sleepy Yountville township. It was 150' x 80' and two stories tall, built of bricks that were baked in a kiln on Groezinger's property. Crushing was done in a wing on the north side. Like many of his peers, Groezinger ran a brandy distillery behind the wine cellar a legal distance away. He sold wine as far away as London,[36] but despite the size and apparent vitality of Groezinger's, it operated for less than 20 years. A bank in Nevada took it over in 1891 and put its 700 acres up for sale at bargain prices.The first buyer built a saloon on the small portion he purchased.[37]

Groezinger's neighbor, G. Pampel, manufactured 150,000 gallons at the end of the '70's, nearly as much as the old German.

The rest of Yountville was given to farming in the 1870's. Other than Groezinger's, the only other big enterprise was a soap factory owned and operated by a man named L.M. Moore, who also sold lumber.[38] Before the Veterans' Home came in 1884 to artificially swell the numbers of residents, Yountville could claim a population of 150. There was one general store, one saloon, two hotels, two blacksmith shops, one tin shopand two "shoe shops," probably for horses, not people.

Up the Valley an American, Henry W. Crabb put in a big winery in 1872 on Walnut Drive in Oakville,[39] not far from the site of the present-day Robert Mondavi Winery. He named his vineyards "Hermosa" (Spanish for "beautiful") and his big wooden cellar "To Kalon" (Greek for "the highest good"). Crabb was a lover of racehorses who must have crossed paths with Nathan Coombs. He

---

[35]*Napa Reporter,* 1-25-1873.

[36]*NCR,* 9-26-1876.

[37]*Napa Register,* 4-24-1891.

[38]*SHS,* 3-22-1878.

[39]*Wine Library, III,* p. 136.

first planted 240 acres of his choice land in grapes and wheat,[40] along with some oranges and Italian chestnuts. When it was apparent that wine might be a better investment, he expanded to 360 acres of grapevines and took out the wheat. Crabb was willing to expand his knowledge, too. Following Crane and Krug's lead, his viticulture hobby became an all-consuming passion, and he boasted of the largest collection of wine grape varieties in the United States at the time. He experimented constantly. He developed "Crabb's Black Burgundy," which turned out to be nearly identical to a Northern Italian grape, the Refosco.

He shared both his expertise and cuttings from his vines with others. One thing he would not share freely, however, were the figures pertaining to his wine production. He was not alone in his disdain for the tax-assessing government. A fellow vintner named Giaque (or Jaaque) in the St. Helena area had his winery seized by the government for shipping wine without paying the taxes on it.[41]

Crabb's neighbor W.C. Watson married a Yount granddaughter.[42] Watson was a Director of Chancellor Hartson's Bank of Napa. The Watsons produced as much as 154,000 gallons of wine a year at their pleasant "Inglenook" resort.

Two Frenchmen, Jean Brun and Jean Chaix, had a winery in Rutherford, the "Nouveau Medoc," where they made wine from cuttings taken from the French region of Medoc. Brun had manufactured olive oil and cider as well as wine in his native country, and Chaix was a horticulturalist. They established a vineyard on Howell Mountain in 1876 and built a tiny winery (20' x 34') by the Rutherford depot. The distance from the vineyard to the winery was inconveniently long, so to expedite communication they built a tower that could be seen on Howell Mountain. They tried to send messages by code to a watchman with a telescope situated in each place. Perhaps it worked: their business expanded. By 1881 they

---

[40]*NCR*, 2-1-1873.

[41] *SHS*, 9-15-1876.

[42]Yount, Loc. Cit.

needed to enlarge the Rutherford crushing and storage facility to 160' x 34', and even that wasn't enough. They built a second winery near the Howell Mountain vineyard to accommodate the 130,000 gallons they produced and obviate the need for watchtowers and telescopes. Their Howell Mountain Winery is still owned by French vintners and now operates as Chateau Woltner. Cajuns in New Orleans were especially fond of the semi-dry, full-bodied wines of Brun and Chaix. Their establishment later came to be known as the "French American Winery."[43]

Vineyards and wineries appeared in many places in the lower half of the Valley in the 1870's, but the most intense action in the infant wine industry took place in the St. Helena area, not only because the soil was good for viticulture, but also because Krug and Crane's voices were heard there the best. There was a concentration of vineyards and wineries south of town before 1880, starting where Zinfandel Road now intersects Highway 29: Sixteen wineries stood within three miles of each other.[44] "Pine Station," as the Zinfandel area was called, was a suburb with its own schoolhouse, a resort, "Inglewood," and its own little literary society, the "Pine Station Lyceam," aka the "Vineland Literary Club." Pine Station was home to the wineries of T.A. Giaque (the tax evader), the Wheeler family and W.P. Weaks, who had a large winery built of stone, cement and wood. Weaks' winery was named "Monongo," and later, "Pine Station Cellar." It sold most of its wine in bulk to Groezinger's. Monongo has vanished, and so has most of Wheeler's, although part of its walls still stand on the corner of East Zinfandel Lane and Highway 29. A 49'er named J.H. McCord also had a winery ("Oak Grove") there. He proudly claimed that his vineyard of mission grapes was the oldest in the Valley. He was making about 50,000 gallons of it by 1890, along with blackberry brandy and "cherry

---

[43]Joseph Henry Jackson, "Nouveau Medoc," *The Vine in Early California, III*, The Book Club of California, SF, 1955.

[44]*SHS*, 3-30-1877.

H. A. Pellet

cordial."[45]

A few hundred yards farther up the railroad track there was another stop called "Vineland Station," or "Thomann," which stood near the road to White Sulphur Springs. John Thomann, a Swiss from Bern, had a large winery there. Relatives of another Swiss, John Sutter, bought it from him. "Sutter Home" was their second winery. Their first vineyard and crushing facility was part-way up Howell Mountain,[46] and they sold it to an Irish family named Ballentine. The Ballentines called their place "Deer Park" in memory of an estate in their native land. Soon people referred to anything near the Ballentines' winery as "Deer Park," and the appellation has stuck.

Crane's winery was just north of Thomann's, and across the street was a large one belonging to G.G. Fountain. Next door to Fountain and across from Crane, a Missouri rancher named John McPike had a narrow strip of land that extended from the County Road to the River. McPike came west on one of Joe Chiles' several overland trips, and partnered with him in a mule-breeding business: an enterprise that would have been very lucrative in the 19th Century. He also raised cattle. Crane's daughter married John McPike. Under Crane's influence, McPike planted wine grapes on his property, which he crushed and sold as grape syrup.

West of Crane's, toward the hills on the way to White Sulphur Springs, was Pellet and Carver's, a modest wooden structure,[47] and near it was a small facility belonging to William Bourn, heir to a silver fortune. Pellet was Bourn's winemaker, and Bourn stored his barrels at Krug's.[48] Bourn was a financier. His father, Will Sr., was a partner in the great Empire Silver Mine. The Bourn family also owned and operated the Spring Valley Water Company, which

---

[45]Wait, p. 118. Yount grew grapes and made wine before McCord did.

[46]The Sutter family sold their Howell Mountain winery to an Irish family named Ballentine

[47] Pellet's winery was later acquired by the Butala family.

[48]Irene W. Haynes, *Ghost Wineries of the Napa Valley*, Wine Appreciation Guild, San Francisco, 1995, p. 16.

supplied the drinking water for San Francisco.[49] Will Sr. was probably introduced to the Napa Valley by summering at White Sulphur Springs. So pleased was he with the vicinity that he bought property near the resort and built a mansion for the enjoyment of his family (now a Christian Brothers retreat house) with cottages for the hired help. Will Sr. died of a gunshot wound that he suffered one morning while preparing to make a payroll run to the digs.[50] His body was found in the bathtub, and it was assumed by the newspapers that he had committed suicide, although the family believed it was an accident, because Will had not been depressed and had no apparent motive. Will Jr. took over the family finances for his father.

Virginia-born Erasmus Keyes had a residence and the "Edge Hill" winery, about 1.5 miles south of town at the end of Sulphur Springs Avenue. It was one of the largest in the county. Before retiring to St. Helena, Keyes had been the first US Commandant of the Presidio in San Francisco and a friend of Jefferson Davis. Keyes hired James Dowdell, an Irishman, to be his foreman; Dowdell went on to make not only wine, but beer, as well.[51] The mansion itself burned down, but the 20th century St. Helena cultural gathering place known to many as the "White Barn" of Nancy and David Garden was its carriage house. Erasmus' son, W. F. Keyes, bought land on John Howell's mountain and built a wood and stone building to house his "Liparita" wines.

When Erasmus Keyes died the winery was taken over by General Richard L. Heath, known during the Mexican War to his soldiers as "strong-arm Dick." Like Keyes, General Heath was a hero to many of the pioneer families, and the family was very highly esteemed by many. But General Heath died in the Spring of 1875[52] and left the

---

[49]Napa's James Goodman was one of its directors.

[50]*NCR*, 8-1-1874.

[51]*Wine Library*, I, p.49.

[52] One of his pallbearers was the millionaire William Ralston; another was the old Donner rescuer and J. C. Fremont stalwart William Le Gros

winery in the charge of his son, Richard S. Heath. Shortly after Richard took over, his sister died in an accident. Perhaps depressed over the loss of his father and sister in so short a time, Richard had trouble keeping up with the winery's needs. The business went bankrupt, and Richard attempted suicide.[53] He failed and went to work for Tiburcio Parrott, the cinnabar magnate. William Scheffler, who ran Pine Station's Monongo winery, bought Edge Hill and made lavish, expensive additions to the Keyes/Heath mansion.

Just north of Crane's there was the wine cellar of E. Heymann, and then the ramshackle Chinatown. Interwoven among the wineries and estates to the south, west and north of Crane's was a 600-acre spread of well-tended orchards and vineyards belonging to John Lewelling, who came to town in 1864 after farming in Oregon and then in Alameda county with a major landowner there named William Meek. He had to fight off a squatter who insisted the orchards were not an improvement on the land.[54] Enology was only one of several agricultural interests for Lewelling. He prepared raisins and prunes in dryers on the premises and made wine in a facility that still stands on Spring Street at the end of Stockton. His farm rivaled those of the Thompson brothers in Soscol and William Nash and his family at "Walnut Grove" near Calistoga.[55]

Enthusiasm for wine skyrocketed in Hot Springs Township, aka St. Helena. St. Helenans established a local viticultural club in 1875, a year before the city itself was officially incorporated. The club built a large bonded warehouse out of lava rock on Church Street, near the site of the Baptist Church. The club provided a forum for the discussion of wine-related topics and allowed the members to share their knowledge with each other. This mutual instruction and

---

Fallon.

[53] *NCR*, 12-5-1884.

[54] *Wine Library*, I, p.135.

[55] Nash's place was sold after the turn of the century to a man named Martin Holje, who manufactured glue. The main residence at Walnut Grove was rechristened "Maplewood."

cooperation proved extremely beneficial in improving the quality of the area's wines.[56] The *St. Helena Star* covered the club's meetings very closely, and in so doing disseminated important enological and viticultural information to the rest of the world. Charles Krug, the former editor and political activist, was a prime mover of the "Vinicultural Club." His early ambition of influencing the masses was realized through the wine industry.

The *Star* also prospered. While newspapers in other small towns struggled, the St. Helena journalists were able to build an attractive stone edifice in 1878. The architect, Ira Gilchrist, also designed a new court house for Napa City.

Many householders added wineries onto their homes to produce wine for their own consumption and sold the remainder to larger manufacturers like Uncle Sam's and Charles Krug's. Some of the old buildings still stand and elicit an intriguing nostalgia for times past. If a building looks weathered and old and is in the St. Helena area, it was probably used to make or at least store wine at some point in the 19th century.

Lewelling and Crane are remembered today only as St. Helena street names. Heymann, Heath, Keyes and even Pellet have been forgotten by all but a few wine history buffs. One early Saint Helena vintner whose memory has lasted was Jacob Beringer.

The Beringers had been prominent vintners in Mainz, Germany, for several generations. The older brother, Frederick, emigrated to the United States and started a brewery in upstate New York. Jacob joined him in 1868 but left two years later with the idea that he could improve upon Krug's wines. Krug agreed and hired Jacob to be his cellarmaster.

Friendly, confident and good-looking, Jacob Beringer quickly became St. Helena's most eligible bachelor. He was also popular with the men, particularly after he showed heroism in dealing with a

---

[56]Ketteringham, p. 144.

dangerous fire that nearly destroyed the Krug winery.[57] The fire started when a cellar worker was fumigating a barrel. Chemical means of sterilizing equipment were largely unknown in the 1870's. Cellarmen removed residue from old casks by wrapping a long stick with a cloth, soaking it in sulphur and setting it on fire, like a huge match. When it was inserted into the bung hole of a cask it cauterized the cask. But in this particular case, there was gas in the barrel, and it created an explosion that shot the cellar worker across the room and ignited some dry evergreens that had been piled up nearby. The fire quickly spread to a vat of proof spirits (alcohol) that Krug used in his vinification process. The vat exploded like a volcano, flinging liquid flame all over the winery. Jacob Beringer ran up on the roof with a hose and tried to extinguish the holocaust, watching in horror through the smoke and disintegrating timbers as barrel after barrel caught fire and burst. Thirty thousand gallons of wine and 7,000 gallons of brandy, much of it on fire, filled up the winery and poured out the door. Beringer was unable to stop the fire, but his courageous attempt was applauded for years.

In 1875 the pioneer David Hudson, plagued by asthma, put his 215-acre parcel up for sale and moved to Lake County. He, too, had planted grapes, and his vineyard foreman was Jacob Beringer. Jacob persuaded brother Frederick to help him buy Hudson's land as a joint venture. Jacob crushed his first vintage the next year. He finally left Krug's altogether in February of 1878,[58] and by March was listed by the *St. Helena Star* among the local vintners who were shipping wine to various markets.

The Beringer brothers built their winery against a hill, using the Vine Cliff/Occidental model. While preparing the road up to the new winemaking facility, Jacob found that the hillside behind it was solid limestone. His neighbor up the road, Jacob Schram, had demonstrated that limestone caves were ideal for storing wine because they maintained an even temperature throughout the year. Like

---

[57]*Napa Reporter,* 7-18-1874.

[58]*SHS,* 2-8-78.

Tiburcio Parrott, the Beringers risked the wrath of the townspeople by hiring Chinese laborers to tunnel into the rock, a task that took several years. The caves that resulted are still in use today. As tour guides at the winery will happily point out, marks from the laborers' picks can still be seen on the sides of the walls.

Frederick Beringer joined his brother in 1883 and began building the Rhine House--a temple of sorts to the cult of elegance that began to surround the juice of the grape. Two years later they planted a row of elm trees along both sides of the County Road.[59] The attitude of old-world refinement that these men portrayed (and in fact possessed) set a style that has continued to the present day in many of the region's wineries.

Charles Krug continued to make wine and train others to do so, but the bearish economy of the 1870's hit the old German rebel hard, and he had to borrow ever-increasing amounts of money to stay in business. He continued, however, to be extremely active in wine-related activites as viticulture and enology became increasingly respectable as subjects for scientific study and erudition.

More wineries went up along the county road leading from St. Helena to Calistoga. J.C. Weinberger, a German, built a large facility just north of Beringer and Krug. His land holding included Glass Mountain (then called "Glass Hill"), the site of the indigenous peoples' obsidian quarry. Weinberger's days were cut short when he was shot dead at the Barro railroad station on Lodi Lane by a young man who was obsessed with Weinberger's daughter. His wife, Hannah, took over operation of the large facility and ran it successfully for many years.

The murderer, an employee named William Gau, committed suicide before he could be tried by a jury of the peers of his victim. Several German-speaking winemakers were to be jurors, among them Charles Krug, Jacob Beringer and John Thomann. It is possible that the trial, had it taken place, could have been conducted at least partly in German. There were so many German-speaking people in St.

---

[59]Landmarks, *St. Helena*, p. 52.

Helena in the 1880's that locals joked about holding the elections in *Hoch Deutsch*, and John York actually requested election materials in German from Sacramento for the 1896 elections.[60] Both Napa City and St. Helena had *Turn Vereins*--German-style social halls. The one in St. Helena was anglicized to "Turner Hall" and was located where Lyman Park is now.[61]

Swiss were also very well represented in St. Helena. Frank Salmina (Italian Swiss) co-owned a dairy near the Occidental winery, as described above. In partnership with his brother John Battista Salmina, he turned part of his pasturage into a vineyard. The vineyard thrived, and Battista was able to sail back to Switzerland to marry. He and his new wife returned to the Napa Valley and set up home in Napa City, where there were many Italians but not enough Italian Swiss. His wife was homesick. He cured this by purchasing the William Tell Hotel,[62] a saloon and boarding house on Spring Street in St. Helena that was owned by another Swiss, Baldisare Tosetti. The William Tell was a magnet that attracted Swiss men: it did very well. In 1890 the Salmina family bought Lillie Coit's "Larkmead."

Antone Nichelini, another Italian Swiss, established a winery in Chiles Valley. According to the historian William Heintz, it sold most of its wine to miners at a nearby magnesite mine.[63] The Nichelini family is one of the very few original Napa vintners still in the business today.

A young man from Bordeaux, Jean Laurent, joined the world-wide

---

[60]John W. York, personal corespondence to the author.

[61] When Napa businessman George Cornwell went back east as a delegate to the Democratic National Convention in 1876 he observed that Germans and wine drinking seemed to go together. "Wherever he saw a sign of California wine for sale,...he was sure to find Germans, and as sure to find them discussing political questions."-*NCR*, 8-5-1876.

[62]Wilhelm Tell was the national hero of Switzerland.

[63] Magnesite contains the mineral magnesium, which is used in the manufacture of a wide variety of products.

rush for California gold in the 1850's. When he was finished being a miner, he became a Napa City vegetable farmer, and, finally, a St. Helena vintner. His winery, built of lava rock from a quarry on his property, was across the County Road from Weinberger's. Today Markham Winery occupies the site. Laurent grew hops as well as grapes

A sea captain named Sayward[64] bought acreage just to the north in the late 1860's. Sayward actually bought two parcels. The first, purchased in 1867, was a large piece with rolling hills on the east side of the County Road. He built a large home, planted vineyards and called the the place "Lodi Ranch."[65] His old barn was used as a schoolhouse and for social events until the end of the 20th century.

The next year he bought the Bale gristmill, and three years later, in 1871, he sold it to the retiring Rector of Trinity Episcopal Church in San Francisco, Reverend Theodore B. ("T.B.") Lyman.[66] Included in the package was the home that belonged to Florentine Kellogg. The Napa Valley lost Kellogg when he attempted to start a town in near the Napa/Lake border, which, had it taken hold, would have been near the junction of Highway 128 and Franz Valley Road. He eventually moved to Goleta to be near his longtime friend, Reasin Tucker, who had been stung in the land grant crisis.

With his son Will ("W.W."), the Reverend Lyman hired Chinese laborers to erect a winery. The design was provided by T.B.'s friend Charles Krug. [67]Their "El Molino" was a hillside-hugging, concrete-and-stone structure. The foreman at El Molino was an Italian Swiss named, appropriately, Molinari. Although not in the original family,

---

[64]Sayward's name is listed variously as William James, William T. and J.W.

[65]Dolly Prchal, "Josephine Marlin Tychson: The First Woman Winemaker in California," in *Gleanings*, Napa County Historical Society, Vol. 3, No. 4, Dec., 1986, p. 9.

[66] Lyman performed George Yount's wedding in Sonoma two decades earlier.

[67]*Wine Library*, I, p.142.

the historic old winery operates again today, providing a super-premium product in limited quantities.

Ten years later Captain Sayward sold the other parcel. This went to a consumptive Dane named John C. Tychson, who married an American widow. Josephine Tychson was widowed again in 1886 when John, perhaps despondent over the progression of his disease, committed suicide.[68] Having lost two husbands, Josephine did not remarry. It was an unusual decision for her era, when women had few rights and little encouragement for autonomy. Instead, she carried out the plans they had begun to start a winery, and soon this independent-thinking mother of two became the first female vintner in California. The widowed Hannah Weinberger probably drew inspiration from Tychson; they were neighbors with mutual challenges. Josephine Tychson produced wine for about eight years, then sold her estate to Nels Larsen, her winery foreman.[69]

Antonio Forni, an Italian from the mountainous Lombardy region adjacent to the Swiss border, bought the winery. He rebuilt it by encasing the original wooden structure with lava rock from nearby Glass Mountain. The Alpino quarrymen--men with surnames like Giugni, Poggi and Bognotti--collected round boulders and hacked them into squares under the supervision of another Forni, Charles.[70] The refurbished winery went by the name of "Lombarda" until it was sold again and rechristened "Freemark Abbey" in the 20th Century.

Jacob Schram was a German. He had been a barber in a major San Francisco hotel, and through the advice of his clients invested in property south of Calistoga. The hillside land that he bought in 1862 up the road from Weinberger and Tychson happened to be composed of limestone, and he was the first in the Napa Valley to tunnel into this soft rock to make aging cellars. The Schrams and their wines were immortalized in Robert Louis Stevenson's *Silverado Squatters*:

Stout, smiling Mrs. Schram, who has been to Europe and

---

[68] Prchal, pp. 11-12.

[69] Ibid, p. 13.

[70] *Wine Library*, II, p. 83.

apparently all about the States for pleasure, entertained Fanny in the verandah while I was tasting wines in the cellar. To Mr. Schram this was a solemn office; his serious gusto warmed my heart; prosperity had not yet wholly banished a certain neophyte and girlish trepidation, and he followed every sip and read my face with proud anxiety. I tasted all. I tasted every variety and shade of Schramberger, red and white Schramberger, Burgundy Schramberger, Schramberger Hock, Schramberger Golden Chasselas, the latter with a notable bouquet, and I fear to think how many more.[71]

William Nash sold his "Walnut Grove" in the early 1870's and may have moved to Napa. He married Mary Patchett (probably a daughter of John Patchett) and had two more children, raising the final tally of little Nashes to 14. Nash had made a small quantity of wine, but his buyers, the Shamp brothers, engaged in the pursuit far more earnestly. The Shamps built 10,000 square foot Victorian mansion and renamed the place "Maplewood." They retained the Nash family's 3,200 square foot home, which still stands, as does the mansion. With 20 rooms, two towers and an 1,800 square foot wrap-around verandah, it overlooks the Napa Valley behind gates that reveal its current name: St. Michael's Villa.

Julius Fulscher established a winery in Calistoga near where Hudson and York had erected their first cabin back in 1845. Fulscher sold out to Louis Kortum in 1880, and the Kortum winery prospered for many years, although they often made their wine with unripe grapes and added sugar to improve the taste.[72]

Sam Brannan's Calistoga winery and distillery were just east of the railroad station. The Donner party's Louis Keseberg worked there. In 1870 Brannan and Keseberg distilled 90,000 gallons of brandy and marketed it in New York. There is no trace of either the winery or

---

[71] Robert Louis Stevenson, *The Silverado Squatters*, Boston, 1895, pp. 56-57.

[72] *Wine Library*, p. 57.

the distilley. They may both have been destroyed when Calistoga burned to the ground in 1901. His stable at Grant and Stevenson Streets still stands, however. After Brannan departed the Valley a vintner named Ephraim Light bought it and used it as a winery, probably after sanitizing it.[73] Not far from Light's stable a farmer named John Hiltel housed his winery in a barn.[74]

Not all the alcoholic beverages produced in the St. Helena area came from grapes. The hop crop was significantly large.[75] Some growers, like James Dowdell, Abram Clock and Charles Story, planted hops and brewed beer. Freshly made steam beer cost 5 cents a glass on tap,[76] and there was a brewery off of "Brewery Road" in St. Helena. The road was renamed "Elmhurst Street" near the turn of the century when a private Catholic school, Elmhurst Academy, was built (now the site of a Seventh Day Adventist church). Among his peers, Dowdell was probably the best-known brewer. Arriving in California via schooner in 1867, he worked in the wine cellar of General Erasmus Keyes and rented land from George Crane, which he planted in hops, grapes, grain and hay. He was able to earn enough money from his two simultaneous careers that eventually he could buy the land he leased. He enhanced his local popularity by hosting social events for the community. His Hop-Pickers Ball was very popular. Partiers paid to attend, and the proceeds went toward funding St. Helena's first public library. Charitable in some respects, the Irish Dowdell was intolerant in others. He disliked the Chinese and refused to hire them.[77]

In 1876, Napa Valley wineries produced 750,000 gallons of wine, some of it very good, much of it not. Despite their poor reputation back east and the reticence of financial institutions to invest in their

---

[73]Ibid., p. 90.

[74]Ibid., p. 92.

[75]Charlotte Miller, *Grapes, Queues, and Quicksilver,*unpublished manuscript, St. Helena, 1966, p. 7.

[76]*Wine Library*, p. 176.

[77]*Wine Library*, III, p. 112.

efforts, the more optimistic among them contemplated unlimited growth for the industry.

Only the most primitive home wineries--if any at all-- used the Spanish method of crushing grapes by foot. Some of the earlier vintners dumped their grapes in watering troughs and smashed them with long wooden pestles. Krug started off with a cider press; the more mechanized wineries used steam-powered presses, and others employed the power of horses to push or pull gears that put the squeeze on grapes.

There was some variation in how the grapes arrived at the press. The luckiest (or perhaps wisest) vintners were those who built their wineries at the bottom of hills. They delivered their grapes by horse-drawn carts to the top story of the winery along a path that led up the hill behind the building. The grapes were presented to the press on the third floor, and the juice flowed down to vats waiting below. Vine Cliff and Occidental operated this way.

The Groezinger winery was a freestanding facility with no hills to simplify the transportation of grapes. Pulleys hoisted the grapes up to the roof, which was flat. The berries were dumped into a crusher that funneled the resulting juice down through a skylight to a fermenting room on the story below. Groezinger's grape pulley handled a 60-pound box every seven seconds. The empty boxes were loaded onto a second platform and pulleys brought them back down. Horses ran the pulleys.

While Krug, Crane, Beringer and the rest were experimenting with *Vitis vinifera*, a creature of an entirely different Order was doing exactly the same thing. Tiny phylloxera lice that were native to the soil east of the Rockies had been making their own trek across the continent and may have already resided in the mission grapevines when Haraszthy planted his first European varietals. They eagerly jumped aboard the more tender *Vitis vinifera*.

Phylloxera lice resemble aphids. The mature adult is about .25 of an inch long, oval and usually wingless (although some have wings). Depending on the health of the vine they infest, the lice can be a vigorous green, anemic yellow or dying tan color. One thing that

238

makes them so troublesome is that there are so many of them. They lay eggs asexually, and all mature adults are female. Moreover each female can spawn several hatches during her long fertile season, which lasts throughout the summer and fall. They multiply, therefore, exponentially--by the trillions.

The bugs make their home in the roots of grapevines. Native American vines don't seem to mind when the lice insinuate themselves into the root system, but European varietals cannot tolerate them. Phylloxera secrete a substance that is poisonous to *Vitis vinifera*. The root swells and forms a node where the louse has burrowed; rootlets beneath the node die of strangulation. Above ground the starving vines produce small, pale grapes, and the leaves turn yellow long before autumn. The entire vine can succumb within five years.

Oakville vineyardist Green Whitton may have had phylloxera on his flame Tokay grapes during the 1872 harvest. He knew there was something wrong with the vines but could not diagnose it. The *Napa Register*, which in the 19th Century was not especially friendly toward the wine industry, reported that "from some unknown cause the grapes are killed by the sun before they mature."[78] Haraszthy identified the bug on his European stock in 1873. Two winegrowers in Carneros--Winter and Duhig--admitted to having the lice in their vineyards, but many less forthright viticulturalists concealed the creatures' presence in their vines and sold out to unsuspecting buyers. In the give-and-take of samples and information that edifies many healthy industries, the French unwittingly imported vines from America that were infested with phylloxera. Confronted with a veritable sea of delicacies, the lice had an orgy in the vineyards of France and devastated them. In time, 80% of France's vineyards died. Napa Valley wine enthusiasts rejoiced, believing that Europe's loss was California's gain, and that Napa Valley wines would fill the gap in the market.

---

[78] *Napa Register* 2-15-1873

Many of the old St. Helena pioneers sank cash into planting grapes, although none of them built successful commercial wineries. Eli McLean York had a small winery ("Lodi Farm") on what became known as York Lane off Highway 29.[79] He was distantly related to the Bear Flagger John York. John himself was listed among the growers at a meeting of the Napa County Winegrowers in 1880. [80] Brothers from another southern family, William and Henry McCormick, moved to town in 1864[81] and became close to the York and Hudson families. Like the Fowlers and Hargraves, the Yorks, Hudsons and McCormicks intermarried and bought, gave or swapped lands with each other. The St. Helena Cemetery holds the remains of many of the York-Hudson-McCormick triumvirate; the Cemetery itself was a gift to the town from Mollie Hudson McCormick. John and Lucinda York reared 10 children (including Dean York, b. 1845, for whom a street is named in St. Helena) and farmed the land, watching their children, grandchildren and great-grandchildren become an important part of one of the Up-valley's three personalities-- the rural, homespun community of interrelated families who watched others sink their money into phylloxera-infested vineyard land.

Just before the annual Independence Day celebration of 1885, the St. Helena Cemetery received forever one of the few Americans who had lived in the Valley longer than the Yorks and Hudsons. More than 100 black carriages made their way down Spring Steet to say goodbye to Joe Chiles. He was almost 75.[82]

The violent streak in the mentality of some of the pioneer families persisted throughout the 1880's. The same rage that once led to the lynch murders of Hamilton McCauley and Manuel Vera in Napa was revealed one warm night in May of 1888 in St. Helena. John Ramos' defunct sherry house at 1478 Railroad Avenue became a bar,

---

[79]John W. York, personal correspondence to the author.

[80] *SHS* 6-18-80

[81]*SHS*, 9-19-1879.

[82]*NCR*, 7-3-1885.

Johnson's Depot Saloon, aka the "Pink Saloon." The building immediately adjacent to it was a brothel operated by an 18 year-old boy named John Wright, whose sister was a prostitute there. Two St. Helena boys of about the same age from pioneer families with southern backgrounds came to the door, drunk, demanding admission. One of them, Budd Vann, threw a rock through the window, and Wright shot a gun at him. The bullet pierced Vann's heart, killing him instantly. Wright was arrested and brought to Napa, but perhaps because of the McCauley and Vera incidents, Wright was transported to the jail on Telegraph Street[83] in St. Helena, where the sheriff thought he would be safer.

Rodney McCormick wrote a first-person account of what happened next:

A goodly number of businessmen and leading citizens gathered together, broke open the jail door, escorted the fellow up to Beringer's Bridge, across York Creek, tied a rope around his neck and pushed him off the bridge, where he was found hanging the next morning. The fellow had a rather doubtful reputation and no one seemed to miss his passing away.

I carried on my dray a clothesline rope, and the day before the hanging had purchased a new one. Rumor had it that the fellow had been hung with a new clothesline rope. Next morning, on hitching up my horse to the dray and getting ready to drive off, I noticed that my clothesline rope was missing, and remarked in a shakey voice to my father who was standing near that my rope was gone. Father said: "Go buy yourself a new rope and keep your mouth shut."

(...)The local authorities, probably feeling that the fellow got his just desserts, did little about it. Therefore, a number of people appealed to the Governor, raised a considerable fuss, and demanded a searching investigation. The sheriff, a Southerner by birth, arrived at St. Helena one fine day and stepped off the train, looked around, noticed my father and remarked: "Come here, Bill, [William McCormick] I want to talk to you."

---

[83]Now Money Lane. The alley across from Hunt Street that led to it was called Telegraph Alley.

I was 17 years of age at this time, still thinking of my good lost rope, and the terrible consquences that might ensue, so I followed Dad and the kindly sheriff around to the back porch of the depot where they sat down to make conversation...The sheriff wound up by admonishing Dad to tell all the boys to keep their "damn mouths shut, and not talk so much, as the Governor was pretty rambunctious about the whole thing."[84]

As McCormick pointed out, "if you wrong one of them, you hurt the whole neighborhood of Southerners."[85]

Before he left town, David Hudson, like many residents of Napa County, joined the temperance bandwagon. The tee-totalling element was nearly as numerous as the wine-bibbing throughout the Victorian period in the valley. Napans met at "Grigsby Hall" near present-day Fuller Park to voice their opposition to alcohol. In an election in 1893, the Prohibition Party succeeded in getting a measure on the ballot that would have banned the sale of alcohol, and it nearly passed.

John Bidwell of the Bartleson-Bidwell overland party of 1841 was the Prohibition Party's candidate for United States President in the 1892 national election, and he campaigned in the Napa Valley. He was resoundingly defeated by Grover Cleveland, who happened to be a good friend of Frederick Beringer's.

The Republican choice for President in that election was Benjamin Harrison, whom Cleveland also defeated. Harrison's entourage dealt Napa Valley vintners a public relations blow in 1891 when the candidate came to San Francisco during a whistle-stop tour of California.[86] They snubbed local producers by offering only French wine on the menu at a major fundraising banquet. Napa Valley representatives quickly protested, and California wines were

---

[84]Rodney McCormick, "My Clothesline Rope," unpublished manuscript, 1939.

[85]Idem.

[86]Heintz, pp. 233-236.

substituted at the last minute, but the damage was done. Whether intentionally or not, Harrison had sent out a message that minimized the importance of California winegrowing, thus tacitly aligning himself with the Prohibition camp.

Another voice that frequently seemed irked with the success of the Up-valley's wine industry was that of the *Napa Register*. It actually complained that because of the publicity the *St. Helena Star* gave to viticulture, tiny St. Helena was getting more state-wide attention than was Napa City, the county seat, which it characterized as "the Oxford of the Pacific." The *Register* suggested that Napa, too, should organize a viticultural club so it could benefit from good publicity. The *Star* shot back a modest proposal that the county seat be moved to St. Helena and the Napa court house be used as a wine-cask. The *Napa County Reporter*, perhaps fearing the loss of business from being left out of this bit of journalistic backbiting, suggested that the *Star* suspend publication and turn their editor into a wine cask.[87]

Temperance was often linked with religion. Carrie A. Nation riveted the American public's attention by laying siege to saloons with a Bible in one hand and an axe in the other. In the Valley, "Camp meetings" with Christian and temperance themes were common. The Disciples of Christ and the Seventh Day Adventist Church each sponsored very large gatherings of the faithful that sometimes lasted as long as a week. One favorite location for these conventions was a piece of land between the Napa River and the Conn Creek bridge northeast of Yountville.[88]

Merritt Kellogg--no direct relation to Florentine Kellogg of the Bale Mill, but a half brother of the founder of Kellogg's cereal company--preached a message in the Valley that emphasized a connection between spiritual and physical health. Kellogg was a medical doctor who received his license to practice after completeing a six-month course. He became friends with a St. Helena bricklayer named William Pratt, a very devout Seventh Day Adventist. An SDA

---

[87]*NCR*, 4-22-1881.

[88]Napa Landmarks, Inc., *Final Report*.

church was built in 1875 off the road to Pope Valley, near Pratt's home. Pratt donated land for a "Rural Health Retreat Association" in Deer Park in 1878, which Kellogg managed briefly.[89] To inspire other Adventists to join him in the healthy environment of St. Helena/Deer Park, Pratt offered more of his land to be developed for residential use. Many accepted. Pratt's resort became a hospital and was renamed the "St. Helena Sanitarium" in the 1890's. Ellen G. White, the former Millerite, bought 10 acres from Pratt. She settled there just after the turn of the century and continued her worldwide ministry.

A few miles farther up Howell Mountain an Englishman, Edwin Angwin, grew potatoes and preached the gospel. A *St. Helena Star* reporter commented on Angwin's land holding:

> This is the Howell, Yount, Smith, Brown place, it belongs to Mr. Angwin now. And we all agree that Mr Angwin has a beautiful place situated in a little valley on the top of the mountain, the land is very rich, an abundance of water, mountain springs, running streams and the healthiest place in the county. Mr. Angwin should make of it a resort for health and pleasure of others and profit for himself and add to the many attractions that surround the pleasant town of St. Helena.[90]

Angwin did, in fact, establish a resort, which later became the site of Pacific Union College.

Abram Clark of Angwin and Pope Valley owned the most acreage in all of Napa County during the latter part of the 19th Century. It was planted not in vines but in wheat.

Christian fundamentalism and a mistrust of outsiders continued to be features of the rural American landscape in the 1890's, as they had been in the middle of the century. In the cities, labor unions were forming to come to the aid of embittered workers. Social reformers like the writers Frank Norris and Ida Tarbell readied to expose the repressive and often rapacious mechanics of unregulated big business.

---

[89]Jakes, pp. 110-11.
[90] *SHS*, 10-29-1874.

Ellen Gould Harmon White was the primary prophet of Seventh-Day Adventism. She was a hundred years ahead of her time in recognizing the strong link between diet and health.

White was inspired by the apocalyptic predictions of William Miller, right. Subject to spontaneous, trance-like visions, she often sounded like an Old Testament prophet, predicting death and desolation to the intemperate and wicked. She believed the 1906 earthquake was the beginning of the end and was discouraged when she learned it was confined to the Pacific Coast.

Once called the "Rural Health Retreat," the St. Helena Hospital is one of several run by the SDA church.

Elizabeth Cady Stanton, Lucretia Mott and Susan B. Anthony used techniques they had honed decades earlier as abolitionists to fight for women's suffrage.

A small but powerful new upper class was also developing in America, with wealth derived not from the "old money" of previous generations, but from successful capitalism. Eager to experience the pleasure, cultural refinement and personal growth that their new money could bring them, the financially fortunate looked toward Europe, where great wine, great food, great art and architecture had long been cultural treasures. The upper Napa Valley, populated by Europeans and European-turning vintners, was becoming associated in the minds of many with elegance: something of an anomaly for an agrarian region. It would suffer a crippling blow in the next century, when the nation vented the energy of its mounting economic and social frustrations on the alcoholic beverage industry.

The last two decades of the 19th Century saw a proliferation of new wineries north of Napa City, these often quite elaborate. A tally of significant wineries in 1886 listed 104 in the Napa Valley, with two more in Conn Valley and one a piece in Pope and Chiles Valleys. More than half of them were within five miles or so of St. Helena.[91] As vintners became more skilled at their craft, the product improved; and as the quality of California wine picked up, so did sales. Winemaking finally became associated with money-making. Despite the bugs in the soil, people who had made fortunes in other pursuits continued to invest part of their wealth in the wine industry, perhaps because they could purchase phylloxera-infested vineyards from cash-poor growers at fire-sale prices and then wait for a cure.

A period of intense building commenced in the city of St. Helena, and though the businesses they housed are gone, the structures are still in use today. Taylor, Duckworth & Company established a foundry for manufacturing wine presses at 1345 Railroad Avenue. Over the years the building has also been home to a leather glove

---

[91]Ketteringham, p. 130.

factory, the St. Helena Electric Light & Power Company and a number of restaurants. A. Goodman, a dry goods dealer, built a brick building on the corner of Main and Spring Streets that has housed, over the years, a clothing store, a specialty shop, a bar, a bowling alley, a theater, a pool hall, a barber shop and a grocery store. The Owen Wade Building at 1347, and the Kettlewell Building at 1381 Main Street went up during this time, as did the Windsor Hotel at 1305 Main Street and the Miramonte Hotel at 1327 Railroad Avenue.

A subdivision of 20 new homes was developed in the late 1870's in the southern part of town, around Charter Oak Avenue. It was known as "Logan's Addition" for its developer, a man who had made his mark not as a vintner but as a mortician. J. I. Logan invented a special embalming process. Another undertaker/embalmer. W.T. Simmons, was a trustee of the town in 1878.

The Bank of St. Helena formed in 1882, with capital derived almost entirely from profits in winemaking.[92] All 11 men on its board of directors were vintners or vineyardists: D.B. Carver, H.W. Crabb, Seneca Ewer, S.C. Hastings,[93] Charles Krug, John Lewelling, W. W. Lyman, Gustav Niebaum, William Scheffler, John Thomann and E.W. Woodward. Carver founded a bank of his own (the Carver National Bank). Its president was another St. Helenan, Daniel O. Hunt, whose building at 1302-4 Main Street stood at the head of a street that also bore his name. A pharmacist named George A. Riggins leased the corner section. He called his place the "Wonderful Drug Store" and embedded his initials, G.A.R, in bronze in the sidewalk. Southerners may well have had a problem with Riggins' monogram, as it also stood for "Grand Army of the Republic." Hunt Street ended in "Hunt's Grove," a park with large formal gardens. Carver's head cashier, Frank Alexander, developed a subdivision of homes just north of town that clustered around a horseshoe-shaped

---

[92] The site of the Bank of St. Helena is now a bar. The vault still stands.

[93] Hastings planted 50 of his acres in vines in 1873. According to the *Napa Reporter,* he grew Franken, Johannisberg Reisling, Golden Chasselas, and Black Malvoise grapes.

court that he named for himself.[94]

Down in Napa City, the entrepreneurial Goodman brothers also entered the wine business in the 1880's. George and James established the "Eshcol" Winery (now Trefethan) north of Napa near Oak Knoll. They hired Smith Brown, the old stage line operator, to manage it. The Goodmans were Jewish, and the name they selected was Hebrew, meaning "Valley of Grapes." It was a very large, well-insulated wooden building constructed according to the design of an architect named Hamden McIntyre[95]

In Rutherford, McIntyre built a stone winery for a former State Senator from Butte County, Seneca Ewer. Ewer's partners in this enterprise were a family named Atkinson, and the cellar that resulted was called the "Ewer and Atkinson Winery." Across the road from the French Americans Brun and Chaix, Ewer and Atkinson's would one day be bought by another Frenchman, Georges De LaTour who would expand it and rename it "Beaulieu." Ewer lived in a mansion just north of St. Helena and incurred the wrath of his neighbors by hiring Chinese workers. To encourage him not to do this, arsonists burned his house down. The Atkinsons' house was spared and today is part of the St. Supery Winery.

A colorful and adventurous genius named Gustav Nybom bought up farmland in Oakville and Rutherford. Perhaps in deference to the many German-speaking vintners in the Valley, he changed the spelling of his last name to "Niebaum." One of his first purchases was "Inglenook," the estate of W.C. Watson, Cashier at the Bank of Napa. He bought up surrounding parcels, including that of Bank of St. Helena director S.C. Hastings, founder of a law school of the same name. Soon Niebaum had an impressive holding.

Niebaum's fascinating life began in Finland, which was then part

---

[94]Napa Landmarks, Inc., *Historical Resources Inventory: City of St. Helena,* Napa, 1978, p.48.

[95]William F. Heintz, *Wine Country,* Capra Press, Santa Barbara, 1990, p. 177.

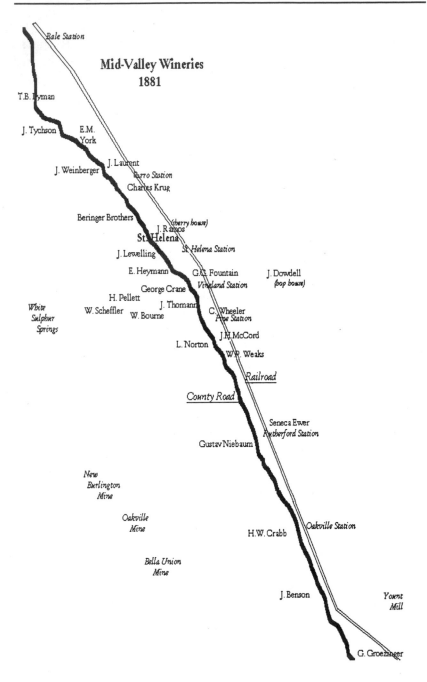

Bale Station

Mid-Valley Wineries
1881

T.B. Hyman

J. Tychson   E.M. York

J. Weinberger   J. Laurent

Barro Station

Charles Krug

Beringer Brothers

(berry house)
J. Ramos

St. Helena

J. Lewelling   St. Helena Station

E. Heymann   G.S. Fountain   J. Dowdell

George Crane   Vineland Station   (hop house)

H. Pellett

White
Sulphur
Springs   W. Scheffler   J. Thomann

W. Bourne   C. Wheeler

Pine Station

J.H. McCord

L. Norton   W.P. Weaks

Railroad

County Road

Seneca Ewer
Rutherford Station

Gustav Niebaum

New
Burlington
Mine

Oakville
Mine   H.W. Crabb   Oakville Station

Bella Union
Mine

J. Benson   Yount
Mill

G. Groezinger

of the Russian Empire.[96] He went to sea, and while still in his 20's achieved captaincy of a vessel. His career took him to the Arctic, specifically to Russian America--Alaska--in the late 1850's. He hunted and traded for fur and explored the region extensively. He arrived in San Francisco with more than half a million dollars worth of furs and immediately attracted the attention of the movers and shakers. Among these was Senator William Gwin, who was laying the groundwork for the US to purchase Alaska. The Civil War put a hold on the Alaskan purchase, but, perhaps through Gwin, Niebaum had become friendly with the tall, athletic Union General, John Miller, of the Indiana State Senate and La Vergne.

Like Sam Brannan, Niebaum knew Europe and developed a taste for good wine. Also like Brannan, he became intrigued with the potential of the Napa Valley as a wine-producing region. Brannan wanted to make money by any means possible, and his ventures into brandy and winemaking were only a fraction of the plethora of activities he undertook in order to reach that end. The aristocrats he wanted to impress saw through him and disapproved of his affair with Lola Montez, as well as of his alcoholism. Niebaum had much more success not only with the "Shivs," but with wine, as well. His interest in winemaking became a sincere passion to which he devoted considerable time. Fluent in five languages and able to read in several more, he taught himself all the world had to say about viticulture and enology. He imported samples of soil from various locations in Europe for comparison with the several types of soil on his estate. He planted cuttings from numerous varieties and made careful records of all he observed. He inspected European winemaking facilities and visited technical schools on the continent.

Finicky but effective, Niebaum believed that everything about a winery should be first-rate, reflecting an attitude of elegance and European taste. His "sample room," where visitors could taste the wine he made, was lavishly appointed with ornately carved oak woodworking, fine crystal and stained glass windows--more like a

---

[96] *Wine Library,* p.203 and ff.

chapel than a place of business.

Niebaum's Inglenook was, in its day, the most technologically advanced winery in California, with particular attention given to sanitation. He was among the first to appreciate the effect that unwanted bacteria could have on vinification and did all he could to guard against it. The wine he produced was world-renowned, winning gold and silver medals at the Paris Exposition of 1889.[97]

Unlike many of his neighbors, who believed that the trick to winemaking was in the skill of the cellarmaster, Niebaum thought that the character of the grape, enhanced by growing in a type of soil suitable to it, determined the quality of the wine. To him the winemaker was less like a chef and more like a midwife, providing the most comfortable conditions possible for the birth of a healthy vintage.[98]

Niebaum was probably the first major Napa Valley vintner to put his wine in bottles. The others kept the beverage in puncheons, or casks, like the barrels of *aguardiente* that Vallejo opened to make the Bear Flaggers tipsy. Restaurants and European-influenced householders served wine in ornate carafes or elegant pitchers. Neibaum's bottles were hand-blown and must have added significantly to the price of the wine.[99]

Inglenook, like Ewer's and Eshcol, was designed by Hamden McIntyre. McIntyre was also responsible for the architecture of a fourth winery, "Far Niente" in Oakville,[100] the venture of a San Francisco real estate tycoon named John Benson. The winery's name means "without a care." It was a getaway place for Benson as well as a serious business project. His nephew, the American artist Winslow Homer, may have designed the label for Benson's Sweet Muscat.[101]

McIntyre masterminded a huge wine storage facility for another

---

[97] *Wine Library* IV, p. 31.

[98] Ibid, p. 16.

[99] Heintz, p. 170.

[100] Ibid, p.179-182.

[101] *Napa Register,* 3-25-1998.

The Tubbs family spent a fortune building their majestic home and castle-like "Hillcrest Winery" in Calistoga.

Brun and Chaix–aka the "French-American Winery"–was a presence in 19th Century Rutherford. Note the watchtower. A signalman climbed it to communicate with Brun & Chaix's Howell Mountain facility in the hills to the east.

important San Franciscan, Morris M. Estee, a lawyer who was heavily involved in Republican Party politics. Estee ran unsuccesfully for US Senator in 1878, but came back to run as the Republican candidate for Governor in 1882. He presented himself as a "gentleman farmer," wore a floppy hat and spoke out against big corporations.[102] He lacked credibility, however. Many farmers doubted he really was what he claimed to be, and those in favor of big corporations were angered by him. The land which he felt qualified him to be called a farmer was 600 acres near John Miller's LaVergne, half of which was planted in wine grapes. He purchased the acreage a year before the gubernatorial race. Estee lost, but McIntyre's big stone building still stands[103].

As more and more people planted vineyards, storage became a problem. William Bowers Bourn, who tired of having to keep his wine in Krug's winery, entered into partnership with E. Everett Wise and built "Greystone," an enormous stone warehouse where local vintners could store and age their product before marketing it. It was the largest wine-related structure in Napa County, and Hamden McIntyre served as a consultant in its design. The mammoth stone building became Christian Brothers winery in the 20th century, and then the Culinary Institute of America.

Another way of storing wine for long periods was to distill it into brandy, in which form it would keep indefinitely, the longer the better. Most of the commercial wineries incorporated distilleries into their plants, a practice which has all but disappeared.

Other very wealthy people chose the Napa Valley as the site of their getaway vineyard villas. Alfred C. Tubbs, who manufactured string in his Tubbs Cordage Company, constructed a winery that looked like a castle, with turrets and crenolated walls.[104] Tubbs was introduced to the Valley through summers at White Sulphur Springs, and his baronial mansion was a second home. Tubbs died in 1897,

---

[102]Palmer, pp. 451-53.

[103]See Heintz, pp. 198-200.

[104]*Wine Library*, p. 164.

and his Hillcrest Winery was out of business by 1899,[105] but it was reborn in the 20th century as Chateau Montelena, keeping many of the magnificent features of the original grounds.

A San Franciscan, Tiburcio Parrott, mentioned earlier as owner of the Sulphur Bank quicksilver mines, broadened his interests by entering the wine business. His "Madrona Villa" was a luxurious sylvan home with a 4,000 gallon winery he called "Miravalle." It later bore the name Spring Mountain Vineyard and was featured on a 1980's television series called "Falcon Crest."

Another San Francisco businessman, F. Chevalier, erected a chateau dubbed "The Castle" on Spring Mountain, west of St. Helena. As its name implies, it was a turreted mansion and, like surprisingly many elegant homes of its day, had a swimming pool. Chevalier kept his family in St. Helena and lived in San Francisco during the week. He commuted by train on the weekends.[106]

A prominent real estate developer named George Schonewald diversified his portfolio, which included a lease on Brannan's Calistoga Hot Spring Resort, by buying up vineyard land in the Napa Valley. He owned much of what is now the west side of town and had a winery on the north side of Hudson called "Esmeralda." Numerous other, smaller vintners also made wine near by.One-time saloon-owner Baldisare Tosetti became a vintner. His water tower and barn still stand on Spring Street. Tosetti sold wine on the premises, both before and after the Volstead Act made Prohibition the law. Across the street a man named Antone Schweinitzer lived in a spacious stone home and crushed grapes in his basement. City maps from the 1880's indicate that Schweinitzer also owned White Sulphur Springs for a period of time. The aforementioned Lewelling winery was also off Spring Street, as was that of a family named Schultz,[107] and Frank Kraft built a square stone winery next to his home at the juncture of Madrona Avenue and Hudson Street, now the site of the

---

[105]Ibid., p. 92.

[106]Wine Library, *Interviews*, I, p.

[107]Ibid, p.10.

Spottswoode winery.

Across the Valley, the Chabot family, who left their prestigious name elsewhere on a college, an observatory and a lake, created a winery/villa not far from where the Wappo mined their obsdian.[108] It is a private residence today.

Farther down the "Road to Conn Valley," which was what the Silverado Trail was called in the 19th Century, several families had moderately large estates. Taplin Road led to the Taplin's home. The Mee family also left their name on a St. Helena lane. George Mee took advantage of the distress in the wine industry and bought up equipment from wineries that had been foreclosed. When phylloxera devastated the vineyard of the Snowball Winery, for example, Mee was able to buy their 500 gallon storage tanks for $30 each.[109] The Mees and Taplins lived in an area at the base of the eastern foothills called "Spring Valley." Today's Meadowood Resort is in the Spring Valley area.

Down in Yountville the scion of Chicago's Chase family, Horace Blanchard Chase, built an extraordinary Spanish-style villa he called "Stag's Leap Manor" on a ridge of lava and ash flow.[110] Like Chevalier he commuted to San Francisco, but unlike the San Francisco businessman, Chase was met at the depot by a coachman in gloves and tails. The Chases entertained constantly and counted among their visitors the King and Queen of Portugal.[111] They also entertained Napa's W.W. Thompson, co-founder of the Uncle Sam winery. Thompson was Horace Chase's uncle. Guests at Stag's Leap had a number of picturesque venues where they could sip their wine. The house itself had two huge fireplaces, one in the drawing room, the other in the 40'-long dining room. There was a smoking room,

---

[108]Haynes, p. 43.

[109]*Wine Library*, pp. 185-192.

[110] Laurie Marcus, "Creation," in *Late Harvest*, California Indigenous Arts Organization, 1984.

[111]Joseph and Rose H. Willis, *Stag's Leap: Biography of a Manor House*, published by the author, 1971, p. 39.

accessed through doors with leaded glass windows, which bore on one wall the family crest, and a music room with a grand piano. There was a small winery associated with the estate.

As businessmen became involved in the wine industry, vintners began to apply business principles to producing and merchandising their product. A marketing group, the Napa Valley Wine Company, formed with the express purpose of packaging and selling certain Napa Valley wines to consumers outside the state.[112] The members sent their wines in bulk to a plant in San Francisco, where they could be blended, aged and bottled. A facility at the corner of First and Market Streets was their home base, and they established branch offices in New York and St. Louis. A similar but larger organization, the California Wine Association, formed in 1894 around the NVWC, consolidating it with Greystone and the Uncle Sam Winery. Some vintners may have resented this select joining of forces, but the result was a greater market reach and more consistent quality in the wine being offered.

But while hopeful vintners were sinking roots into Napa County's soil, the little phylloxera lice were there to suck them dry. The epidemic spread unchecked throughout the 1880's and '90's. Vintners whose lands lay near water tried drowning the pests by flooding their vineyards, but the bugs were able to reproduce underwater. Some tried, unsuccessfully, to kill them with sulphur concoctions.[113] Others dug up up their vines and replanted them in sand, but this was prohibitively costly and didn't really work either, because the trouble resided not in the dirt but in the roots of the vines themselves.

At last it was determined that the only way to save the wine industry was to plant native American rootstock that was resistant to the ravages of the lice--*Vitis rupestris St. George* in particular--and graft onto these roots the European varietals that made such good wine. This meant tearing out all the existing vines and completely

---

[112]*NCR,* 12-7-1872.

[113]*NCR,* 4-29-1876.

Most of downtown St. Helena's stone buildings were in place by the turn of the 20th Century.

Greystone Winery (above), Far Niente (left) and Charles Krug (below) were already venerable institutions by the turn of the 20th Century.

replanting, a task that forced many wine growers into foreclosure. Very wealthy people and winery owners who had diversified into other endeavors were not necessarily ruined by this exigency. But growers who had already extended themselves as far as they could suffered badly. Many quit the grape-growing business and planted prune and walnut orchards.

One family who felt the full force of the problem was that of Charles Krug. Krug strongly advocated replanting with resistant root stock and attempted to salvage his own business by doing so. Perhaps because of the stress of the Krugs' mounting financial crisis, Carolina Bale Krug plunged into despair and was finally hospitalized at the new asylum in Napa, and in 1883 she died. Charles suffered a stroke two months later. The next year the bottom fell out of the wine industry, and in 1884, he joined his wife. St. Helena held an enormous funeral for Krug, similar in size and in sentiment to that which Napans had held for Nathan Coombs.

The following year, the *Napa County Reporter* declared Krug's estate insolvent and listed his many debtors.[114] Krug had loans from both the Bank of Napa and the Bank of St. Helena, and had borrowed heavily from fellow vintners. He was indebted to George Crane, D.B. Carver, Seneca Ewer, A.L. Tubbs, Eli York, John York and John Tychson, as well as to a long list of individuals as varied as Jacob Levi, Sr. (of Levi-Straus) and two Chinese men, Ah Bam and Ah Cook Doon. Gustav Niebaum was his largest creditor. Krug owed him $30,000, almost all of which was secured by his wife's inheritance.

The other great pioneering vintner, George Crane, died in 1898, leaving Frank a widow for the second time. A year before his death, Crane donated a portion of his land to be used as a public school. Frank requested that Crane be remembered in the naming of the school, but this wish was not granted by the town government.[115] In many ways, the premium wine industry in California can be said to

---

[114]*NCR*, 6-26-1885.

[115]*Wine Library*, p. 29.

have roots in Crane's experimental vineyard, on the ground that is now the campus of St. Helena High School.

As families sold out, others bought in. Many more small, low-volume wineries appeared on the side-roads, their walls built of rock that long outlasted the memory of their owners. Two German vintners, H.W. Helms and Charles Brockhoff, established minor wineries off of what is now West Zinfandel Lane, and two Scottish brothers named Rennie built one just to the north.[116] The remains of Helms' place--a wall and part of the floor--are a picturesque gothic ruin on the property of a small modern-day premium cellar, Livingston Wines. Brockhoff's is now a residence, a destiny shared by many of the more attractive stone facilities. The Rennie Brothers' winery sees life again as the present-day Flora Springs Wine Company.[117]

William Scheffler also felt the impact of the wine industry's financial crisis. Scheffler was a Prussian who served as an aide-de-camp during the American Civil War. After a stint in the insurance business he started working for David Fulton, who had built a home winery on what is now Fulton Avenue. Fulton owned a saddlery and was one of St. Helena's earliest arrivals, coming to the little town in 1852. Fulton died in 1871 at the age of 47, but Scheffler continued running the operation for David's widow, Mary, and also took over control of the big winery at Pine Station, "Monongo Cellar." [118]

He then bought Edge Hill winery from the suicidally depressed Richard Heath and invested a lot of money into its beautification. Saying nothing of the quality of the wine, a contemporary wrote that "there is probably not a vineyard and home in St. Helena where more money has been used than at Edge Hill."[119] The place had its own water works, stables and cooperage as well as the requisite

---

[116]Haynes, pp. 67-69.

[117]Idem.

[118]*SHS*, 5-21-1880.

[119] Frona Eunice Wait, *Wines and Vines of California*, Berkeley, 1973, p. 120. Originally published in 1889.

offices and other wine-related structures. In 1881 Scheffler contracted with the widow of Will Bourn Sr. to lease her vineyard, too, which put him in charge of about 205,000 grape vines altogether. He also built a distillery. Now a major player in the industry, he became a director of the Napa Valley Wine Company.[120]

Phylloxera lice slowly infested Scheffler's rootstock just as they had everyone else's. Desperate for funds to finance replanting his extensive acreage, he began a frantic effort to acquire cash. He talked the domestic help of his San Francisco friends into investing their life's savings in his winery projects.[121] In 1885 he purchased White Sulphur Springs[122] in the hope, perhaps, that he could draw moneyed people back to the resort and recoup his losses. This final venture may have been his undoing, because in 1887 he was declared insolvent.[123]

Scheffler's Edge Hill was one pearl in a string of estates in St. Helena's elite section. Sulphur Springs Avenue--known to all as simply "The Avenue"--started at the County Road and ended at White Sulphur Springs Resort. Social and cultural events among the wealthier residents of The Avenue may not have been as splendid or as frequent as might be imagined. The *St. Helena Star* complained that the local citizenry were "not...a very good party-going community."[124]

Churches were important gathering places. They were especially important for the women, who had few other acceptable outlets for expression. Mrs. Bourn, Mrs. Heath and Mrs. Pellet were friends and initiated social events through Grace Episcopal Church, which they founded, named and more or less ran through their Ladies' Guild. Sometimes the Guild held their parties at the spacious homes of winery executives. The Pellets hosted a "Gypsy Encampment"

---

[120]*SHS*, 8-21-1883.

[121]*Wine Library* I, p. 277.

[122]*SHS*, 5-11-1885.

[123]*SHS*, 7-1-1887.

[124] *SHS* 1-4-1878

festival that attracted almost 900 people and featured an entertainment program followed by dancing. They put on a similar fete in 1895 at the Rutherford estate of the Atkinsons (near the Ewer and Atkinson Winery). The grounds were lit by hundreds of Japanese lanterns suspended from the trees. The Stewart Banjo Club and Miss Nita Beringer were among the performers during the entertainment that preceded the "social dance."[125]

One year The Guild organized a New Year's Eve gala at the National Hotel in St. Helena. Details of the extravaganza were big news for the *Star*. Miss Dixie Chiles (presumably a good Baptist) seems to have stolen the show in her black camel's hair dress with a black fringe, although Miss Burbank must also have been lovely in her dress of "ashes of roses, elaborately trimmed with knife pleating."[126] The managers of Scheffler's distillery blew the factory whistle at midnight, and the Methodists rang their church bell for a solid half hour. On New Year's Day the Guild presented an art exhibit at the hotel. Mrs. "Frank" Crane showed her first husband's portfolio, *Birds of the Pacific Slope*, a very valuable collection that was inspired by Jackson Grayson's affection for the works of Audubon. Mrs. Richard Heath displayed her most prized piece of art: a signed lithograph of her hero, Senator William Gwin.

If a traveler could time-warp back to the Napa Valley a hundred years ago, he or she would see a gently sloping alluvial plain whose southern end was given to agricultural grazing land and orchards. There was a tiny train-stop town there, and a busy pier by the Napa River where sidewheelers deposited their passengers. Homes were going up in a section called "American Canyon," and children walked to a little school nearby.

A gravel thoroughfare and the Southern Pacific Railroad led to the city of Napa, a modest Hometown, USA kind of place with

---

[125]Charles Pope Rossier, *History of the Parish of Grace Church*, Grace Church, St. Helena, 1975, p. 26.

[126] *SHS*, 1-4-1878.

The lovely Genthe sisters of Napa City get ready for the Fourth of July parade.

The Ladies' Guild at St. Helena's Grace Church hostessed big social events.

St. Helena's original Baptist Church was the church of
Church Street. It stood on the corner of Church & Hunt.

handsome Victorian homes and wide streets that were sprinkled regularly with water from the new Rector Reservoir to keep the dust down.

Buggies and carts drawn by one or two horses would be hitched to brand-new telephone poles while their owners shopped, paid to bathe in a new invention called the "bathtub," visited saloons or did their banking. Many stores had bicycle racks out front. Cobblestone crosswalks and new stone sidewalks made crossing the dirt streets less distasteful for the ladies, who wore long, bustled dresses even on hot summer days and often carried parasols. Many of the stone or brick buildings that now stand on Main, Brown, First, Second and Third Streets were standing then.

Businesses with some history behind them grouped along both sides of the very polluted Napa River, each with piles of manufactured articles ready for shipping. There were three tanneries producing gloves, harnesses and shoe leather. There was a shoe factory (home of the then-famous "Napa Tans"); a glove factory, a woolen mill, a planing mill and a flour mill; a cannery; a fruit dryer, and Uncle Sam's winery and distillery. The factories sent up puffs of steam and poured streams of effluent into the river. Boats with tall masts were moored often three-deep to the many piers that jettied into the brown water, ready to transport lumber, barrels of wine, sacks of flour and wares from Napa's little industrial center.

At night the city's streets and homes were illuminated by gaslight powered at the Napa City Gas Light Company at Fifth Street on the west bank of the river, J. H. Goodman, President. The gas came from coal that was shipped to town by barge or horse-drawn wagon.[127] Giacomo Migliavacca's handsome brick winery was across the street.

Most of the Chinese had left East Napa, but the Italian population was thriving. Antone Carbone, merchant, had been appointed to the new Grand Jury. He served beside second-generation Napans like J.W. Grigsby, David J. Brown and J.J. Swift. Caleb Gosling, John Burg and W.R. Stearns were some of the Grand Jury members from

---

[127]Hanrahan, p.140.

Knoxville, a mining community. Hot Springs, which included both St. Helena and Calistoga, was represented by Will Lyman, William Cole, F. A. Crouch, H.J. Lewelling, J.R. Kettlewell and Edwin Angwin (among others). Henry Tiederman was one of the representatives from tiny Yountville, population 300.

Napa City's favorite native son had just been made a Federal District Judge. Frank Coombs followed his father's footsteps by winning seats in the California legislature four times. St. Helena's favorite son was the District Attorney, Theodore Bell. The Valley became aware of Bell when he shot, helped capture and then prosecuted Buck English, a notorious stage coach bandit who menaced the rugged road behind the sleepy town of Calistoga.

Tourists came in large numbers a hundred years ago. They came to breathe the sweet air and taste the fine wine. They fled the Industrial Revolution to absorb health in a climate that seemed both European sophisticate and American provincial. Neat, new orchards of prune and walnut trees checkered the landscape, alongside seas of vineyards that changed colors with the seasons. They caught glimpses of stone mansions tucked in the hills to the east and west.

Most folks just came for a visit. Some came for the summer. A few left their pasts behind them and moved in for good. The 20th Century was waiting for them, full of surprises.

BIBLIOGRAPHY

Published Works:

Archuleta, Kay. *The Brannan Saga*. St. Helena: Illumination Press, 1977.

Bancroft, H.H. *California Inter Pocula, 1848-1856*. Berkeley: 1888.

Bartlett, John Russell. *Bartlett's Narrative*. Chicago: Rio Grande Press, 1965.

Bean, Walton, and James J. Rawls. *California, an Interpretive History*. New York: McGraw-Hill, 1988.

Beard, Charles and Mary. *The Rise of American Civilization*. New York: Macmillan, 1936.

Beard, Yolande S. *The Wappo--A Report*. St. Helena, CA: Published by the author.1977.

Bryant, Edwin, *What I Saw in California*. Palo Alto: Lewis Osborne. 1967.

Busch, Briton Cooper, ed., *Fremont's Private Navy*. (In which is Phelps, William Dana, "The1846 Journal of William Dana Phelps,") Glendale CA: Arthur H. Clark Co., 1987.

Camp, Charles. *George C. Yount and His Chronicles of the West*, Denver: Old West Publishing Company. 1966.

Campbell, James. *Economic Survey of Napa County*. Napa: Napa County Planning Commission. 1960.

Carr, John. *Pioneer Days in California*. Eureka, CA: Times Publishing Company, 1891.

Chinn, Thomas. Ed. *A History of the Chinese in California*. SF: Chinese Historical Society ofAmerica, 1969.

Colton, Rev. Walter. *The California Diary*. Oakland: Biobooks, 1948.

Curti, Merle, *The Growth of American Thought*. Harper & Row, New York, 1964.

Dana, Richard Henry. *Two years Before the Mast*. New York: P.F.Collier & Sons, 1909.

Davis, William Heath. *Seventy-Five Years in California*. SF: J.Howell, 1929.

DeNevi, Donald. *Sketches of Early California*. San Francisco: Chronicle Books. 1971.

Dutton, Joan Parry. *They Left Their Mark*. St. Helena: lluminations Press, 1983.

Emparan, Madie Brown. *The Vallejos of California*. USC: Gleeson Library Associates, 1968.

Forbes, Alexander. *California: A History of Upper and Lower California*. San Francisco: John Henry Nash, 1937.

Gilbert, Bil. *The Trailblazers*, NY: Time-Life Books, 1973.

Goode, Kenneth G. *California's Black Pioneers*. Santa Barbara: McNally and Loftin. 1973.

Goss, Helen Rocca. *The Life and Death of a Quicksilver Company*. LA: Historical Society of Southern California. 1958.

Green, Floride. *Some Personal Recollections of Lillie Hitchcock Coit.*. SF: Grabhorn Press, 1935.

Gregory, Thomas Jefferson. *History of Solano and Napa Counties*. Los Angeles:

Historic Record Company. 1912.

Griffen, Helen S. *Trail-Blazing Pioneer*. San Francisco: John Howell Books. 1969.

Gunn, Harry L. *History of Napa County*. Chicago: S.J. Clarke Publishing Co. 1926.

Haynes, Irene W. *Ghost Wineries of Napa Valley*. San Francisco: Wine Appreciation Guild, 1995.

Heintz, William H. *San Francisco Mayors, 1850-1880*. Woodside, CA: Gilbert Richardson Publications, 1975.

Heintz, William H. *Wine Country: A History of the Napa Valley*. Santa Barbara: Capra Press, 1990.

Heizer, Robert, ed. *The Destruction of California Indians*. Lincoln and London: University of Nebraska Press, 1974.

Heizer, R.F. and M.A. Whipple, *The California Indians--A Source Book*, University of California Press, Berkeley, 1971.

Hinckley, Thomas. *Transcontinental Rails*. Palmer Lake, CO: Filter Press, 1969.

Hoover, Mildred, Hero and Ethel Rensch. *Historic Spots in California*. Stanford:Stanford University Press, 1966.

Ide, Simeon, *Who Conquered California? The Conquest of California by the Bear Flag Party,"* Rio Grande Press, Inc., Glorieta, NM, 1967.

Jackson, Joseph Henry. *The Vine in Early California*. SF: The Book Club of California, 1955.

Jakes, Warren, and Richard H. Utt, *The Vision Bold*. Washington, DC: Review and Herald Publishing Association, 1977.

Josephy, Alvin M. *The Civil War in the American West*. NY: Alfred A. Knopf, 1991.

Kanaga, Tillie. *History of Napa County*. Oakland: Enquirer Print, 1901.

King, Norton L. *Napa City: An Historical Overview*. Napa: Napa County Superintendent of Schools, 1967.

Kraus, Michael, *The United States to 1865*, Ann Arbor: University of Michigan Press. 1959.

Larkin, Thomas O., in *The Larkin Papers*, Vol. II, University of California Press, Berkeley and LA, 1952.

Lerner, Gerda, ed.. *Women's Diaries of the Westward Journey*. NY:Schocken Books, 1982.

Lewis, Oscar. *Here Lived the Californians*. NY: Rinehart & Co.1957.

Lyman, George D. *John Marsh, Pioneer*. New York: Charles Scribner's Sons, 1930.

Lynch, James. *The New York Volunteers: With Stevenson to California*. Glorieta, NM: Rio Grande Press, Inc.,1970.

Menefee, Campbell. *Historical and Descriptive Sketch Book of Napa, Solano, and Lake Counties, 1873*. Fairfield, CA: James D. Stevenson, 1993.

McGlashan, C.F. *History of the Donner Party*. Palo Alto: Stanford University

Press. 1968.

McLeod, Alexander. *Pigtails and Gold Dust*. Coldwell, ID: Caxton Printers, Ltd. 1947

Montgomery. R.T. *The Narrative of R.T. Montgomery*. Berkeley: Bancroft Library, 1871.

Mora, Jo. *Californios*. Garden City, NY: Doubleday. 1949.

Morgan, Dale, *Overland in 1846: Diaries and Letters of the California-Oregon Trail*. Georgetown, CA: Talisman Press.1963.

Murphy, Virginia Reed, *Across the Plains in the Donner Party*, Golden, CO: Outbooks. 1980.

Nevins, Alan. *Ordeal of the Union*, NY: Chas Scribners Sons, 1947.

Noorbergen, Rene. *Ellen G. White: Prophet of Destiny*. New Canaan, CT: Keats Publishing Company, 1972.

Olmsted, R.R., ed. *Scenes of Wonder and Curiosity*. Berkeley: Howell-North, 1962.

Palmer, Lyman. *The History of Napa and Lake Counties*. Napa:Slocum & Bowen, 1882.

Patent, Dorothy Hinshaw, *The Way of the Grizzly*, New York:Clarion Books. 1987.

Potter, David M. *The Impending Crisis, 1848-1861*. NY: Harper and Row, 1976.

Powers, Stephen. *The Tribes of California*, Berkeley: University of California Press. 1976.

Price, Harold *The Vine in Early California*. SF: The Book Club of California. 1955.

Richman, Irving Berdine. *California Under Spain and Mexico, 1535 - 1857*, NY: Cooper Square Publishers, Inc., 1965.

Rose, Viviene Juarez, *The Past is Father of the Present*. Vallejo, CA: Wheeler Printing, 1974.

Rossier, Charles Pope. *History of the Parish of Grace Church*. St. Helena: Grace Church, 1975

Russell, Andy, *Grizzly Country*, New York: Lyons & Burford, 1967.

Sanchez, Nellie Van de Grift. *Spanish Arcadia*, San Francisco: Powell Publishing Company, 1929.

Smilie, Robert S. *The Sonoma Mission*. Fresno: Valley Publishers, 1975.

Smith, Clarence, and Wallace Elliott, *Illustrations of Napa County, California, with Historical Sketch*, Oakland, 1878.

Sorensen, Lorin. *Beringer: A Napa Valley Legend*. St. Helena: Silverado Publishing Company, 1989.

Steed, Jack and Richard, *The Donner Party Rescue Site*, Graphic:Publishers, Santa Ana, 1991

Stellman, Louis J. *Sam Brannan, Builder of San Francisco*. NY: Exposition Press, 1953.

Stone, Lois Chambers, "Biography of Andrew Jackson Grayson," in *Andrew*

263

Jackson Grayson, Birds of the Pacific Slope, SF, Arion Press, 1986

Swett, Ira L. and Harry C. Aitken, Jr. *Napa Valley Route*. Glendale, CA: 1975.

Taper, Bernard ed., *Mark Twain's San Francisco*, New York:McGraw-Hill Book Co., 1963.

Thompson, Virgil L. *Wine Industry in Napa County Past, Present, Future*. Napa: United California Bank, 1971.

Wait, Frona Eunice. *Wines and Vines of California*. Berkeley: Howell --North Books, 1973.(Originally published in 1889.)

Watson, D. S., trans. *The Spanish Occupation of California*. SF: Grabhorn Press, 1934.

Whipple, A.B.C. *The Clipper Ships*, Time-Life Books, Alexandria, Virginia, 1980

Unpublished Works:

Beales, John T. *The Saga of Locoallomi*. ND.

Boggs, Hugh Francis. "Family History." ND

Gregory, Edith. "Pioneers of Las Posadas." Berkeley:1938

Hanrahan, Virginia. "Forgotten Spas of Napa County." ND

Hanrahan, Virginia. *Historical Napa Valley*. Napa: 1948.

Hardin, Mrs. Y. M. "Early History of Pope Valley." 1950.

Hutchinson, Fred C. *T.B.Hutchinson of Napa*. ND

Kerr, Capt. William, ed., *History and Bibliography of the Mexican Ranchos of Napa*, San Diego.ND

Ketteringham, William J. *The Settlement Geography of the Napa Valley*. Palo Alto: Master's Thesis, 1961.

Kingsbury, Ralph. *The Napa Valley to 1850*. LA: Master's Thesis, 1939.

Larios, Rodolfo, *The American Invasion of Mexican Alta California, 1842-1847*, 1983.

Lyman, W.W. "Memoirs." ND.

Maccantelli, Bruna Haegele. "Family Tree and Heritage." ND.

Mallett, Fowler. *Geneological Notes and Anecdotes*, Berkeley, 1953.

McCormick, Rodney, "A Short Story History of Grandfather York." September, 1938.

Miller, Charlotte T. *Grapes, Queues and Quicksilver*. St. Helena:1966.

Myers, Jourdan George. *Tiburcio Parrott, The Man Who Built Miraville-Falcon Crest*. Deer Park: 1987.

Sheffer, Genevieve. "History of White Sulphur Springs." ND

Tucker, George. "Old Mill." ND.

Turner, Maggie. "The Oak Knoll Ranch." Handwritten manuscript. ND

Wallace, Zaidee A. "How Pope Valley Prospers." ND

Willis, Joseph and Rose. *Stag's Leap: Biography of a Manor House*. 1971.

Wright, Elizabeth. *Early Upper Napa Valley*. Calistoga: 1924.

York, John W. "Enoch York." 1989

<u>Resource Works:</u>
Bancroft, Hubert Howe. *The History of California*, Vols. XX, XXII, XIX. Berkeley, 1886.
Board of State Viticultural Commissioners of California., *Directory of the Grape Growers, Wine Makers and Distillers of California*.Sacramento: 1891.
California Division of Mines. *Geologic Guidebook of the San Francisco Bay Counties*. Bulletin 154, 1951.
Napa Landmarks, Inc.. "City of St. Helena." *Historic Resources Inventory*. 12-1-1978
Napa Landmarks, Inc.. "City of Napa." *Historic Resources Inventory*.12-1-78
Napa Valley Wine Library. *History of Napa Valley: Interviews and Reminiscences of Long-time Residents*. St. Helena: 1974.

<u>Articles:</u>
Ault, Philip H. "Pioneer Nancy Kelsey: Where My Husband Goes, I Go." *The Californians*. March/April, 1992.
Bradley, Walter W. "Quicksilver Resources of California." *California State Mining Bureau Bulletin # 78*. Sacramento: 1918.
Carpenter, E.J., and Cosby, Stanley. "Soil Survey of the Napa Area, California." Series 33, No.13. University of California, January, 1938.
Department of Mines.*Geology of Northern California*. Bulletin 190,. 1966.
Driver, Harold "Wappo Ethnography," *University of California Publications in American Archaeology and Ethnology*, Vol. 35, No. 3, Berkeley, 1936.
Gore, Rick. "The Most Ancient Americans," *National Geographic*, Vol. 192, No. 4, October, 1997.
Heizer, Robert F., and Adam E. Treganza, "Mines and Quarries of the Indians of California," in *California Division of Mines Report*, v.40, no. 3, Ballena Press, Ramona, CA,1944.
Heizer, Robert F. "The Archaeology of the Napa Region," *Anthropological Records*, Vol.12, No. 6, 1953.
Issler, Anne Roller. "Silverado." *First Annual Report of the Napa County Historical Society*. Napa: May, 1949.
Jackson, W. Turrentine. *Stages, Mails and Express in Southern California: The Role of Wells, Fargo & CO. in the Pre-Railroad Period*. Historical Society of California. Fall, 1974.
Lyman, George, MD. "The Scalpel Under Three Flags," in *California Historical Quarterly*, IV, no. 2, June, 1925.
Marcus, Laurie. "Creation," *Late Harvest: Napa Valley Pioneers*.. California Indigenous Arts Organization, 1984
Adrian Michaelis, "Jacob Primer Leese--Founding Father of Yerba Buena." *Antepasados*. Vol 2. Los Californianos, 1977.
Neelands, Barbara, "Reasin P. Tucker: The Quiet Pioneer," *Gleanings*, V, no.

2, Napa County Historical Society, March, 1989.

Owen, Frank. "Early Days of Zen Zen." *First Annual Report of the Napa County Historical Society.* May, 1949.

Prchal, Dolly. "Josephine Marlin Tychson: The First Woman Winemaker in California," in *Gleanings.* Napa Historical Society, December, 1986.

Roberts, Effa White and Mattie White Hutchison, "Father White and His Blue Tent," in *Second Annual Report of the Napa Historical Society.* February, 1951.

Scalf, Henry P. "Overland California Letter Carried by Prestonburg Man," *Floyd County Times,* Prestonburg, KY, June 28, 1962.

Scott, Sarah, "Los Californios," in *Late Harvest: Napa Valley Pioneers,* California Indigenous Arts Organization, 1984.

Silver, Jonathan M., "Neuropsychiatric Sequelae of Traumatic Brain Injury: Assessment and Management," in *Currents in Affective Illness,* XIV, no. 10, October, 1995.

Skjele, Sheila, *Edward Turner Bale, A Pioneer Miller in the Napa Valley,* California Department of Parks and Recreation, August, 1976.

Toledo, Charlie et al, "Native Americans," in *The Valley of Legends,* Napa, 1997.

Verardo, Jennie and Denzil, "Dr. Edward Turner Bale and His Grist Mill," *Napa Historical Society Gleanings,* vol 2, no.3, June 1979.

Watson, Douglas S. "The Great Express Extra of the California Star of April 1, 1848." California Historical Society Quarterly XI. 1932.

Wey, Nancy. "A History of Chinese Americans in California,"in *Ethnic Historic Site Survey for California,* Office of Historic Preservation, Sacramento, 1988.

Wichels, John. "Railroads in Napa County: Why They Came and Why They Failed." *Napa County Historical Society,* series two, number 3.

Wichels, John. "John Lawley: Pioneer Entrepreneur." *Napa Historical Society Gleanings.* February, 1982.

Newspapers:

Napa County Reporter	*Napa Register*	*St. Helena Star*
Napa Daily Journal	*San Francisco Examiner*	*Weekley Calistogan*
Napa Echo	*Solano Times-Herald*	

Index

271

277